Essays in Canadian Business History

edited by
Tom Traves

McCLELLAND AND STEWART

McClelland and Stewart Limited
The Canadian Publishers
25 Hollinger Road
Toronto, Ontario
M4B 3G2

Canadian Cataloguing in Publication Data

Main entry under title:
Essays in Canadian business history

(The Canadian social history series)
Bibliography: p.

ISBN 0-7710-8570-2

1. Canada – Commerce – History – Addresses, essays,
lectures. 2. Canada – Economic conditions – Addresses,
essays, lectures. I. Traves, Tom, 1948-
II. Series.

HF5349.C2E88 1983   380.1'0971   C83-099292-8

Printed and bound in Canada

Contents

Abbreviations

BCS	*B.C. Studies*
CHAR	Canadian Historical Association *Report*
CHR	*Canadian Historical Review*
HP	Canadian Historical Association *Historical Papers*
HS	*Histoire Sociale/Social History*
JCS	*Journal of Canadian Studies*
L/LT	*Labour/Le Travailleur*
OH	*Ontario History*
PAC	Public Archives of Canada
RHAF	*Revue d'histoire de l'amérique française*

Introduction

Business history has not yet become an academic specialty in Canada. There are no journals, no academic associations, and almost no conferences dedicated to its systematic study. A decade ago, the first and last of the two Canadian collections of essays explicitly identified with the field were published, but their impact was marginal.[1] Yet, paradoxically, over the last ten years our knowledge of the Canadian business system has increased enormously. This seeming contradiction derives from the fact that much of what we know now has come to light as a result of examinations focused on other subjects of study. In the course of their work, historians concerned with labour studies, political economy, social structure, and politics have inadvertently opened a new field of enquiry without attempting to specify and define its contours.

Such intellectual antecedents create both opportunities and hazards. On the one hand, the risk is that a valuable intellectual enterprise will get lost in the shuffle of other concerns and the analytical gains that derive from systematic and focused study will disappear. By contrast, if the field does develop, it will be defined broadly because of its origins and its obvious relationship to other subjects of scholarly interest. Given the occasional attempts elsewhere to limit business history to the study of entrepreneurship or business administration, attempts which ultimately have proven to be too restrictive, the intellectual pluralism inherent in the Canadian case will doubtless come to be seen as a marked advantage.[2]

Like women's and labour history, the two most recent notable fields of historical specialization in Canada, business history offers a new window through which to look at and concentrate on a fundamental feature of human activity. Introducing the "new" labour history to Canada, Kealey and Warrian claimed that

> labour history ceases to be simply a category of political economy,
> a problem of industrial relations, a canon of saintly working class

5

leaders, a chronicle of union locals or a chronology of militant strike actions. Instead it becomes part of the history of society. Workers are no longer seen as isolated figures engaged only in trade unions, strikes, and radical politics; instead they are studied in a totality that includes their cultural backgrounds and social relations, as well as their institutional memberships and economic and political behaviour.[3]

With obvious appropriate substitutions this manifesto would serve the cause of business history equally well. One important caveat must be noted, however. The initial enthusiasm that propelled labour and women's studies to the forefront of contemporary historical writing was often connected to the explicit ideological goal of linking the search for a usable past to current struggles for social change. It would be naive to assume that any important field of social enquiry, let alone one so potentially contentious as business history, could escape this impulse, but it would be regrettable indeed if the goal of writing about businessmen came to be inextricably linked to either of the hagiographical or muckraking traditions that have prevailed in the past. Neither simple-minded social theories nor uncritical analytical practices will serve to advance our understanding or the field very far.

It is a commonplace to observe that industrialization marks a turning point in the transition to "modern" social structures and practices; certainly the institutional character of the business firm was not exempt from change. Canadian historians have written very little of the kind of organizational history that characterizes business history elsewhere, in part due to a paucity of sources, but surprisingly we know more about the pre-industrial era than the more recent past. From the early histories of the great fur-trading companies to more recent studies of the mercantile business world, it has become quite clear that pre-industrial commercial enterprises were subject to different external constraints and were organized and managed along quite different lines than their industrial counterparts. The first two essays in this collection, by Douglas McCalla and Dale Miquelon, explore the essential features of this pre-industrial business system and should be read together.

McCalla's article raises a host of important issues by way of introduction to some of the more recent studies of the nineteenth-century economy. In particular, he analyses briefly the transformation of the commercial economy, questions the utility of the concept of entrepreneurship as an explanatory model of historical change, and describes the business structures within which the mercantile firm operated. In addition, he assesses the constraints, opportunities, and development strategies these structures allowed businessmen. These issues are explored in greater depth in his excellent study of the Buchanan business, *The Upper Canada Trade, 1834-1872*. Finally, McCalla's article serves as a helpful introduction to Miquelon's detailed case study of the eighteenth-century Quebec merchants, Havy and Lefebvre. As McCalla notes, "Until at least 1850, the scale and structure of Canadian business might, but for a variety of institutional factors, be said to have been eighteenth-century in nature."

Miquelon's study of the operations of two prominent French merchants in Quebec provides a wealth of data about the structure and character of colonial commerce. François Havy and Jean Lefebvre served as the factors or agents of Robert Dugard and Company of Rouen for more than a quarter of a century and as such they played a crucial role in linking the small merchants of the interior to the great metropolitan trading interests of France. Read in conjunction with José Igartua's study of the pre-Conquest Montreal merchant community and John Bosher's detailed analysis of French interests trading with Canada,[4] Miquelon's discussion of Havy and Lefebvre's affairs highlights the essential features of the French mercantile system in Canada. In particular, Miquelon explores the character of the standard colonial marketing strategies, explains the basis of the credit system, without which neither the colony nor the merchants could survive, and analyses the structure of the import-export trade in which Havy and Lefebvre specialized. As well, he briefly discusses alternate investment opportunities that such merchants could seize upon if they were anxious to diversify their interests.

Above all, however, Miquelon's study serves to illustrate the material basis of imperialism in this period. Quebec was a colony and men such as Havy and Lefebvre embodied the metropolitan urge to economic expansion. Their mercantile careers read like a précis of colonial economic history and their decision to close their careers by returning to France underlines the essential dynamic of their activities. Comparisons with the contemporary multinational corporation, which some analysts have characterized in terms of modern neo-mercantilism,[5] are obvious and point to important questions about our own business system, some of which are explored in the essay by Graham Taylor in this collection.

While the structure and operations of the mercantile firm are well known, at least in outline form, it is astonishing, given its overwhelming importance, that we know so little about the business system in the early stages of industrialism in Canada. Economic historians have mapped out the broad contours of the industrial landscape, largely based on an analysis of the census, but such macro-economic discussions have generated few insights about the nature of the industrial firm in the last half of the nineteenth century. This lacuna has been filled somewhat in recent years by historians from other fields, principally those concerned with labour studies.

Ian McKay's study of the Halifax baking industry is an excellent example of this trend. Although McKay is concerned ultimately with the development of class relations within the industry, his analytical framework requires first a careful study of the industry itself. Combining Marx's insight that industrial capitalism developed in three stages – handicraft, manufactory, and factory – with Raphael Samuel's finding that these stages often overlapped one another in many industries, thus leading to a revised view of the "concurrent phases of capitalist growth," McKay offers a detailed analysis of combined and uneven development within the baking industry. His concern, of course, is to show "the effect of the evolution of the productive forces on the workers in the industry" and to discuss their consequences for labour struggles between 1868 and 1896, tasks which he accomplishes admirably. From the perspective of the business historian, however, what is also fascinating is McKay's analysis of market forces and competitive strategies, technological developments, the financial basis of the first modern industrial corporation within the industry, the process of vertical and horizontal integration pursued by the industry leader, and, finally, the different patterns of organizing and managing the work force at different stages of industrial development. McKay's discussion of class consciousness and the limits of class formation within different or overlapping modes of production is also important for the obvious parallel questions it suggests to the historian of the business community.

Whether viewed as an instance of class struggle or a problem in industrial relations, the management of a large, diverse work force continues as one of the central tasks in the modern corporation. Businessmen have developed a wide range of techniques and strategies to this end over the years, but most of them can be traced back to the "scientific management movement" that emerged around the turn of the twentieth century. It is appropriate, given the development of the large corporate bureaucracies inherent in the scientific management approach, that Graham Lowe's essay examines this phenomenon by focusing on the organization and supervision of the large office staffs that became an increasingly common feature of modern business organizations. As Lowe asserts, "we are suggesting that in order for administrative control to be exercised *through* the office, managers also had to apply the same principles of control *over* the office." To demonstrate this proposition, Lowe examines the occupational and organizational dimensions of what he styles the "administrative revolution," locates these changes in the context of the transformation of the Canadian economy after the turn of the century, and analyses the rationalization of office work itself. Finally, in yet another demonstration of the value of an interdisciplinary approach to business history, Lowe discusses the origin and meaning of these changes from the perspective of the divergent Weberian and Marxian perspectives on the dynamics of corporate capitalism.

In addition to the problems analysed by McKay and Lowe, the rise of the modern corporation also entailed significant financial dislocations and innovations. The transition from small-scale enterprise to monopoly capitalism sometimes was financed by retained earnings, but, over time, corporate owners had to look increasingly beyond their narrow circle of relatives and business associates to new sources of credit and investment capital. The stock market, recently examined by Christopher Armstrong, and the creation of new financial institutions such as trust and insurance companies, studied by Michael Bliss, played an important role here.[6] The banks, however, remained the major source of ongoing outside financing for most businessmen. Most of the major banks have published or been the subject of institutional histories, and the financial system as a whole has received scholarly attention, but these treatments have told us too little about the banks' investment strategies and their role in the process of industrialization. As a result, some serious misconceptions about the banks' lending policies to industrial concerns have arisen.[7]

James Frost's study of the Bank of Nova Scotia, then, is an especially valuable addition to our knowledge of the role of the banks in the business system. But while Frost's article tells us a great deal about Scotia's lending and investment policy during a crucial phase of development, as well as detailing the bank's organization and the network of customers it serviced, the thrust of his argument lies elsewhere. Frost's concern is to examine the cause for and impact of Scotia's transition from a largely regional bank into a national financial institution, especially in the region it "deserted," the Maritimes. His evidence that bank policy ultimately led to a net flow of funds out of the region confirms previously impressionistic conclusions on this score, but his detailed discussion of the banks' relationship to local efforts to industrialize demonstrates that simplistic conclusions about the role of "commercial capital" in regional underdevelopment must be examined more critically.

Regionalism and underdevelopment are persistent features of the Canadian political economy. Tom Traves picks up on these themes in his analysis of business-government relations concerning the automobile tariff in the 1920's and early 1930's. The role of the state in the Canadian economy has been discussed frequently in scholarly studies and the business press alike, and while the latter is usually filled with businessmen's complaints about government policies that hobble free enterprise, the reality of the situation is a good deal more complex than such accounts sometimes allow. As Traves's study demonstrates, the business-government relationship is a dynamic process. In a capitalist society divided by class and region, with a business system fragmented by inter- and intra-industry competition, the state becomes both an arena where social and economic conflict is further articulated and the object of such conflict insofar as it bears on the control of public policy. Traves locates the political strategies of the various economic groups he examines – the automobile manufacturers, parts producers, import dealers, and consumer groups – in relation to the structure of the auto industry and its place in the broader political economy. Changes in structure led to revised political strategies.

At the same time, Traves does not see the state as a neutral arbiter or a passive reactor to social change. The structure of the state, the character of its representative institutions, the make-up of the party system, the strength of public opinion, and the personal ambitions of the politicians themselves are all examined in relation to the debate over tariff policy.[8] While the tariff and the National Policy have long been staple items in the diet of Canadian historians, their discussions of its impact have usually remained at the level of macro-economic generalizations. Traves's study, however, examines the issue at the industry and firm level and incorporates the impact of uneven development into the history of the automobile industry.

By the 1920's all the major automobile producers were foreign-owned corporations, and this fact was not irrelevant in the debate over tariff policy. Since then, of course, the debate over the consequences of foreign ownership has broadened. Like the economic controversy surrounding the tariff, however, much of the analysis of the impact of foreign ownership has been carried out at the macro-economic level. In part, this has been a result of the obvious difficulty in gaining access to appropriate corporation records. As a result, Graham Taylor's study of Canadian Industries Limited (CIL), which was jointly owned by major British and American chemical interests between 1927 and 1951, is especially valuable because it offers a relatively rare glimpse of the internal operations of multinational capital in Canada. Taylor concludes that CIL enjoyed a considerable degree of independence in its relations with its foreign parents. He attributes this to the unusual fact of joint foreign control, the special circumstances faced by its American parent in the 1940's, the parent firms' attitudes toward decentralization and managerial autonomy, and finally, the skill with which the Canadian managers played off their foreign parents against one another to achieve a degree of independent decision-making authority. In many ways, as Taylor notes, this makes the CIL case untypical of the situation facing most branch plant managers. Readers should also pay special heed to the nature of the autonomy sought and achieved by the CIL executives. Thus the debate that started with the first era of imperial control of Canada, when merchants such as Havy and Lefebvre were designated as "forains" and distinguished from native-born businessmen, will continue. If historians can produce more studies like Graham Taylor's, however, the debate will at least move on to a new level of precision and sophistication.[9]

These essays represent a fair sample of the interests and approaches in recent years of those studying the history of the Canadian business system. A great deal remains to be done, of course. For a start, more businessmen have to be persuaded to save and open their records to historians. It would also help if more economists and business administration professors appreciated the value of studying the origins of the institutions that occupy their attention. The old cliché about those who ignore the past being condemned to repeat it bears notice here. On a more positive note, however, these studies indicate clearly that Canadian scholarship in this area, although perhaps focused on somewhat different issues than those currently in vogue elsewhere, has matured to the point where one can hope with some confidence that the birth of a clearly defined new field will soon be a fact rather than a wish.

Tom Traves
York University

1

An Introduction
to the Nineteenth-Century
Business World

Douglas McCalla

It was once the task of the student of business history, like his
counterparts in political and military history, to study great men, to
identify the heroes who, it was assumed, were the makers of history
and of the modern world. Peter Newman, for example, has often
depicted in such terms the businessmen who "transformed Canada
from a community of traders and land tillers into one of the world's
economically most advanced nations. They changed history and the
face of their country."[1] At the other extreme, but in fact with a
similar orientation to great men, were those who searched for villains.
Unfortunately this has seemed to some, who would suspect the
approach in any other field of history, still to be a legitimate avenue
to understand the history of business in Canada; there is even a
school of thought that depicts Donald Smith, Lord Strathcona, as a
kind of arch-villain, almost single-handedly dominating and manipulating more than half a century of Canadian history.[2] Such approaches as these, however, by their emphases on businessmen's
individual qualities, have tended to over-simplify the past and have
insufficiently explored the context in which their individual stories
should most appropriately be set. Even without Newman's particular
collections of businessmen, after all, other western economies have
undergone the same transition, which suggests structural rather
than individual explanations.

Reprinted from *The History and Social Science Teacher*, 18, 2 (1982), with the
permission of the author and editor.

Recognizing this difficulty of the great-man approach, Canadian historians have increasingly sought to focus on political, economic, and social structures and their ordinary and typical institutions and behaviour, rather than on the heroic exceptions. Although much of the research of business historians has continued to focus on individual firms and businessmen, the questions posed have very much reflected this concern with structures. Because of the importance of business institutions in Canadian economic life, their roles have become of considerable interest to a much wider historical community, including regional, urban, labour, economic, social, and political historians.[3] From all this work has come a growing sense of the shape and significance of Canadian business history.

I

One fundamental role of recent research has been to combat anachronism by sharpening our knowledge of the chronology of the transformation of business organization in Canada. Until at least 1850, the scale and structure of Canadian business might, but for a variety of institutional factors, be said to have been eighteenth-century in nature. The largest businesses were mercantile and did general rather than specialized trades. The widespread industry of the society was small of scale by the standards of the leading industrial societies of the day, very much oriented to local markets, and, in a variety of ways, quite traditional in the organization of work.[4] More modern financial institutions had been organized, including incorporated banks, insurance companies, and even mortgage loan companies; but even the largest such institutions did business on a scale and in a way familiar to the eighteenth century.

Although Canadian railroads have thus far been studied more in terms of promotion and construction than of subsequent operations, it would not be unreasonable to hypothesize that in Canada as in the United States, it was railroads which from the 1860's or 1870's first began to epitomize the structure of more modern business. Not only did they develop a growing appetite for fixed capital, but they needed to confront the physical and accounting problems of depreciating such capital. They needed larger and more bureaucratic organizations and specialized skills in fields such as engineering. Their labour problems took on new levels of complexity, and management became generally divorced from ownership.[5]

The railroad also, with the steamship, the telegraph, and the Atlantic cable, began to change the significance of distance, as the risks hitherto associated with slower movement of information diminished. This permitted major expansion in the trade volumes of some firms, especially in bulk trades, and a bypassing of some links in the chains of middlemen that earlier characterized the structure of business. Increasingly, such changes in communications would also permit effective management and supervision from a distance, an important prerequisite for the development of larger and more complex organizations.

Such changes were not immediate; rather, throughout the second half of the nineteenth century, in a gradual and cumulative process marked by the end of extensive agricultural growth in eastern Canada, the rise of urban centres, and the workings of comparative advantages in the industrial sector, Canada developed an economy characterized by a larger and more urbanized industry, a very much enhanced and commercialized service sector, and an increasing predominance of incorporated and larger firms, as measured in terms of capitalization, number of employees, and volume of output. Because the scale, swiftness, and simultaneity of these interrelated transitions can readily be exaggerated, there is great need for research on the history of individual business sectors to permit generalizations more precise than these.[6]

It was not until about 1900, however, that market forces, the capital and other business requirements of new technologies such as electrical power, and the cumulative example and experience of successful incorporations in various economic sectors began to produce in Canada something like the "big business" that we tend to associate with late nineteenth-century capitalism. Only after 1900 did the Toronto Stock Exchange, for example, take on the characteristics of an important component of the workings of the Canadian business system.[7] Even by 1914 the predominance of bigger business was anything but complete or comprehensive.

Throughout the nineteenth century, in short, the Canadian business world was one of relatively small-scale firms, usually owner-operated, functioning in competitive markets. It was a world of growing specialization and complexity of business institutions and, increasingly, an urban business world in which fewer and larger centres dominated in most areas of economic activity. But not until virtually the end of the period, in 1914, could the modern bureaucratic, multi-branch, multi-product company be said in any sense to have typified Canadian business.[8]

II

Traditionally, one central concern of the business historian has been to identify and consider the significance of entrepreneurship as a factor in economic development and change. Entrepreneurship, something in a culture or at least in some individuals within the culture, was the quality that led the independent, risk-taking, profit-seeking economic agent, the entrepreneur, to innovate by combining economic resources in new ways. This, it was argued, was an essential part of the process of economic progress, and to many it was the key variable that explained varying growth patterns in different regions or countries. Such behaviour needed to be differentiated from what was thought of as merely managerial behaviour, in which the businessman simply responded to economic stimuli in predictable ways. Failing this distinction, "entrepreneur" became merely a synonym for businessman.

Thus, for example, Atlantic Canada's relative economic stagnation after about 1870 has been attributed in part to the failure of the region's entrepreneurs to make appropriate investment decisions, especially in the previous two decades. When they persistently invested in traditional trades such as timber and wooden shipping, they ignored the chance to encourage or invest in secondary industry, and thereby "they contributed to the retardation of a viable industrial base" in the region.[9] On the other hand, the large-scale quantitative investigation of entrepreneurial behaviour that is being carried out by the Atlantic Canada Shipping Project is enabling us to see more clearly the rationality of Maritime businessmen in the shipping industry. Wooden shipping continued to be a most reasonable investment, in a number of ports, until the 1870's. Moreover, "when new markets and new opportunities appeared in the domestic economy, shipowners and their sons responded, not in undue haste, but with the same prudent calculation which earlier had guided them into the ocean trades of the North Atlantic."[10]

More generally, it seems implausible that one region of a society in which there is much mobility of population should lack such a cultural quality as entrepreneurship unless other, prior factors caused the migration away from the region of some of those possessing it.[11] There is in fact great danger that the often met concept of entrepreneurial failure will be little more than a label employed to explain why a particular economy did not take a road that it was never destined to take. As H.C. Pentland once tartly and succinctly put this point, "it seems to me that in societies of a northwest European type (at least), development is dependent upon supplies of resources, capital and labour, but not upon promoters, who are always in excess of supply."[12]

Even if this is true and the use of business history to study entrepreneurship is something of a dead-end street, the approach has reflected and helped to highlight the importance of cultural and organizational factors in the economic world. The significance of such factors is suggested also by the failure in the last twenty-five years of so many efforts at economic development, both within some of Canada's less developed areas and elsewhere in the world and by the relative success of some economies not notably better endowed with measurable and quantifiable resources than others.

It is an important virtue of business history that it considers economic change and development at a less abstract level than economics; in so doing it can reveal much about the mechanisms of economic change in a society. The same point can be made in sociological terms: if one wishes to understand, investigate, indeed, see at all the role and influence of a dominant class in society, rather than simply to assume and assert, then examination of the institutions and the inner workings of that class can be very much to the point. With this perspective in mind, let us review briefly a few contributions of relatively recent work in nineteenth-century Canadian business history.

III

An appropriate starting point lies in the structure of commercial enterprise, the dominant business form of the period. That structure has often been misunderstood, and it has tended to be seen largely through the eyes of its critics. One of the first of these was John Graves Simcoe, who was convinced that a merchant monopoly was obstructing his plans for Upper Canadian prosperity by holding up prices of wheat and flour to the government, yet paying the farmers only a small proportion of such high prices, keeping the rest for themselves.[13] Doubtless the merchants wished for such power to control prices and margins, but in fact Simcoe, and those who have echoed his opinion of the merchant class in the almost two centuries since, blamed the individuals who visibly represented the business system, entirely ignoring the underlying structure of trade and the inescapable realities of the market forces that actually determined prices.

The mercantile firm depended on credit, from suppliers, banks, and other mercantile intermediaries, in order to acquire and ship its goods to the colonies, where it sold them, also on credit. The usual retail term was twelve months, reflecting the economy's harvest and timber marketing cycles. The entire world of credit focused on the metropolitan centres of Britain – London and, especially important in the Canadian context, Glasgow and Liverpool. There, in expansionary times, competition meant that credit was liberally available, at least to appropriate borrowers, and this prevented the formation of monopolies such as Simcoe feared.

When the business cycle turned downward, credits were tightened or withdrawn. Because trust was central to the granting of credit, easiest and earliest access to it in expansionary times and preferential treatment in contractions went to those on whom the creditor considered he could rely most fully, that is, to people whose characters he knew and to those personally recommended or guaranteed by those he knew and trusted. Thus the commercial world was structured not only in the competitive yet mutually supporting business communities of individual cities, with which research has made us increasingly familiar in recent years, but also, in some respects more importantly, along international chains of personal connections.[14]

As work progresses in Canadian business history, the reality of risk for businessmen is repeatedly emphasized. In a commercial world that required the merchant to decide what to buy as early as the autumn of one year to obtain goods to be sold in the summer of the next and on which payment would not follow until the ensuing summer, much could happen to undermine a business. Too little or too much expansion, a wrong estimate of future wheat and timber supplies and prices, extension of credit to the wrong people, or a sudden commercial collapse in Britain could all bring serious loss. Bankruptcy, especially in the recurrent cycles of credit stringency, was a frequent and normal feature of the business world.[15]

These risks, plus the personal nature of business, in which death or retirement could bring a change of business partnership and name, meant that relatively few enterprises spanned multiple generations, although we are likely to hear most about the exceptions that did survive. If the departure of firms left opportunities to be grasped, it was likely that the business world would produce successors, either through the formation of new firms or the expansion or adaptation of existing ones. Where opportunity had shifted, would-be successors either did not appear or did not succeed; such was the case, for example, as independent wholesaling declined at Hamilton after the 1850's.[16] These general points on the nature of the Canadian business world in the merchants' age help to explain the shifting fortunes of competing nineteenth-century urban centres, and they have much to say about larger social changes in the period.

IV

One of the crucial issues in the interpretation of the Conquest and the development of Quebec and its élite thereafter has been the takeover of the St. Lawrence economy by English-speaking, notably Scottish, merchants in the generation after 1763.[17] How and precisely when did this happen, what did it have to say about British policy and practice and about French-Canadian business abilities, and, of course, what did it mean for French-Canadian society to have at the head of its business system a Scottish-dominated mercantile élite? While a variety of answers have been offered to these questions, it is our interest to view them in the perspective of business history. From this angle, it comes as no surprise that the economy of a colony that became dependent on British supplies, markets, and credit was increasingly dominated by those with superior access to the metropolis.

Such a transition did not occur all at once, because the French-Canadian merchants had knowledge of their local markets and of the indigenous credit mechanism, which was of real advantage in a competitive world. But as the normal turnover of firms took place, the successful among the aspiring replacements were very likely to be those with more immediate connections in Glasgow, Liverpool, or London than any Lower Canadian could have. After 1800 this probability was still further increased by the fact that the Upper Canadian frontier region, now almost entirely English-speaking, was the most dynamic commercial sector in the St. Lawrence valley.

It has not usually been recognized that the Lower Canadian situation was in many respects paralleled in Upper Canada, where commercial leadership soon fell largely into the hands not of men of Loyalist, military, or American background, as the composition of the population might have suggested, but into those of newly arrived merchants, especially Scots, with solid connections to the Montreal, Quebec, and Glasgow commercial worlds. As Bruce Wilson has argued this point in his excellent account of the enterprises of Robert Hamilton, the Niagara area's leading merchant at the beginning of the nineteenth century, economic power in the first generation in Upper Canada stemmed directly from the ability to be part of that commercial and communications system.[18] Even in the 1830's and 1840's, it is clear that suitably connected Scots had better opportunities for commercial leadership in Upper Canada than the native born.[19] Thus it was that the economic leadership of the St. Lawrence economy acquired and long retained its markedly Scottish character, and this in turn had real consequences in determining the personnel of its business élite.

Related to, yet distinct from, the question of domination of the Lower Canadian economy by English-speaking merchants was the question of the entrepreneurial spirit and values of French Canadians. It was once usual to contend that, either through decapitation of the society, that is the removal of its commercial élite by the Conquest, or because it was a Catholic-peasant-seigneurial-professional culture that was inimical to entrepreneurship, French Canadians lacked the business values and commercial drive that produced great entrepreneurs. Recent research has made that view difficult to sustain. Certainly in those areas of trade and business where connections in the French-speaking community gave an advantage, French Canadians were much involved in business enterprise. They were, for example, active in a venturesome and risk-taking way in the domain of urban land development and associated real estate speculation, where international ties mattered less than local ones.[20]

At the same time, economic historians are increasingly noting contrasts in the basic resource endowments for agriculture between Upper and Lower Canada, thereby revealing the basis for the lower per capita output and income of French-Canadian farmers. Of course, this in turn left a smaller and less dynamic market, one that experienced real economic crisis and decline in at least the second quarter of the nineteenth century, as the basis for French-Canadian commerce.[21] Here, in short, is a classic case where observed differences in economic behaviour have in the past been attributed to that elusive quality, entrepreneurship, when they should probably have been attributed to quite other factors.

Given the merchants' concern with the problems of credit, aspects of their business and political behaviour also become more explicable. It was one of the merchants' earliest priorities to improve the banking and insurance systems in order to obtain assistance in carrying credit burdens, controlling risks, and effecting interprovincial and international transfers of funds. Needing and knowing these financial services, which could, moreover, be built up incrementally, they were very ready to establish the appropriate institutions themselves, though the state had a role to play in chartering such companies. By contrast, they consistently avoided personal investment, except in certain promotional stages or when given ample government aid, in such desirable but capital-consuming and altogether unsafe investments as the shares of most canals and railroads. For these ventures, they predicted large returns to society and urged and often obtained state support in such forms as subsidies, share purchases, loan guarantees, and land grants.

At the same time, merchants were markedly involved in politics and legal efforts to develop and improve other aspects of a credit-based society, such as laws relating to promissory notes and currency, bankruptcy, the role of the courts in enforcing contracts, land tenure (important in terms of securing debts), etc.[22] In all of these, merchants were at once debtors and creditors and hence as a class they had a particular interest in the certainty and efficacy of procedures. Given their awareness of the importance of maintaining and increasing the stream of British-based credit, they were naturally attentive to the worries of overseas lenders. Indeed, the Canadian businessman's often met litany of fear of giving offense to foreign creditors and investors had a genuine basis in his actual economic activity, particularly in this early period.[23]

We have in the twentieth century come to view with suspicion the intertwining of politics and business engendered by these and other merchant concerns. We have also, perhaps paradoxically, both pursued a wide variety of state interventions in business and economic life and enacted laws (e.g., on conflict of interest, public tendering, political party funding, etc.) to separate the two domains in an effort to reduce what we see as undesirable links between business and politics. We are, however, liable to misunderstand the politics of the nineteenth century if we apply our current standards on these matters anachronistically, or, alternatively, if we assume that the interrelationship of business and politics is largely a modern phenomenon.

The nineteenth-century spheres of government, politics, and business were not discrete or separate from each other; they overlapped in wide areas and it was altogether natural that businessmen and politicians should have many connections. If, as politics developed, this common ground led to situations in which political capital could be made by opponents of one or another element in the process, the consequence was the gradual buildup of a set of political and institutional barriers attempting, seldom successfully, to separate the spheres. As often as not, however, the issue in political debate in such cases was not the appropriateness of links between politics and business, but inappropriateness of particular links, especially ones that appeared to favour one set of development ambitions over another. This most often happened when the interests of one generation of businessmen collided with another, or of one city with another, or of one element in the business community with another, or of established business institutions with newer ones.[24] Only gradually did debates of this kind create a more general sense of the need for limits beyond those supplied by the common law. But it is not helpful to apply those standards moralistically to the business-political world of most of the nineteenth century.

As Keith Johnson has shown so well, especially in his perceptive studies of John A. Macdonald's earlier years, the aspirant local politician and the aspirant local businessman had much in common, and it is artificial and harmful to our understanding of the behaviour of either to separate one sphere too much from the other. The leaders of the age, as Johnson notes, spoke a "common legal-entrepreneurial language," which also had clear equivalents in French, as the careers of Cartier and others indicated.[25] Certainly an understanding of how the world looked to a typical Kingston businessman has much to say about Macdonald's guiding tenets in politics as a whole. That the state existed to promote economic development and the interests of businessmen (a distinction easier to make now than then, and easier to make even now by the observer than by the businessman) was not really in question; politics was, in significant part, about how that would be done.

These then are among the conclusions and perspectives raised by a focus on the commercial world of business in nineteenth-century Canada. As they indicate, that earlier world deserves understanding in its own terms, and not merely as a distant prelude to the real world of big business today. Indeed, while bigger business, with its far more complex structure and its greater wealth, power, and institutional permanence, has overlaid that earlier structure, it has not completely overwhelmed it. Traces of that earlier period can, after all, be found almost everywhere in Canada.

Thus, some sense of its outlook can be gained from the boosterism that even now characterizes the business outlook of most local business communities in Canada. The intricate connections and barriers among our government and business institutions can be given historical roots once an idealized, usually *laissez-faire*, model of the past is abandoned and the actual history of nineteenth-century business behaviour is considered. Entrepreneurial failure and inadequacy, on which so much historical research has focused, continue to be cited frequently as explanations for why something in the Canadian economy or business world has not happened as the observer would have preferred, just as entrepreneurial skill and success are often assumed to be explanations for the growth of new areas of the economy.

Finally, as is vividly exemplified still in the financial districts of Canada, where one finds the headquarters of, for example, most of the country's resource-extracting companies, the history of nineteenth-century Canadian business illustrates clearly the centrality of credit and the institutions by which it is managed in the overall structure and functioning of an economy.

2

Havy and Lefebvre of Quebec: A Case Study of Metropolitan Participation in Canadian Trade, 1730-60

Dale Miquelon

"Galants & aimables hommes . . . aimées et honnêtes gens."[1] So a contemporary described François Havy and Jean Lefebvre, who came to Canada in 1732 as the factors of Robert Dugard and Company of Rouen and remained prominent Lower Town merchants for more than a quarter of a century. Of Norman, Huguenot families of modest means, Havy probably twenty-three years old and Lefebvre only eighteen, they were young provincials resigning themselves to the colonial exile that had been the foundation of many metropolitan fortunes.[2] Representatives of a company that was of uncommon importance in Canada in the 1730's and 1740's, they have a certain intrinsic historical importance. But in all European colonies, as in all areas where European trade was significant, there were men like them, backed by businesses comparable to Dugard and Company. The social and economic historian therefore finds their importance as much in what they shared with others as in their individuality, seeing each, in the words of Phillippe Wolff, "le représentant d'un groupe sociale plus ou moins vaste, de son régime économique, de son statut juridique, des ses habitudes mentales...."[3] In this perspective, Havy and Lefebvre are representative Lower Town factors through whose letters and accounts the trade of colony and metropolis in the world of the eighteenth century may be apprehended.

Reprinted from *Canadian Historical Review*, LVI (1975), pp. 1-24, by permission of the author and University of Toronto Press.

In eighteenth-century Canada merchants were classed as *forain* or *domicilié*, the seasonal trader from across the Atlantic and his settled counterpart, attached by the interest of property or family to the colonial community in which he lived. But the traditional categories obscure the situation of the factors, one of the most important merchant groups, which came into existence because the needs of a metropolitan company's Canadian business could not be met by the services of transient supercargoes or *capitaines-géreurs*. The character of their duties and their little attachment to the colony might be such that they were scarcely distinguishable from the *marchands forains*. "Ils viennent passer ici deux ou trois an ou plus," wrote the intendant Bigot, who characterized them as "des marchands forains qui vont et viennent …."[4] But many factors stayed longer, marrying Canadians and founding families, although never cutting the transatlantic ties that were their *raison d'être* and that drew them back again to France. Men such as Antoine Pascaud in the seventeenth century and Denis Goguet in the eighteenth were *domiciliés*.[5] Many other metropolitans, including François Havy, were among the seventeen "principaux négocians" of Quebec who gathered at the *palais* to elect a syndic in 1740.[6] But the most important thing about them was not that they were *domiciliés*, but that they were Frenchmen backed by French businesses and aspiring to careers in France. In 1735 the intendant Hocquart estimated that Frenchmen, *forains* and *domiciliés*, were responsible for two-thirds of Canada's import/ export trade. The economic importance of this Lower Town enclave is known to have been considerable; its significance in the development of colonial life is a matter of conjecture.

Dugard and Company, or the Société du Canada as they formally called themselves (their bale mark, SDC, could stand for either), were a group drawn from five Rouen families, both Protestant and Catholic. Their company had begun with the building of a small ship, the *Louis Dauphin*, in 1729. The following year the ship made its first colonial voyage, visiting Quebec at St. Pierre de la Martinique with François Havy aboard as supercargo, a *marchand forain par excellence*. Havy and the *Louis Dauphin* returned to Quebec again in 1731. Risking only very small cargoes, the company in this way investigated the nature and potential of Canadian trade. They were optimistic. In 1732 they greatly increased their outlay on merchandise, began building up a fleet that numbered eight in 1740, and decided to establish Havy and his cousin Lefebvre at Quebec as permanent representatives.[7]

For Havy and Lefebvre, Robert Dugard, chief and inspirer of the company, was a kind of protector, a co-religionist willing to super-intend their start in life.[8] He hired these young and inexperienced men for a modest wage. Havy was satisfied with 1,000 livres per annum until the end of 1736 and 1,500 thereafter, while Lefebvre was originally hired at 600 livres per annum and may have received as much as 1,200 in his later years in Canada.[9] This was probably an anomalous arrangement as far as Canadian trade was concerned. According to Havy, most companies were represented in Canada either by commission agents earning 5 per cent on sales of incoming cargo and 2.5 per cent on the value of the returns they provided, or by traders associated with their European suppliers for a one-third share, alternatives more lucrative than salary.[10] As Havy remarked in his later years, "Il falloit Payer Mon aprentissage."[11] But there were other benefits to being a factor: a measure of independence, the keeping of large amounts of money and merchandise, the enjoyment of influence and of a certain reflected prestige. Havy and Lefebvre would make the most of these as the years went by.

Beginning with the first appearance of their corporate signature "Havy & Lefebvre" in 1734, while still employees, their living ex-penses charged to the company, they were also a business partner-ship, whether in relation to their employers or others. Under this signature they became involved in many enterprises for their own account. This was not uncommon among factors, although as Havy later denied having had private ventures in Canada while working for the company, Dugard may have forbidden it.[12] If so, his decrees were without effect. Nevertheless, until Dugard and Company with-drew from the Canada trade in 1747, the factors were concerned primarily with company business, the sale of French merchandise and the purchase of Canadian furs, bills of exchange, and produce for export. The letters and accounts of Robert Dugard, Havy and Lefebvre, their customers, and their competitors make possible a detailed understanding of these exchanges with regard to prices, profits, marketing practices, credit, and the relative market positions of metropolitans and colonials.

The Quebec merchants' busy season was framed by the arrival and departure of ships from France, Louisbourg, and the West Indies. The ships began to arrive in July and continued steadily through October. Furs from the hinterland as well as ships from France often came late to the town, and there was always a concen-tration of activity in the late summer and the autumn. In addition to cargo, the ships carried the mail, including letters and invoices for Quebec and Montreal merchants.[13] The mail was brought to town by messengers long before the ships arrived in port, some of it being forwarded to Montreal by freighters, travellers, or government couriers.[14] News of prices, shortages and oversupplies, prospective war and political changes passed swiftly among the merchants. Much of the commercial news was of a confidential nature; and as Havy and Lefebvre passed it on to their Montreal correspondent, Pierre Guy, they enjoined the strictest secrecy, "ne voulant pas passer pour auteurs de Gazettes de cette ville."[15] They supplemented postal communications with France by frequent visits, one of them always remaining behind at Quebec.[16] Visits to Montreal during the slack season of winter and early spring were also essential to efficient business operations.[17] The merchant was always a writer and a traveller, a specialist in communication.

The cargoes sent out from France and committed to the care of Quebec factors were transferred from merchantmen to small bateaux that carried them to the beach or directly to Montreal. Portions of Dugard and Company cargoes intended for specific customers, frequently in Montreal, were baled and marked accordingly in France, thus reducing handling to a minimum. It was up to the factors to oversee disembarking and forwarding, to ascertain the condition of the merchandise, and to declare imports of dutiable tobacco, wine, and spirits.[18]

Each year the Montreal merchants descended upon Quebec when they had been informed of the arrival of the ships.[19] Money and merchandise began to change hands, and in the classic manner prices soon found their level in response to the market. Of course, the market required a little prompting to arrive at a suitable price. The French invoices upon which the Canadian wholesale prices were based were always slightly inflated. This was generally known, and buyers compared the invoice prices of different importers, refusing to buy where they found prices too enthusiastically increased. According to Gilles Hocquart, the intendant of Canada, the invoices of Pascauds Frères of La Rochelle were always taken as the standard.[20] The level of inflation for the company cargo of 1743 can be measured because both the invoices sent to Robert Dugard by the suppliers of the cargo and invoice prices quoted to Pierre Guy for the same merchandise at Quebec are extant (see Table 1). These increases ranged from 2.5 per cent on eight-point blankets to 25 per cent on some steel items. The data also permit the calculation of an estimated increase of 5.88 per cent for the entire cargo.[21] The figure is low because the 1743 cargo, like all those of the company, consisted primarily of textiles. It corresponds to the 5 to 6 per cent estimated

Table 1
Inflation of Invoice Prices in Canada, 1743

Commodity	Price quoted in Canada	Original invoice	Per cent increase
Textiles			
Calmande rayé	29s	27s 6d	5.5
Calmande couleur	31s	29s 6d	5.1
Carisé	26s	25s	4.0
Beaufort	33-35s	29s	13.8
Blanket, 3 point	8#	7# 10s	6.7
Blanket, 8 point	20# 10s	20#	2.5
Toile d'allemagne	11# 15s	11# 6d	4.0
Other			
Spiggots	9# 10s	7# 14s 6d	18.0
Plowshares	20# cwt	17#	17.5
'Bottes d'acier'*	50#	40#	25.0
Candles	340#	312# 16s	8.8
Wax	120#	117#	2.6

*Identity of this item in doubt. Perhaps it refers to tied bundles of steels for use with flints.

SOURCE: SHM, Collection Pierre Guy, factures, especially item 24; AN, 62 AQ 41, 14e cargaison, Aller, factures.

as normal by a prominent Canadian businessman of the time, François Etienne Cugnet.[22]

However anomalous the inflation of the invoice might have been, it had come to be regarded as a prescriptive right of the seller. The profit, or *bénéfice*, determined by the market at Quebec was a percentage calculated on this inflated base (see Table 2). A normal peacetime *bénéfice* fell between 20 and 30 per cent.[23] For a given season, the *bénéfice* was uniform throughout the city. Each item in invoices made out for Canadian buyers was listed at the price of the false French invoice. As the *bénéfice* was usually the same for all kinds of merchandise, it was calculated on the total and added at the bottom. Practice sometimes deviated from this norm: different rates for certain commodities, a sale based on the rate of some future date, or a special price resulting from close bargaining (*à prix fait*).[24]

Wines and spirits were a thing apart. Neither were their invoice prices inflated nor were they sold at the *bénéfice* that prevailed for

Table 2
Level of Profit in Excess of Invoice Inflation
(*Bénéfice*), Quebec, 1740–47

Year	per cent
1740	18-25
1741	25-30
1742	20
1743	20
1744	55
1745	
Jan.	60
March	60
Sept.	80
Oct.	80-100
Nov.	80-100
1746	
Aug.	100-120
Oct.	120
Nov.	100-180
1747	
Oct.	100

SOURCE: SHM, Collection Pierre Guy, factures; PAC, Collection Baby, lettres de Havy et Lefebvre, 548-1102; ASQ, Polygraphie 24.

other merchandise. The prices Pierre Guy paid Havy and Lefebvre for wines in 1743 exceeded those of the original invoices by 128 per cent for red and 160 per cent for white.[25] These rates may have meant the difference between profit and loss on outward voyages, given that markups on most cargo items (invoice inflation plus *bénéfice*) fell in the modest range of 26 to 36 per cent. However, even in eighteenth-century Canada, demand for wines and spirits was not infinitely elastic. For example, these commodities constituted ony 6 per cent of the 1743 cargo, which grossed a profit of no more than 33.5 per cent. An anonymous "Mémoire sur la Domaine d'Occident en Canada (1736)" suggests that wines and spirits may have played a more significant role in the operations of other shippers, that they were "même à présent la principale occasion des armemens qui se font pour la colonie."[26] The memorial states that dry goods were usually included in *pacotilles* shipped for the account and risk of colonial traders, yielding only commission and freight to the metropolitan shippers, who reserved wines and spirits as *cargaison* – that is, to be shipped and sold for their own account. This distinction is not made in the accounts of Havy and Lefebvre and Robert Dugard, but it serves to underscore the crucial role of alcohol for all shippers.[27]

Havy and Lefebvre, like other Lower Town merchants, always stocked a wide range of goods that made it possible for a customer to satisfy all his needs at their warehouse. Failure to stock a proper *assortiment* reduced a merchant's ability to demand the current *bénéfice*. Havy and Lefebvre recount how "les mag^{sins} desassortis ont vendu a tous prix" and that a competitor's low prices reflected his lack of *assortiment*.[28] On one occasion Pierre Guy informed another Lower Town metropolitan factor, Jean-André Lamaletie, that he would only give him his business if Lamaletie could fill his order in its entirety.[29] By late winter nearly everyone in the Lower Town was usually *déassorti*, and the orders of Montreal customers could only be filled if the factors bought from each other.[30] The colony's capacity to absorb European goods varied according to economic and political conditions. Temporary shortages and gluts were common, and these had to be anticipated. The composition of their annual *mémoire*, or order for the following season's goods, may therefore be regarded as Havy and Lefebvre's most basic responsibility.

The credit system was closely linked with the practice of maintaining an *assortiment*, in part explaining why the latter was so important for gaining customers. Credit was extended in return for volume purchase. It was necessary, in the words of Governor Beauharnois, that the traders "trouvent de quoi s'assortir de tout ce qui est necessaire."[31] Having been enabled to make a large purchase, the customer "n'en paye souvent que la moitié et il luy est donné credit de l'autre." The Canada of Havy and Lefebvre was not a rich country. "L'indigence domine," wrote the governor and intendant. "On cherche à s'en tirer et à se procurer un peu d'aisance."[32] To finance their fur-gathering voyages and other enterprises, many Canadian traders turned not unnaturally to the Lower Town mandarins of the import-export trade for needed credit. The metropolitans, at once suppliers and creditors, clearly had the upper hand in such arrangements.

The debtor often signed a negotiable promissory note, or *billet à ordre*. Sometimes this was not considered sufficient guarantee, and Havy and Lefebvre required that an obligation be drawn up before a notary. Fourteen fur traders' obligations to the favour of Havy and Lefebvre are extant in the Quebec Archives.[33] They consist of a general encumbrance on the debtor's possessions "présent et à venir" and a special claim on the anticipated return of furs. While a specific date of maturity was agreed upon, the debt was considered due as soon as the fur canoes reached Montreal. The documents pertaining to Havy and Lefebvre suggest that in spite of its obvious merit in the eyes of creditors, the obligation did not displace the promissory note as the most common credit instrument among merchants, perhaps because it was not negotiable.

Taken together, the signers of obligations and *billets à ordre* accounted for no more than half of Havy and Lefebvre's total sales. Analogy with European practice suggests that considerable business was done by current account, a conjecture borne out by the fragmentary records extant. The Séminaire de Québec still possesses accounts showing the sale of agricultural products to Havy and Lefebvre and their purchase from them of French merchandise.[34] The accounts of Pierre Guy provide yet another example. But while there is an essential element of credit in the current account, it is not to be thought of in the same light as debts secured by notes and obligations. Credit by current account was short-term, being in principle settled on an annual basis; low-risk, being confined to stable business friends; and most important of all, it was reciprocal. Debit and credit transactions were continually cancelling each other out. In itself, the web of reciprocal accounts rendered Canadian business more efficient and stable rather than adding to its fragility. Of course, its outermost threads were invariably attached to the brittle twigs of a second or third party's own debtors, for example the fur traders outfitted by Guy at Montreal.

Credit was thus crucial and, next to the adjudication of the needs of the market, it was probably the extension of credit that most exercised the factors' judgement. While the misfortunes that befell their correspondents might have repercussions on Havy and Lefebvre's own business, the risks of credit can only be apprehended in the case of loans secured by notes and obligations. Only for the period 1730 to 1738 are the identities and liabilities of the total body of these debtors known.[35] Most of their loans were small, 80 per cent of them under 2,000 livres, although most credit extended by value was accounted for by larger loans, over 2,000 livres. A mere 4 per cent (those over 5,000 livres) accounted for almost half of the credit extended. Still, few of the debtors were remarkable for the large size of their borrowings. Only four – Foucher, Gaudet, d'Auteuil, and Volant d'Hautebourg (himself a front man for Havy and Lefebvre) – carried the five-figure loans that were common and frequent among

Europeans such as Robert Dugard and his circle. Over the years the character of the debtor group changed such that the small debts were concentrated at the beginning of the 1730's and the larger ones at the end. Extant obligations from the 1740's add five names to the catalogue of men of substance – Montford, D'Ailleboust, Texier, Auger, and Béner.[36] This tendency toward large figures would seem to be an indication of concentration and hence a reflection of the maturation of the Canadian economic community.

Were all these debtors prompt in redeeming their notes, the advances made by the company in one year would be offset by the redemption of the previous year's debt. The extension of credit would not interfere with the factor's ability to prepare a return cargo equal to or greater than the value of the outward cargo sold in Canada. In the jargon of the time, they would be able to make their returns. However, a significant proportion of debts was paid very slowly. Of the 144 advances against notes and obligations made by Havy and Lefebvre in the 1730's, ninety or 62.5 per cent were redeemed within one year. An additional 7 per cent were redeemed within two years. The remaining 30 per cent were redeemed in various lengthy terms such as one-half in six months and one-half in six years or one-third in one year and another third in two years with a final payment in three years. One was outstanding for nine years, and many became lost debts. Over the years the unpaid debts mounted up and the percentage of the total debt returned each year was usually much less than 62.5 per cent (see Table 3). Debt was thus

Table 3
The Accumulation of Debts Owing
(Promissory Notes and Obligations), 1730–38

Year	Debts owing paid	As % of debt owing	Debts owing carried	New credit extended	Total extended
1730				2,835	2,835
1731	2,835	100	0	3,025	3,025
1732	1,603	53	1,422	22,652	24,074
1733	18,831	78	5,243	43,208	48,451
1734	26,426	55	22,025	27,501	49,526
1735	22,061	54	27,465	46,837	74,302
1736	33,393	48	40,909	23,707	64,616
1737	37,496	58	27,116	37,818	64,934
1738	16,974	26	47,960	57,171	105,131

SOURCE: AN, 62 AQ 40, Comptes de gestion à Québec 1730-38.

a factor that served to slow the return on investment in the Canadian trade and hence to reduce its profitability.

As the trading season advanced, Havy and Lefebvre's warehouse filled with return cargo. The most important single item was, of course, fur. A third area in which they were called upon to exercise skilled judgement was therefore the appraisal and pricing of furs. All furs other than beaver were sold on an open market. The manner in which quantities and prices are entered into accounts suggests that once the price of a good-quality pelt was determined, a specific lot was examined for quality. If the furs were inferior in whole or in part, the lot was regarded as equal to a lesser number of perfect pelts and their total value was computed on that basis.[37] Sometimes the valuation might be decided by arbitration.[38] In any case, it was a buyer's market. Jean-André Lamaletie's adviso to Pierre Guy, "Jaye passé vos Martres a 40s ... quant ala mitraille Je n'en ay pas fait encore le pris ...." shows how little say the seller had in price determination.[39] All extra charges were passed on to him, just as all those on incoming French merchandise had been assigned to him as purchaser by the adjustment of the *bénéfice*. In another letter Lamaletie explained to Guy, "Il ne seroit pas juste que je vous la payasse. Le meme prix des annees precedentes puisque le fret et les assurances ont considerablement augmenté."[40] That the Canadian trader rather than the ultimate metropolitan purchaser of fur goods should have borne the brunt of these charges indicates that the colonial fur sellers were unable to curb supply or otherwise influence the market in their favour.

Bills of exchange were another important export. A large part of these was given to Canadian traders in exchange for beaver pelts by the Compagnie des Indes, which held a monopoly on their export. These bills thus represented purchasing power gained in return for a commodity export. Other bills drawns on the French government and received in exchange for Canadian paper money were exported because Canada could not provide sufficient exports to balance its foreign trade. As their continued use was a measure of Canadian economic underdevelopment, it is significant that the proportion of Havy and Lefebvre's "returns" constituted by bills of exchange declined from between 37 and 44 per cent in the period 1730 – 32 to 4 to 13 per cent in the years 1741 – 43 (see Table 4).[41] The quantity and range of Canadian export items was increasing.

In the case of Havy and Lefebvre, ships were a very important new item of export. Between 1736 and 1745 they launched six ships for the company, having a combined value of almost 300,000 livres.[42] The first of these, the *Alçion*, was begun in 1734, the year after a revised system of royal bounties for Canadian-built ships was estab-

Table 4
The Declining Importance of Bills of Exchange in returns
from Quebec, 1730-44 (percentage of returns constituted by drafts)

1730	37
1731	44
1732	38
1733	19
1734	24
1735	24
1736	13½
1737	10½
1738	10½
1739	11¾
1740	9½
1741	5
1742	13
1743	4
1744	44

SOURCE: AN, 62 AQ 40, Comptes de gestion à Québec, 1730–44; Compte de balance de Havy et Lefebvre, Québec, 15 juil. 1746.

lished.[43] While bounties could not fully offset the high cost of labour in an underpopulated country, the Rouen company persevered in building ships because they were yet another item of export, providing the means of repatriating outlays in Canada.

Dugard and Company also maintained an extensive trade in the West Indies.[44] Imbued with the same concept of self-sufficient mercantilist empire that moved colonial administrators, solicitous of the Caribbean market's need for a proper *assortiment*, and alive to any new profit potential, the company not surprisingly attempted to tie together their Canadian and West Indian trades. To this aspiration Louisbourg was the key, and there Dugard and Company maintained permanent relations with a commission agent, Léon Fautoux. The soldier and fisherman population of Louisbourg depended to a considerable extent upon Canadian provisions, and most company ships stopped there on their return voyages from Quebec. Canadian cargoes of wood and grain were also suitable for the West Indian market when their profitability was increased by the addition of dried cod available at Louisbourg. However, the sugar island trade remained marginal as Canada could surrender its major export of

fur only in exchange for French manufactures to supply the fur trade
and could neither absorb a large quantity of Caribbean produce nor
provide a sufficiently large and dependable supply of provisions and
forest products in return. Thus, of the sixty-eight voyages to Canada
and the West Indies undertaken by the company between 1730 and
1755, only ten were triangular.

If none of the voluminous correspondence that passed between
Robert Dugard in Rouen and Havy and Lefebvre in Quebec is
extant, nonetheless there remain many accounts that provide an
outline history of the Quebec factory.[45] The company's volume of
trade in Canada may be judged from the accounts recording Havy
and Lefebvre's receipts for each year from the sale of French cargoes
as well as the payments made by customers moving freight on
company ships and the value of their annual "returns," which consisted of cargo, bills of exchange, paying freight, newly built ships,
and the year's expenses (see Table 5). Dugard and Company's commitment to the Canada trade, indicated by the establishing of the
factory in 1732, was reflected in the increased volume of trade in that
year. For the next seven years receipts clustered around the 200,000-

Table 5
Receipts and Returns of the Quebec Factory, 1732-45
(numbers rounded off to nearest whole livre)

Year	Receipts	Returns
1732	150,081	109,370
1733	225,148	211,785
1734	153,513	130,283
1735	203,091	205,395
1736	195,535	199,200
1737	220,212	217,578
1738	276,589	217,885
1739	234,673	213,414
1740	334,563	329,800
1741	362,570	410,257
1742	193,666	155,000
1743	232,684	215,931
1744	104,357	118,571
1745	119,275	212,593

SOURCE: AN, 62 AQ 40, Compte de balance de Havy et Lefebvre, Québec, 15
juil. 1746.

livre mark. The next notable change occurred in 1740, when they were boosted to the level of 300,000 livres, there to remain until suddenly reduced in 1742 to what they had been prior to 1740.

If these figures are compared with those very rough estimates of the value of French merchandise annually imported into Canada prepared by the Canadian intendancy, the relative importance of Dugard and Company's Canadian trade becomes apparent.[46] From 1733 on it usually accounted for an eighth or a tenth of the colony's import trade, rising to a sixth in 1738, a seventh in 1740, and a fifth in 1741.

In its essentials the task set Havy and Lefebvre was to receive and sell the cargoes sent by Dugard as advantageously as possible and to provide the best possible returns. Their performance may thus be judged by how well they succeeded in providing returns equal or superior in value to their annual receipts. Figure 1 illustrates this for the period from 1730, when Havy first brought a cargo to Quebec, to 1743, year of the last cargo received before the war of the Austrian Succession radically changed the conditions of Atlantic commerce and the fortunes of Dugard and Company. Specifically, it shows by what percentage returns exceeded or fell short of the factory's receipts for a given year; for convenience, it may be termed the curve of returns. It is an index of the performance of a business

Figure 1
The Curve of Returns, 1730–43

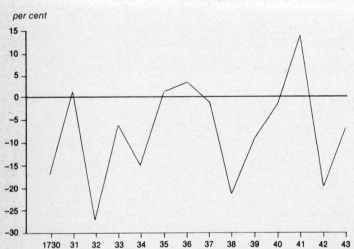

house as well as an indicator of the fortunes of the Canadian economy, reflecting its capacity to support an export trade and to pay its debts abroad. The close correspondence of the curve to other economic indices lends credence to all. As the economic history of this period has been interpreted in terms of the vicissitudes of the money supply, the fur trade, and the production of wheat, it is with these that the curve of returns is compared.[47] Similarity to or a tendency for the curve to indicate greater buoyancy than these indices can be taken as a demonstration of the competent management of the Havy and Lefebvre-Dugard business, because it would be the result of the maximization of possibilities. The nature of the articulation of the import-export trade to other economic sectors is also illuminated.

Although France's monetary policy with regard to Canada was never satisfactory and both local officials and merchants continually clamoured for an increase in the money supply, sound money was probably more available in this period, especially the later 1730's and the 1740's, than in any other time in the colony's history.[48] It is, however, possible that the drop in returns evident in 1732 and 1734 is related to the inadequacy of the supply of bills of exchange on France. In each of these years Havy and Lefebvre were left at year's end with substantial sums of money in the cash box and owing by current accounts. There were 19,909 livres listed under this heading in 1732 and 29,044 livres in 1734. These balances were responsible for the significant drop in returns in those years.[49] The relation between the balance in 1734 and the inadequacy of the bill market, in the colonial setting largely dependent upon government redemptions, would seem to be confirmed by Hocquart's report to Maurepas that in that year he could not redeem all the paper brought to him and was forced to return one-fifth of it to the merchants in the form of cards.[50]

Yet if capital were in short supply and hence a brake on economic expansion, the want of it was at least a constant. After 1734 the unavailability of metropolitan exchange appears to have caused no annual variation in the returns of Havy and Lefebvre. Returns were articulated to the possibilities offered by the money supply; what is chronic can at least be depended upon.

With fur holding pride of place among Canada's exports, it is to be expected that there would be a notable correspondence between the ability of Havy and Lefebvre to make returns and the fortunes of the fur trade. The latter may be traced by means of tables of the amount of beaver in pounds accepted by the Compagnie des Indes from 1729 to 1745 and the value of *menus pelleteries* entering La Rochelle in livres *tournois* for the years 1729 to 1741, both long since compiled by Jean Lunn. These have been used as an index of the vicissitudes of the fur trade.[51]

Although there is no correspondence between the fortunes of the trade and the first three years of company operations in Canada, it is very marked for the next five trading seasons, 1733-37. For 1738, the correspondence is broken and the relation even inverse. Although beaver is down in 1739, other furs are up, maintaining the similarity. The trends compare in 1740 and perhaps in 1741, although the fortunes of fur in the latter year are by no means clear. There is no figure for pounds of beaver accepted; and the drop in the value of all furs imported to La Rochelle may be so great because of large exports to Le Havre for Dugard and Company, 1741 being the year of Havy and Lefebvre's greatest return, both in absolute terms and relative to sales and freight payments received. However, the definite increase in pounds of beaver delivered in 1742 is not at all paralleled by the curve. Indeed, in that year returns are in complete disarray. The continued rise in pounds of beaver delivered in 1743 and 1744 conforms to the rise of the curve of returns.

The third index, the state of the harvests, is reflected in the curve of the price of wheat established by Jean Hamelin, a price rise reflecting the poor harvest of the previous year.[52] The general downward trend in the price of wheat, 1730-35, parallels the general upward trend of the returns. The price of wheat, 1739-41, which is indicative of an adequate supply, corresponds with another upward trend. But the outstanding correlation is between the plummeting returns and the skyrocketing wheat prices of the years 1737-38 and 1742. The crop failures of 1736, 1737, and 1741 have completely upset the steady upward trend of the curve of returns.

Havy's returns for 1730 and 1731, years before the founding of the trading factory marked by a very small investment, demonstrate no correspondence with the indices of money supply, fur, and wheat. The failure to make a full return in 1732 is most easily explained in terms of a shortage of bills of exchange. But once the factory was established and the regular expansion of the money supply assured (after 1734), the ability to make returns closely paralleled the fortunes of the colony's twin economic foundations, fur and wheat. The importance of wheat to the well being of a large trading company is unexpected. So significant were the setbacks of 1738 and 1742 and so long was the period of recovery, that regular crop failures were the single most important factor retarding the orderly growth and profitability of the company's trade. This can be shown in yet another way. The percentage of debts owing to the company as of 1738 that were paid in that year was only 26 per cent, the smallest for any year of the decade (see Table 3). The business undertaken for Dugard and Company in Canada by Havy and Lefebvre was obviously not confined to fur. Although wheat occupied but a modest place among exports, the data suggest, nevertheless, that it supplied the consumer needs of the colonists, who depended upon wheat to provide payment that by the time of its remittance to France, at least, was no longer grain. It is also possible that by some indirect means crop failures hampered the capacity of fur traders to pay their debts, but the present case study throws no further light on this question.

By 1743 the fortunes of Dugard and Company had reached their zenith. The company's investment in trade was enormous both in Canada and in the West Indies. At Quebec, when Hocquart was forced to commandeer the crew of the company's *Centaure* to man the *Vaisseau du Roi*, he did everything in his power to help Havy and Lefebvre find replacements, his intention being "de favoriser une comp^{ie} qui soutient depuis quinze ans des entreprises considerable et utiles ala Colonie."[53] Given equally appreciative comments penned by officials at Versailles, it is surprising that the coveted reward of the contract to supply the king's warehouse in Canada should have escaped the company.[54] They were a serious contender for the award, but were ruled out by an old enemy, geography. As Hocquart explained, "Les Srs. Pascaud meriteroient la préférance, ils sont plus a portée que M. Dugard de remplir à votre satisfaction leurs engagemens avec Le Roy par le Voisinage dela Rochelle du Port de Rochefort Et par la Relation que ces négocians doivent avoir avec M de Ricouart" [intendant at Rochefort].[55]

It was with this disappointment, as well as the loss of two ships, the *Alçion* and the *Louis Dauphin*, to heavy seas, that the company entered the period of the war of the Austrian Succession. The war did not spare the company. Between 1744 and 1747, the *St. Mathieu*, the *Imprévû*, and the *Fleury*, as well as a chartered vessel, the *Thétis*, were captured. The *Union* was shipwrecked in a storm; and the *Trois Maries*, carrying company cargo from Canada and owned in part by some members, was sunk in a collision. Because of the dearth of shipping in Canada, Havy and Lefebvre launched a company ship, the *Astrée*, that had long lain on the stocks for want of cargo. The *Astrée* was so badly mauled on its stormy maiden voyage that its repair took two years.[56] It is therefore understandable that the company shared the views expressed by one member, that it was time to liquidate "toutes nos affaires et cesser un commerce si declaré contre nous."[57] Thus, late in 1747 Havy and Lefebvre, who had reeived very little merchandise during the war, were informed that the company had decided to wind up its Canadian business.[58] From November 1, 1747, the company would cease to pay the rent of the warehouse and the room, board, and wages of their former factors. As the company still possessed three ships, all too old to fetch a good price, they continued to use them as sugar haulers in the West Indian trade. But this was little more than a caretaker operation. The great days of the company were over, and the Canadian chapter of its history definitively closed.

Havy and Lefebvre were thus on their own. The last strands of their tie with Dugard and Company were cut slowly, as for some years they continued to sell off a residue of merchandise on the company's behalf.[59] In the 1750's they owned a ship, the *Parfaite Union*, in company with Dugard, acting in his own right, and a fourth party, probably Jean Jacquelin, whom Dugard had sent to Quebec to help them in the 1740's.[60] While the entrepreneurs of the Société du Canada were being drawn into many other enterprises, so too were Havy and Lefebvre. Even during the war they had small interests of their own in schooners and bateaux sailing to Louisbourg and the West Indies.[61] Released now from their close liaison with the Société du Canada, they also acted as commission agents for at least two other metropolitan shippers, Jean Gardère of Bayonne and a Sieur Garisson of Bordeaux.[62] Much of their capital was invested in houses and properties in and around Quebec and in mortgages, providing them with some immunity against the fickle ups and downs of trade.[63]

Havy and Lefebvre's most important investments were in sealing/ trading stations on the lower North Shore and the coast of Labrador. Almost all of the more than twenty posts in the region were established in the eighteenth century, over half of them after Utrecht. Havy and Lefebvre's investment began in the 1730's, the decade of the greatest number of new foundations.[64] The buildings, ships, and hired labour required by the sealing industry were expensive. There was a high element of risk resulting from the vagaries of migrating seal, the depredations of Eskimos, and, in wartime, Anglo-American privateers. Even in good years the profits were not inordinately high. But seal oil had a special attraction because, unlike wheat and lumber, it was destined for the French market. It thus filled the holds of ships that would have returned to the metropolis mostly in ballast, earning precious credits to help pay for Canadian imports.

From 1737 to 1748 Havy and Lefebvre held a lease on a post at Mingan, exploited on their behalf by Jean-Louis Volant D'Hautebourg to whom they advanced 37,500 livres in merchandise on credit in 1737 and 1738. It was an advantage of their position that as representatives of Dugard and Company they were able to extend credit to themselves. In the same capacity they bought the oil produced.[65] In 1737 they began exploitation of a post at Baie des Châteaux on the Strait of Belle Isle for a one-third share along with Louis Fornel and the post's concessionaire, Louis Bazil.[66] They also sublet a two-thirds interest in the concession of Grand Saint-Modet in 1740.[67] Although a third of the 100,000 livres invested at Baie des Châteaux was lost when the coast of Labrador was cut off from Quebec during the war, Havy and Lefebvre appear to have maintained an interest there until 1754, when the post's ship and sealing equipment, described as belonging to them, were sold at public auction.[68] The original lease on Grand Saint-Modet ended in 1747, but there is evidence that they sent a ship there as late as 1758, this being their last known sealing venture.[69]

Before the war, Havy and Lefebvre's associate, Fornel, had explored the Labrador coast beyond Baie des Châteaux, partly at their expense, and had discovered and laid claim to an excellent site for sealing and trade, the Baie des Esquimaux.[70] Fornel had died in 1745, but Havy and Lefebvre maintained close business relations with his widow, Marie-Anne Barbel. With access to the coast again free, Widow Fornel claimed the post for herself, Havy, and Lefebvre. On September 20, 1749, they were given the concession for twelve years.[71] At the same time, under the name Veuve Fornel et Cie, they also received a six-year lease of the King's Posts.[72] This they relinquished in 1755, fearing war losses. They were the last lessees of the Old Régime.[73]

In the careers of François Havy and Jean Lefebvre a complete evolution appears to have taken place between 1730 and 1755. They first appeared in the colony as typical *marchands forains*. In the next few years they linked their fortunes with Canada through a variety of investments. They undoubtedly were then to be classed as *domiciliés*, and their stay in the colony would be a long one. Then there was the break with Dugard, and the former factors elected to remain in the colony, evidently the seat of their strongest economic attachments. How surprising, then, that in 1756 they began the transfer of their economic interests from Quebec to La Rochelle. In fact, their removal was a foregone conclusion; only the time and the manner were determined by the play of events. If Catholic merchants who had established families in Canada returned to the metropolis when they could do so with economic advantage, how much more must it have been the rule for Huguenots such as Havy and Lefebvre, free neither to marry in the colony nor to bring to it established families.

The occasion for departure was the war that broke out at the forks of the Ohio in 1754. Under hazardous but potentially profitable wartime conditions, Havy and Lefebvre decided that one of them should return to France to supervise their export of merchandise to Canada as well as to prepare for their eventual re-establishment in France. In January, 1756, having "échappé à la griffe des anglais," Havy arrived at La Rochelle.[74] There commerce was at a standstill. In 1757 two years' supply of Canadian fur remained unsold and money was of surprising rarity.[75] French policy was to let French shippers take care of themselves while neutral shipping was depended upon to supply the colonies. "N'est-il pas terrible," wrote Havy, "que la Cour ne donne aucun secours ni protection au commerce."[76] In 1758 Louisbourg fell to the English, leaving them poised on the threshold of Canada. By February, 1759, there were few ships available, even fewer seamen, and no insurers. Havy believed France to be lost in lethargy and feared the loss of Canada itself, "Cette grande et Belle Colonie," dragging in its train the collapse of the Marine and the loss of the West Indian colonies.[77] It was his pious hope that God in his infinite goodness would preserve "tout le Pauvre Canada et singulierement son Brave et Pauvre peuple."[78]

In 1758 Havy announced his intention to remain permanently at La Rochelle.[79] His marriage into the François family of Bordeaux, "Riche et de bien honnettes Gens," had probably already taken place.[80] In business, however, nothing was succeeding for him and Lefebvre. He was quarrelling with Robert Dugard, who was only then winding up the affairs of the Société du Canada, which had continued modest operations in the Caribbean until the loss of its last ship in 1756. It was difficult for Havy to find justice in the world about him. So many had been enriched in Canada, while he wagered that there had been no metropolitan merchant in the colony who had worked as hard as he.[81] The worst was yet to come. The Battle of Quebec on September 13, 1759, and the government's suspension of payments on all colonial paper on the 15th of October following consummated the ruin of the House of Havy and Lefebvre. "La prise du Canada," Havy reported to Dugard, "nous a [,] au Sr. Lefebvre et moy [,] Emporté Touts Les fruits de nos immence Travaux parce quil nous restoit gros En divers Etablissements de Toutte Espece surtout des pesche Pour le loup marin des debte hypotesque sur des maisons

[.] Tout cela a esté detruit et par consequent tous est perdu et depuis que je suis en France Je nay fait que perdre et rien ne ma reuisi [.] Les Banqueroutes dans lesquelle je me trouve Les lettre de Change du Canada qui ne se paye point &c Tout cela menes aux abois."[82]

The siege of Quebec had left the town, in Havy's words, a heap of stone and debris.[83] There Jean Lefebvre spent the difficult winter of 1759-60. In the spring he found more comfortable accommodation on the Ile d'Orléans, where he remained until October along with François Levesque, a cousin of himself and Havy who had earlier come out to work with them. When he learned of the surrender of the colony, Lefebvre prepared to rejoin Havy at La Rochelle, writing of "mon voyage projetté pour Europe que je desire Longtems, notamment depuis le Boulversem^t arrivé dans ce pays cy, dont je voy une triste fin."[84] In October, leaving his affairs in Levesque's hands, he left Canada forever aboard the English warship, *Trident*.[85]

From the middle of August, 1760, until the end of the following January, François Havy struggled with a long illness. When fully recovered, he was advised of the death of Lefebvre during his return voyage, news that had long been withheld from him. He confessed that it broke his heart. He had counted on the great pleasure of their being together again, but he wrote: "Dieu na pas voulu Nous donner Cette Cestisfaction Son Saint Nom Soit Beny a Jamais."[86] Havy accepted no new obligations of trade.[87] In 1762 or 1763 he and his family moved to Bordeaux, where he could be advised and helped by his in-laws.[88] There are indications that he was no longer mentally fit for business.[89] It was at Bordeaux that he died, at the age of fifty-seven, on December 12, 1766.[90]

From 1732 to 1760 either Havy or Lefebvre was always at Quebec. They were part of that Lower Town community of metropolitan merchants that constituted an intrusion of the French bourgeoisie into the Canadian colony. But Lower Town was not a ghetto. Havy and Lefebvre's letters bear witness to their continuous interaction with the native Canadian business community and to warm friendships with Canadians. Lending their services to some, bestowing their friendship upon others, how much did Havy, Lefebvre, and their fellow metropolitans transmit something of their own bourgeois attitudes and habits of mind to the colonists? In this regard, the most promising area for investigation is that of commercial practice.

Trade in Canada being to such a large degree dependent on credit extended by metropolitans, its occurrence naturally brought with it the whole European apparatus of promissory notes, personal bonds, mortgages, the taking of interest, and redress through the courts for commercial causes. Indeed, it is impossible to see how trade could have been effectively maintained without the demands of trade leaving their mark on the legal system through the use of the *Code Marchand* (1675). Many of the letters of Havy and Lefebvre instructing Guy on how he in turn should instruct the notaries representing them in Montreal courts seem to presuppose its application. For example, in a remarkable letter of February 8, 1747, they explain that a customer had given them a *brevet* in place of a bill of exchange and that therefore "quand aux interets en qualité de marchands nous avons droit de les exiger parce que ce qui est pour fait commerce emporte les interets dautant que ce Brevet nous a esté donné au lieu et place dune Lettre dechange il ni a pas doute qu'on paye le retard et le Rechange dune Lettre . . . ."[91] The *greffes des notaires* and the records of the Canadian courts will, of course, have to be the object of more considerable research than heretofore if the extent to which the bourgeois mind impressed itself on the Canadian legal system is to be measured.

In this same letter, Havy and Lefebvre go on to expound their refreshingly modern and pragmatic views on money and interest, surprising to a present-day reader who may think of eighteenth-century ideas on these subjects in terms of the theorizing of schoolmen or physiocrats. "Quels sont les outils dun Marchand(?)" they ask. "Cest de largent[.] Sil nen a point Il ne peut travailler." They explain that they charge the common French mercantile rate of 6 per cent for their advances, defending the practice in terms of the above analogy of money with tools: "Si quelqu'un retient les outils dun ouvrier et que cela Lempesche d'exercer son art Celui qui en est cause ne doit il pas payer le retard(?)" There is, however, a certain tone of self-justification in this letter that suggests that their arguments did not enjoy universal acceptance. Perhaps they found they had to press such views on colonials, just as they had to exert pressure (along with the government) to have their suppliers sift grain intended for export, higher metropolitan standards exacting that it be clean.[92] What a burden of impatience with things colonial is implicit in such a rare and unexpected outburst as Havy's excuse to Dugard that errors in his accounts were understandable "surtout de la fasson dont le commerce ce fais en Canada."[93]

The Montreal merchants are a group that will amply repay study by historians. They came into existence to connect the metropolitans at tidewater with a hinterland beyond their reach, demanding trading techniques of a special nature. With regard to this question of mentality, it is important to ask to what extent they were capable of receiving the impress of metropolitan values, to what extent they really did dominate Canada's central economic activity, and whether their place in society was such that they were a ready instrument for the transmission of values to Canadian society as a whole. Were they and their counterparts of Lower Town dominant or too weak to influence a society established on norms other than their own, evolving through the interaction of other, more pertinent aspects of French society with the imperatives of a new and singular environment?

If the question of the extent to which men like Havy and Lefebvre influenced Canadian mentality is an open one, there is no doubt that Canada itself influenced the hearts and minds of Havy and Lefebvre. Havy's reference to Canada as "Cette grande et Belle Colonie" and to Canadians as "son Brave et Pauvre peuple" have already been quoted. To these may be added his protestation in a last letter to a Canadian, "Jay toujours aimé votre Pays et ses habitans."[94] According to traditional mythology, these are strange sentiments for a metropolitan, even if he were not exactly a *marchand forain*. The sojourn of Havy and Lefebvre in Canada was no rapacious visitation. Their solid investments in real property, shipping, and sealing stations tied their own prosperity to that of the colony. In 1744-48 they scorned excessive wartime profits as immoral ("Le Bien General et plus a souhaitter que le nostre particulier"),[95] and warned that in the long run such windfall profits did nothing for the country or its trade: "Ils nous faudroit une Bonne paix pour travailler solidement a lagrandissement du commerce de ce pays."[96] "Travailler solidement" captures the spirit in which Havy and Lefebvre had come to Canada. In the best romantic style, they were there to seek their fortunes, but Fortune was to be wooed by hard work. "Il n'y ait eu aucun marchand foreign qui ait autant travaillé que Moy," wrote Havy toward the end of his life.[97]

While in Canada, Havy and Lefebvre did manifest a high degree of identification with the colony. In 1747 they were sufficiently Canadianized that they could refer to French itinerants derisively as "ces petits Messieurs Les forains."[98] But Havy and Lefebvre were not immigrants. At the end of their history is the return to the metropolis. La Rochelle still dominated the trade of Canada. Dugard and Company, while having first depended upon La Rochelle, had been powerful enough to break this link eventually and swing a significant portion of Canadian trade north to Le Havre-Rouen.[99] In this they had almost no imitators and when they withdrew from

Canadian trade, La Rochelle was left a primacy challenged only by Bordeaux.[100] Thus, in an age when provincial identities were exceedingly strong, this metropolitanism within a metropolis drew these two Norman traders to Saintonge.

The main lines of a trading system were not easily disrupted. Montreal, Quebec, La Rochelle – each was a link in a chain from hinterland to metropolis. Each was also a rung on a mercantile ladder of preferment that led from colonial obscurity to European positions of wealth and prestige. The life of a colonial trader was not to be preferred to the promises of a commercial metropolis, least of all by men like Havy and Lefebvre, for whom the road from yet another obscurity, that of provincial Normandy, led not to, but via Canada.

3

Capital and Labour in the Halifax Baking and Confectionery Industry during the Last Half of the Nineteenth Century*

Ian McKay

Introduction

Industrial capitalism developed in three stages. In the handicraft stage, associated in Europe with guilds and in both Europe and North America with small workshops, production was carried out by small groups of journeymen working under a master, or by small masters in isolation. At a certain stage, "where the minimum sum advanced for production greatly exceeds the maximum of the middle ages," the increase in the size of the workshop and its labour force effected a dramatic change in the conditions of the labour process. This second stage, "manufacture," came about in two ways: by the gathering together of workers belonging to various independent handicrafts, who each contributed to the completion of the product, and by the bringing together of a number of craftsmen who each did

*I should like to thank Judith Fingard, David Frank, Craig Heron, Greg Kealey, Larry McCann, Del Muise, Bryan Palmer, Nolan Reilly, and David Sutherland for comments on an earlier draft of this paper. Newspapers mentioned in the notes were published in Halifax, except where otherwise noted. This paper was first presented at the Atlantic Canada Studies Conference, 1978.

Reprinted from *Labour/Le Travailleur*, 3 (1978), pp. 63-108, with the permission of the author and of the editor. © Committee on Canadian Labour History.

the same thing, but whose craft was broken down into its successive manual operations. The third stage in the development of industrial capitalism was that of "modern industry," which in its primitive form meant the replacement of the tool of the craftsman by the machine, and in its more developed form involved the evolution of the "collective machine," an organized system of many machines. The end point of the process was the performance by the machine of the same operations that had been done by the workman with his tools.[1]

Although these ideas from *Capital* have long formed the basis of critical study of the logic of capitalist development, they have suffered a curious neglect from labour historians. Part of the reason for this may be the inherent conservatism of a "labour" history content with the study of the *results*, but not the *process*, of capitalist development. Another reason why this model has had little apparent resonance is the misconception that each stage in the development of capitalism corresponds to a chronological period. As Raphael Samuel has recently demonstrated, a "mainly hand technology" dominated many sectors of the nineteenth-century British economy. Moreover, he points out that even in those sectors dominated by machinery, the machine itself might create more skills than it destroyed. He proposes that the stages be seen as concurrent phases of production, and that the classical antithesis of labour-power and machinery be qualified by a recognition of the complementary roles of both. It would be difficult to accept the view that no periodization can be elaborated from Marx's analysis, for it should be possible to say that in certain periods the workshop unquestionably dominates, or that in others mass production has relegated prior phases of production to the periphery. But Samuel's notion of "concurrent phases of capitalist growth" is a useful corrective to the chronological approach, in that it leads one to analyse the precise configuration of combined and uneven development within the capitalist mode. One effect of such analysis must be the questioning of the well-rooted theory that "artisans" were generally confronted by the "factory." It would rather appear, given the acknowledgement of concurrent phases, that industry both created and destroyed crafts; that many craftsmen responded not to factories but to manufactories; and that the ideological orientation of class struggles of craftsmen was determined by their precise position vis-à-vis the workshop, manufactory, and factory.[2]

In the Canadian setting further distinctions must be made between those industrial establishments imposed by mercantile or industrial capital with the purpose of substituting Canadian for British or

American manufactured goods, and those factories that emerged from workshops and manufactures. In the first instance, one might conjecture, the absence of native craftsmen would have a deadening effect on the workplace struggles that could emerge. Another distinction that must be made is not between phases of industrial capitalism, but between modes of production themselves: the production of use-values within households remained an important feature of many nineteenth-century communities. Thus we have a complex period of concurrent modes of production in certain sectors and places and concurrent phases of industrial production.[3]

The inner logic of the period was, to be sure, the emergence of industrial capitalism as the dominant mode, and many craftsmen did confront manufactures and factories as threats to their livelihood. This confrontation took place in at least five ways. Outright proletarianization forced craftsmen into advanced industrial production: the individual craftsman was brought to the machine. This would seem to be the situation of many North American shoemakers.[4] The second way involved a period of uneasy coexistence of the handicraft, manufactory, and factory, each within the same category of production (as was the case of bakers). Third, the handicraft might be slowly made irrelevant to the wider economy without any significant transfer of craftsmen to industry. Here one thinks of sailmakers and shipwrights. Fourth, the craft might remain dominant in its field, primarily within manufactures, and thus be in a strong position to create monopolies of skill and job control. This would seem to be the case of the printers, machinists, and patternmakers. Finally, the craft might easily adapt itself to the industrial age, or even to factory production directly, without any significant alteration of skills. This may have been the case of barbers, who seem to have been largely unaffected by industry, and of plumbers, who both in workshops and factories continued to enjoy the privileges of craftsmen.[5]

Historians have been slow to develop the theoretical framework to evaluate the relative importance of each of these paths and the effects of each on class struggle and class consciousness. It does not appear unlikely that the second path of "concurrent phases" was of critical importance. Whatever the most important type of craft evolution, the sheer diversity of craft experience renders somewhat questionable any fixation on either primitive rebellion against the factory or elementary job control as *the* key to working-class experience. Crafts were spawned and died in diverse ways, and each generated its own discrete history. Perhaps this sheer diversity, the absence of any common "massifying" experience, allows one to begin to explore the curious stability of the Victorian class structure.[6]

This essay on the Halifax baking and confectionery industry concerns the second path, in which craft production coexisted with the manufactory and the factory. Journeymen in this situation confronted the factory and manufactory either directly from within, or indirectly by suffering from the effects of competition. From this conception of the ensemble of productive forces one may derive a hypothesis about class struggle: that the permeability of the line between small master and journeyman created an ambivalent sense of class consciousness in both groups, which turned both sides into allies against the emergent factory. A related hypothesis would suggest that journeymen were unable, for objective and subjective reasons, to unite with the permanent factory labour force, and that the manufactory and factory thus divided the mass of workers in the industry. Thus the factory produced a stratified labour force whose unity both within and outside the factory was highly vulnerable.

Portrait of an Industry

The baking and confectionery industry in Halifax was composed of four separate elements: candy production, fancy or pastry baking, bread-baking, and the manufacture of crackers, ship's biscuit, and pilot bread. These separate activities were often combined within one establishment.

In Halifax confectionery production was favoured by the historic connections of the city with the West Indies trade. Of the four activities, candy production was the most susceptible to mechanization, particularly after the discovery of the Van Houten process, which made it possible to use cocoa butter for manufacturing chocolate in solid form. However, until Moirs turned to confectionery in the late 1870's, candy manufacture was an outpost of domestic production and retained strong links to retailing.[7]

Confectionery shaded into pastry-making, which was far less susceptible to mechanization. Many bread bakers produced fancy goods on the side, and fancy bakers as a category showed few signs of going beyond the stage of handicraft. The production of crackers, ship's and pilot bread, and related products was a quite different proposition. Because of its importance to the commercial economy and the greater ease with which the product could be preserved, the cracker industry was more technologically developed than any other sector of the industry. The product had never been made at home to any significant extent before the emergence of the bakery, which left wide scope for product innovation and the early emergence of the brand name. The National Biscuit Company in the United States typified the early and successful domination of the industry by large corporations. Since the manufacture of such articles depended from the beginning on specialized wholesale distribution through ships chandlers' shops, jobbers, and commission merchants, it is not surprising that cracker and related products were marketed on an international scale by the end of the nineteenth century.[8]

Of the four activities, the baking of bread was unquestionably the most important. Of all the urban crafts, it had the closest links to the vital issues of working-class subsistence. Fragmentary evidence gathered by Canadian social historians (and the parallel researches of British historians) buttresses the thesis that bread and potatoes played a vital role in the diet of nineteenth-century workers. This is why bread prices were so often drawn into the debate on the tariff, which was an important class issue in Victorian Canada.[9]

The most important feature of bread-baking was its strong links with household production. The bakery had only just emerged in Canada by 1850, and throughout the last half of the nineteenth century it felt the unseen competition of the kitchen. In Nova Scotia in 1871 there were no bakeries in such rural census districts as Kings, Annapolis, Digby, Shelburne, Queens, Colchester, Guysborough, Inverness, and Victoria; one bakery in Richmond, Cape Breton, Antigonish, Cumberland, Halifax East, and Hants; and only two in all of the census district of Yarmouth. Only Halifax and Pictou could claim a larger number (14 in Halifax, 6 in Pictou). This pattern confirms that previously noted in Britain and the United States.[10]

The implantation of the bakery was so gradual that it provoked little commentary in the press, although complaints about the quality of bread provided by the bakeries often led to comparisons between domestic and craft production. One writer complained, "To be sure there is one remedy left us, that is, to have our bread made at home, but all cannot well do this, and such fall into the hands of the baker, (we almost said poisoner.)" A rare commentary on the coming of the bakery was provided by the regular city columnist of the *Acadian Recorder* in 1893: "I am told that in the city the home baking of bread has fallen off very greatly within a few years. Time was when there was a regular distinction between home-made and bakers' bread; and a piece of the latter was considered by the average juvenile as something in the nature of a treat. . . ." He concluded by lamenting the death of "many pleasant home industries" he thought constituted "a healthy occupation and fillip for both mind and body."[11]

Because of its great social importance, the production of bread was subject to a wide range of traditional controls in many western countries. Although the repeal of the Assize of Bread in England marked the formal termination of a traditional economy that had already been undermined, vestiges of pre-capitalist control lived on. According to the Halifax *Charter* (and this was in line with many other North American cities) bread had to be sold at a certain weight and strict penalties were prescribed for violations. There were also provisions for the marking of bread so that the baker could be identified, and bread sold underweight was to be dispensed by the Stipendiary Magistrate to poor people. Although this ordinance was often not observed, it was sufficiently important to bring the occasional baker into police court and to spark a full-scale debate on the subject of bread controls in 1897. As a consequence of this debate, fancy bread was excluded from the ordinance, and master bakers were thereby given free rein to violate the spirit if not the letter of the law. Less scope was provided, apparently, for the adulteration of the product, which in Britain was an essential aspect of the growth of capitalism in the trade. There is little hard Halifax evidence to suggest adulteration as a means of allowing bakeries to survive in an intensely competitive business. Coupled, then, with the formal traditional constraints of the ordinance, was the limit placed on product innovation, both by legislation and by the inherent conservatism of diet.[12]

Three limitations to a fully industrialized bakery emerge from this discussion of "traditional" controls. First, the baker was confined to the city and its immediate hinterland both by the survival of baking within the household and by consumer resistance to products that might have overcome the problem of perishability; second, he was similarly confined to the production of a customary loaf within socially defined limits of profitability; and finally, his proximity to and competition with household production ensured that the predominant form would be the small neighbourhood bakery with low requirements for fixed capital and a limited market. We must add to this "traditional" structure of controls, the more prosaic obstacles to industrialization presented by perishability, technological bottlenecks, and competition. Perishability obviously confined the baker to his immediate area; Halifax bread bakers seem to have expanded no further than neighbouring Dartmouth. Distribution was confined to the bread-cart (which sometime in mid-century supplanted the hawking of bread by the master himself), regularized bread routes for home delivery, and retailing through corner groceries. Technological bottlenecks took many forms, from the uncertainty of local flour supplies that forced bakeries to carry large stocks of flour to the uncertainty of barm or ferment that (compared to compressed yeast) was unsuited to large-production schedules, to the design of the baker's oven, although the early deficiencies of the peel oven were resolutely attacked by a small army of designers who by the turn of the century had popularized the revolving reel oven (with trays for hearths pivoted between vertical discs revolving in a large baking chamber). This invention largely eliminated the problem of "hot spots," which had so plagued the bakers using peel ovens, but it was a long way from a design to ensure continual process and a fully mechanized system of loading and unloading. Finally, there was little progress in any country on the question of packaging and marketing the product. Advertising in Halifax emphasized cleanliness, wholesomeness, and tastiness, but failed to produce a popular brand name. Packaging meant, by and large, wrapping the product in anonymous waxed paper, and product identification involved little more than the legal requirement that the baker stamp the loaf. Perhaps the most important obstacle to full mechanization was competition itself. Although there is fragmentary evidence in Halifax of collective price-setting and organization (especially the Halifax and Dartmouth Master Bakers' Association), such manifestations of the protective impulse paled beside the evidence of bread wars in 1884 and 1897 and the high number of bankruptcies.[13]

These general constraints to industrialization applied to all countries with a free market in bread. Only in the area of mixing machinery could one draw some comfort. Traditional craft baking involved the baker adding yeast to a pailful of water and, after straining it through a seasoning sieve, emptying it into a hole in a mass of prepared flour. After the dry flour was poured over the top, the mixture (of the consistency of thick batter) was left for three or four hours until swelling began. After the pouring of additional water came the hard labour of kneading. The whole of the flour was worked up into one mass, blocked by a pin board to one end of the kneading trough, and left for an hour to prove. Then the dough was scaled off, cut into masses to be weighed, moulded, and set into the oven. There were countless variations on this pattern: the use of potatoes for ferment, for example, was common by the mid-nineteenth century and we have at least circumstantial evidence of their use in Halifax. Innovation in the mixing process came primarily in the form of mechanical dough-kneaders, which by the end of the nineteenth century had spread to all but the smallest bakeries in England. The most important of the machines was the Stevens Patent Dough Making Machine, which consisted of a mixer, feeder and duster, and a scoop. Fitted out with a double bottom for containing hot and cold water, the machine allowed the regulation of the speed of the process of fermentation. The machine either came "attached" with the motive power supplied, or "detached," with a separate cast-iron framework to which steam or water power could be applied.[14]

Of all mechanical inventions associated with the trade, it was this machine that made the most impression on Halifax. Although only perfected in 1858, it was present in the city as early as 1864, when W.C. Moir adopted it for his bakery. Across North America the machine was taken up enthusiastically and became increasingly sophisticated. This was a genuine achievement, but it must be weighed against the small amount of dough that the machines could use at one time and the differences in the quality of bread which were said to result.[15]

This set of factors – "traditional" constraints, perishability, technological bottlenecks, and competition – explains the wide disparity in the size and sophistication of bakeries in many countries. When bread-baking is taken in conjunction with the other three elements of the trade, it is apparent that we are dealing with a complex structure of relationships of production that necessarily had a distinctive articulation in each locality.

Halifax produced a baking and confectionery industry of unusual importance. Census data reveal that in 1871 the city ranked below all other major Canadian cities save Montreal and Saint John in terms of the ratio of bakery and confectionery workers to population; in 1881 and 1891, however, the city was second in Canada, and it was third in 1901.

These ratios are not unambiguous, for a large proportion of Halifax production went to the military, and this may have been the most important factor. Moreover, a technologically advanced bakery or confectionery factory would create the same impact as a primitive resistance to the bread bakery, and the spread between large and small firms could only be traced through complete runs of the manuscript census. Perhaps the most important qualification that one must attach to these statistics is that they underestimate the number of bakery and confectionery establishments. The 1871 census and the manuscript for that census neglect a large number of establishments, probably as many as twelve. Such reservations must also be made about the statistics on raw materials and value of production (Table 1).

Table 1
Raw Materials and Value of Production,
Halifax Baking and Confectionery, 1871-1891

	1871	*1881*	*1891**
No of bakeries and confectionery establishments	14	17	18
Value of raw materials	$260,250	$388,712	$286,025
Total value of products	$327,500	$564,674	$455,410

*Combines separate baking and confectionery census categories.

SOURCE: *Census of Canada*, 1871, 1881, 1891, Table III.

Table 2 shows the effect of the change of census definition on the statistics of the trade. By changing the census definition to employers of more than five workers, the census removed at a stroke some ten bakery and confectionery establishments.

Table 2
Raw Materials and Value of Production,
Halifax Baking and Confectionery, 1901
(establishments with five or more employees)

No. of establishments	3
Capital	$267,350
Cost of materials	$340,500
Value of products	$508,000

SOURCE: *Census of Canada*, 1901, Table III.

These aggregate statistics do not tell much about the internal differentiation of handicraft, manufacture, and factory production within the industry. A slightly more penetrating source is the city directory. Table 3 is compiled from a reading of Halifax city directories for the period 1871-1900. The unrevised data reflect directory listings year by year; the revised data incorporate evidence from probate records, newspapers, and an allowance made for disappearances from the directory of three years or less provided that the firm reappeared at the same address. Both listings probably underestimate the number of establishments in Halifax, since many masters are incorrectly listed as journeymen in the directories, but there is no reliable way of assessing how widespread this is. On the other hand, the number of proprietors incorporates successions within one family, transitions to partnerships, and changes of name.[16]

This table testifies to the precariousness of the livelihood of many master bakers, particularly those who had no confectionery or fancy trade to fall back on. Yet despite this precarious existence, the ranks of the small masters were replenished. Only in 1898 do we see a diminution in the number of proprietors, and this is probably an effect of the bread war of the previous year. The small bakery was a permanent fixture, but the small proprietor was not. A study of the locations of bakeries yields the same conclusion. Of 102 bakery locations in Halifax in this period, forty-one were on what one might consider major business streets (Barrington, Gottingen, Argyle, and Upper Water), but the remainder were spread throughout the city, many on streets that were impeccably residential. The bakery belonged as much to the north-end neighbourhoods as it did to business thoroughfares.

A final point must be made about the aggregate portrait of the Halifax industry: from 1863 to 1900 we have data on twenty-four female proprietors (9.6 per cent of the 1860's proprietors, 14.9 per cent of those from 1871 to 1901). Of the women in the 1860's, four were plain bakers, and these were all married to male bakers. In some cases this involved the woman taking charge of the firm from her husband, and in other instances it reflected a sharing of responsibility between husband and wife. Of the twenty female proprietors of the later period (one of whom was present in the 1860's as well), thirteen were fancy bakers and seven were plain bakers. Nine of these women were definitely connected by marriage or other family ties to a male proprietor; in four cases the linkage to a male proprietor is probable but not certain; and in seven cases the woman was clearly on her own. This again illustrates the domestic origins of the trade and the importance of small family workshops – for it is difficult to find examples of women in other sectors (except brewing) who headed establishments within crafts.[17]

Table 3
Number of Bakeries and Type in Halifax Per Year, 1871-1900

| Year | Unrevised Data | | | Revised Data | | |
	Plain	Fancy	Mixed	Plain	Fancy	Mixed
1871	12	4	1	17	8	1
1872	19	5	1	21	11	1
1873	12	3	1	13	9	1
1874	15	5	1	16	9	1
1875	21	4	1	24	7	1
1876	14	9	1	17	10	1
1877	16	8	1	18	8	1
1878	12	4	1	14	7	1
1879	10	4	1	13	5	1
1880	8	6	1	9	8	1
1881	9	5	1	9	8	1
1882	11	4	1	12	6	1
1883	14	6	1	14	7	1
1884	10	3	1	10	5	1
1885	11	3	1	11	5	1
1886	10	5	1	11	5	1
1887	10	5	1	12	6	1
1888	9	3	1	11	6	1
1889	12	4	2	14	5	2
1890	14	2	1	15	3	2
1891	16	3	2	17	5	2
1892	14	3	2	16	4	2
1893	13	3	2	18	4	2
1894	17	5	2	20	6	2
1895	23	4	2	25	4	2
1896	18	5	1	18	5	1
1897	13	4	1	14	5	1
1898	7	3	1	8	5	1
1899	6	2	2	6	4	2
1900	7	4	2	7	4	2

Number of proprietors: 134; plain bakers: 101; fancy bakers: 29; mixed: 4.
Average years for plain baker: 4.61.
Average years for fancy baker: 6.37.
Average years for mixed baker: 9.75

SOURCES: McAlpine's *Halifax City Directory*, 1871-72 to 1900-01; *O'Flaherty and Walsh's Halifax and Dartmouth Business Directory*, 1876-88.

Handicraft, Manufactory, and Factory

All three stages of production coexisted in the Halifax baking and confectionery industry. The handicraft bakeries (which may be defined for the purposes of our analysis as those employing fewer than five people) were, as the previous analysis has shown, a continuing feature in the landscape of the industry. The manufactories, employing five or more employees, utilizing mechanical improvements to a greater extent, and with access to steam power, may be distinguished from the handicraft bakeries by their aggregate output, but it is difficult to draw a hard and fast line. I have included as manufactories those establishments that in 1871 had an output valued at more than $25,000, which establishes two firms as manufactories. On largely circumstantial evidence I have also included four other firms as manufactories, which emerged at the end of the century when documentation is less available. Finally, this categorization leaves us with one factory, Moirs, whose 1871 output was over $100,000.[18] Although arbitrary, our operational definitions conform to Marx's own insistence on the manufactory as an expanded workshop and also seem to conform to the distinctions made by contemporaries.

The Handicraft Firms. Fugitive, primitive, harried by competition from manufactories and from other small establishments, the handicraft bakery and confectionery establishments were marginal in every way except in social importance. The extremely crude and impressionistic figures of the 1871 census present a portrait of this sector already outproduced by larger firms: handicraft bakeries produced under half the aggregate value of production of the factory and manufactory. This result must be treated with caution, as the manuscript census neglects so many small bakeries (including some well-known and well-established ones), but at the least one is left with the impression of a sector whose share of output was being severely threatened. In confectionery, the balance of output was rather more than even, largely because the National Policy had not yet turned Moirs toward candy production. Nonetheless, this parity itself was an interesting indication of the balance of the forces of production. This outdistancing of the workshop by the manufactories should not lead us to suppose, however, that the handicraft had lost its social importance or had become irrelevant. Those bakeries that remained handicrafts were without exception restricted to the production of bread ("Soft bread for families," wrote the census-taker), while those that had grown larger had expanded into biscuits, cakes, and "bread of all descriptions." Similarly, the confectioners were differentiated along the lines of mere production of cakes and sweetmeats (the handicraft shops) and the production of candy and syrups (the manufactory).

What can be said of the lives of the small masters? From the 1871 manuscript census we gain important insights into the precariousness of their livelihood, especially when we look at the extremely low profit margins reported and the high amounts that had to be invested in that most volatile of commodities, flour. In all cases the amount reported for the aggregate value of raw materials (notably flour, occasionally butter, sugar, and meal) surpassed the total of fixed and floating capital. Indeed, the difference was almost always double, and in one instance the aggregate value of raw materials exceeded the total of fixed and floating capital by a factor of seventeen. Similarly, the profit margins (excepting one aberrant case of $10,000, which is difficult to credit) ranged from $600 to $5,000. Nothing from the manuscript census qualifies our impression of the uncertain livelihood of the small masters.[19]

The manuscript census gives us only a hazy impression of levels of fixed capital, although we may obtain a figure of $1,357 as a rough estimate of the average in handicraft bakeries. Yet it is clearly important to know whether or not machinery came into this sector. Table 4 provides a rough idea of the types of production in handicraft bakeries.[20]

What is interesting about this table – with all the obvious problems of typicality acknowledged – is the evidence it provides for the view that even the handicraft stage was far from static. Although clearly a small master, John Mahar had invested $10 in a rudimentary biscuit machine. Ten years later, the inventory of Charles Sullivan shows his investment in a much more sophisticated biscuit machine ($300) and dough mixer ($50). It may be conjectured from such details that mixers and some machines were entering and altering the workplace even at the level of the handicraft bakery. The impression that flour played a key role in the costs of the bakery is amply sustained by these probate records.

It will not do to romanticize the life of the small master baker. He was independent, employing at the most himself, his family, and perhaps an apprentice and a journeyman; his work might be rather varied, with responsibility for distribution as well as baking; and the familial context would have softened the harshness of the craft. But all in all, he led a life perched on the abyss of financial collapse.

The Manufactories. From the handicraft bakery came the manufactory. Some struggled to make the transition and failed. The

Table 4
Inventories of Small Bakeries Contained in
Halifax County Probate Records

Year	Proprietor	Description of Equipment	Raw Materials	Total Value (inc. real estate)
1854	James Brutcher	64 bake pans, 34 bread pans, beam and scales, 1 lot bread shovels, 1 iron shovel, wagon, bread carts, 2 sets horses: £57.2.0	116 bbl. flour £290	£1,096.9.3
1861	Wells Boardwell (sold off to pay creditors)	4 bread boxes, 10 empty butter containers, 1 stove and pipe, 2 bread troughs, 25 bread pans, 1 set scales and weighs, 4 biscuit dockers, 1 barrel and potato pounder, 3 peel handles, 1 set wagon harness: £68.15.2½	n.a.	£817.12.1
1862	John Mahar (sold off to pay creditors)	2 troughs, 22 bread pans, 10 cake pans, 6 bread boxes, sundries, scales, pans, sieves, biscuit machine ($10), empty barrels: $277.45	13 barrels flour ($91); 11 cord soft wood ($17.60).	$8,169.05
1872	Charles Sullivan	1 biscuit machine ($300), 1 small ditto ($80), 1 dough mixer ($50), bread pans, 1 box cake pans, 40 biscuit boxes: $585	n.a.	$6,585.10
1890	Hugh Montgomerie	Stock in shop and fixtures ($30), 1 portable iron oven ($75): $115		$302.00

SOURCE: Halifax County Probate Court, Warrants of Appraisement.

prerequisite for success was a heroic degree of self-exploitation, necessary to accumulate the capital for the first investment in machines. It was not something that occurred suddenly but rather took place in establishments in existence for three or four decades. Bakeries that made the transition were those with decades of prior accumulation that took advantage of a favourable economic conjuncture in the 1860's and early 1870's.

Three structural aspects of the city's economy aided the establishment of manufactories. First, the presence of the garrison ensured a large demand for bakers' bread: the baker who won the military contract could invest heavily in fixed capital and expand into biscuit manufacture and confectionery. The existence of a guaranteed mass market assured by the garrison both incited intense competition among small masters to get the contract and eased the effects of competition once the contract was secured. This, of course, was not the sure route for success for the small master. When James Miller, holder of the contracts for supplying both the commissariat and the navy with bread in 1888, fled from his creditors, the *Acadian Recorder* remarked,

> Miller, it appears, was another of the aspiring individuals who were not content till they became "contractors" with the Imperial authorities. These contracts are generally taken at lower figures than ordinary trade prices; and it is rather a curious fact that dozens have held such contracts, particularly in the beef line, but few have escaped a scorching.[21]

Despite this pessimistic analysis, one cannot avoid the conclusion that both in the history of Scriven's (a manufactory) and Moirs, the military contract was of great importance.[22] A second feature of Halifax that favoured the growth of the manufactory was its role as a port. The new manufactories replaced the specialized ship bakeries that had existed on the waterfront in the 1850's, and, as we have seen, production of biscuit and ship's bread was more susceptible to mechanization than that of bread. Finally, Halifax's rise as the leading city and one of the leading industrial communities of the Maritimes increased the size of the local market for both bread and confectionery products.

In confectionery four manufactories were established, two in the 1860's, one in 1889, and one in the 1890's. G.J. Hamilton came to Halifax from Pictou, where he had built up his firm through decades of accumulation. O'Brien and Adams were relative newcomers, by comparison; in their establishment in 1889 one found a range of machinery that would appear to put them beyond the workshop stage. The Allen Brothers (the largest producers in 1871) founded the Halifax Steam Confectionery in 1868. They were responsible for introducing the large-scale pulverizer to Halifax and lasted until about 1877. The case of M.J. O'Brien indicated a more common transition from fancy baker to candy manufacturer. Established in a small way as early as 1864, the firm by 1888 had a modest inventory of manufactured stock ($887.25) but a much larger sum invested in machinery, boilers, and engines ($4,491).[23]

In bread-baking, two manufactories were established in the nineteenth century. The Scriven bakery followed the classic pattern of evolution from handicraft. Founded in 1821 by Joseph Scriven, inherited by J.J. Scriven in 1852, and by George Scriven in 1876, it was a well-rooted Halifax family business. In 1830 it was assessed (real estate and all else included) at a mere £250. In the 1860's it turned to steam technology, with the importation of "some of the latest improvements in the apparatus of biscuit-making now in use in the United States." By 1875 the firm was advertising three separate locations and produced biscuits, crackers, bread, fruit cake, and pastries. When J.J. Scriven died in 1871, stock on hand, shop furniture, and bakery machinery was valued at $3,171.73.[24]

If some sort of transition to the manufactory is evidenced in the 1860's, only in 1891 was dramatic progress visible. The firm moved to a new bakehouse, equipped with two ovens from a well-known Toronto firm, a dough mixer, a moulding machine, rounding off machinery, a mechanical divider, an overhead prover, a steam-proof box, and a tempering tank that weighed and measured water automatically. In 1896 a modern reel oven was installed. By the end of the century this firm employed twenty men.[25]

The other manufactory grew out of the oldest Halifax bakery, Liswell's. If by 1881 some progress toward becoming a manufactory had been made (the inventory of that year mentions two iron biscuit machines worth $800), the bakery was nonetheless little more than an important and prosperous workshop. Only in 1899, after the business had been acquired and moved by Thomas O'Malley, did the bakery become a full-fledged manufactory. It is the one instance in the nineteenth century of an outsider bursting into the trade and establishing himself as a small manufacturer – and it occurred within the context of the most traditional bakery in the city.[26]

The small manufactory, while a heady sign of progress to contemporaries, seems to have been a minor affair. Yet it was not unimportant. Work in such a situation might be in small groups and in a paternalistic setting, but it involved less manual labour, more machine-tending, and less independence than the labour of the small master. Investment in fixed capital gave the manufactories stability – of the three bakeries that endured throughout the period, all three were manufactories or factories. Yet the door to such stability was not wide open, and after 1871 only one establishment managed the transition.

The Factory. Moirs alone of the Halifax baking and confectionery establishments became a factory. With the ropeworks, sugar refineries, and cotton factory, Moirs was evidence of Halifax's growth as an industrial city. In at least one sense Moirs was more important than the other industries: it remained in the city as a flagship of indigenous capital and survived the initial onslaught of the merger movement.[27]

The factory evolved in the classic pattern, from a modest bakery established by Benjamin Moir in 1815 to a joint-stock company working in tandem with Eastern Trust in 1903. The bakery from 1815 to 1864 was a prosperous workshop. When Benjamin Moir died in 1845, he had built up a modest competence: the value of real estate was £530, with an additional £617.7.6 tied up in the bakery itself. Compared to the amounts invested in flour (£220) or cash on hand (£270), the sum given for the bakehouse apparatus (£2) was small indeed. The total value of the estate was £1234.15.7½, a solid basis on which a new proprietor could build.[28]

Benjamin's son, William Church Moir, took control immediately after his father's death. His most important act was the winning of the garrison contract in 1858, after which he held it most of the time. The growth of the firm after this point was remarkable. After moving to a new location on Argyle Street in 1862, Moir introduced steam technology. In 1865, an informant for R.G. Dun thought him a well-respected entrepreneur and described him as "making money rapidly, enlarging premises and employing Steam." In 1866 Moir went into partnership with E.C. Twining, but this partnership was dissolved in 1871, perhaps because Twining brought little additional strength to the business. With profits rolling in, Moir turned to the wholesale distribution of grain, flour milling, and speculation in mining stocks and real estate. In 1876 the R.G. Dun informant described him as ". . . the principal of the firm. He owns a great deal of R[eal] E[state] in this City and fine Mills that he is building 8 miles from the City. Owns val[uable] farm." By 1876 Moir was building a little industrial complex in Bedford near Halifax, complete with large flour mill and elevator, spool factory, a sawmill, and a woodworking establishment. Having expanded too quickly, Moir and his son, James W., suspended payment in 1881, saddled with capital that was plentiful but frozen in real estate and the Bedford enterprises, but the firm survived both this and a fire in 1891. By the time of his death in 1896, William Moir could pride himself on having founded a major industrial enterprise. James W. Moir then steered the business into incorporation as a joint-stock company in 1903 and the issuance of bonds with the Eastern Trust Company as trustee.[29]

Moirs was unique in the Halifax baking and confectionery industry because it achieved a great measure of vertical and horizontal integration. The decision to go into flour production was a classic case of vertical integration. The flour mill, built in 1865 as an adjunct to the main bakery, relied on Ontario and American wheat. Flour milling was the centrepiece of the expansion at Bedford, which took place under the aegis of the Bedford Grain Importation, Milling and Manufacturing Company, incorporated in 1878.[30] It would appear that this scheme was adversely affected by the National Policy, which eliminated the use of American breadstuffs and forced Moir to rely on unreliable shipments of the domestic article.[31] Other forms of vertical integration worked far better. The expansion into box-making was highly successful, for instance, and Moirs in the early twentieth century was said to use over 200,000 feet of boards annually for making boxes for biscuits.[32]

Horizontal integration was typified by the critical expansion of the bakery into the confectionery trade. By the early 1860's the bakery was already specializing in biscuits and hard bread, but it does not appear that it turned to confectionery manufacture until the mid-1870's at the earliest. Certainly confectionery had become important by 1881. Part of this shift can be accounted for by the National Policy, for this established a 35 per cent *ad valorem* duty in addition to a 1¢/lb. special tariff.[33] By the 1890's Moirs turned out over 500 different varieties of confectionery. Possibly this shift in emphasis may be explained by the interests of James W. Moir, who certainly approached the problem of quality control and innovation with enthusiasm and skill.[34] It was this integration within the boundaries of a single company of so many diverse activities that made Moirs unique. In some ways, it was a highly sophisticated example of economies of scale; the diverse operations in Halifax, for example, could be powered by the same source. In other ways, the effect was rather the reverse: even within the factory itself one could argue that there existed such a wide range of activities that it almost resembled a series of little workshops.

Moirs devoured new technology. In bread-baking, the decisive step was the importation in the early 1860's of "a Steam Engine, Boiler, etc. with a large lot of machinery of the latest and most approved kind" for baking hard bread and crackers, and also a Stevens Mixer for dough for soft bread.[35] The new machinery required construction of a new brick three-storey factory in 1865. This mechanization allowed Moir to dominate both the cracker and bread trade by 1871: he turned out $118,000 worth of biscuits, cakes, and bread of all descriptions, $48,000 more than his nearest competitor, J.J. Scriven. By 1876 Moir had "two Side Furnace Ovens of the largest capacity, and one very large Reel Oven." Servicing the huge military contract was a prime motive in this restless drive for fixed capital. In 1891, it was claimed that 3,000 lbs. were required daily for the troops. At the end of the century, the ovens of Moirs stretched several storeys high, and each of his two reel ovens had the capacity of turning out 2,000 town loaves. This restless technological drive was carried into biscuit manufacture, but in confectionery the firm relied more on unskilled manual labour than on extensive mechanization.[36]

The financing of the company also set it apart from other establishments, both in its scope and complexity. In its early years the firm relied on short-term credit from banks but had no long-standing relationship with any one financial institution. The bulk of indebtedness in the financial crisis of 1881 was to other businessmen. In the 1890's, this relationship with banks changed. An entry in the financial statement of 1895 shows the People's Bank of Halifax holding collateral on the bakery building of $30,000. When, after complex legal battles, the company was incorporated, the directors were empowered to borrow upon the credit of the company to the extent of $100,000 to issue 200 bonds of $500 each, all maturing in twenty years after bearing 6 per cent annual interest. Eastern Trust Company was designated the trustee. So the firm that had grown out of the accumulation of capital in the handicraft phase entered the period of finance capital.[37]

Moirs differed from other establishments in the industry in a fourth respect: the acquisition of a regional market. From Schedule A of the Deed of Assignment, drawn up in the crisis of 1881, we can infer the geographical pattern of Moirs' trade. Out of a total of $93,571.12 in debts listed in this deed, Halifax customers account for $41,282.69 and those outside the city $16,460.09. (Excluded from the analysis, and accounting for the remainder, are the real estate and other fixed assets owned by the company.) Of the customers outside Halifax, 67.8 per cent were in Nova Scotia, 6.1 per cent were in New

Brunswick, and slightly under 1 per cent were in Prince Edward Island. Substantial totals appear for St. Pierre (2.1 per cent) and St. John's (1.6 per cent). The range of Moirs' penetration of the provincial market is interesting. The largest percentage was accounted for by Sydney (7.2), followed by North Sydney (5.9), Liverpool (3.4), Lunenburg (3.1), Antigonish (2.2), and New Glasgow (1.7). It is also interesting that the absence of rail links with communities did not hinder Moirs doing business with them, and this may explain the references to shares in steamship companies that surface in the Moir papers. Every major community, and a large number of hamlets, comprised the 108 Nova Scotia communities with which Moirs did business, almost entirely through general dealers.[38] Yet this table almost certainly understates the cause. In 1898, Moirs was reported to have acquired a large market for biscuit and other provisions in Puerto Rico and Cuba, and with the opening of the Canadian West, Moirs made a determined and successful bid for a share in that market.[39]

The city itself captured the lion's share of Moirs' attention, and the firm remained the city's largest bread producer. A reporter counted 11,280 loaves delivered throughout the city on one Saturday in 1896. By the 1890's Moirs was buying up other bread routes and bakeries.[40] Perhaps because of the industry's obvious importance as a bread supplier and employer, the city relented to the company's demand for special consideration on water rates and exempted the firm from taxes by special legislation passed in 1903 to enable it to recover from a damaging fire.[41]

These five aspects – vertical and horizontal integration, technological sophistication, incorporation as a joint-stock company under the aegis of a trust company, a regional market, and civic prominence – set Moirs apart from any other competitor in the industry. It never monopolized the trade; but the logic of its evolution prefigured the growth of monopoly. It did not eliminate the primitive small bakeries, but it surely must have cut into their markets and rendered their existence even more precarious.

We may now arrive at conclusions about the configuration of capital in this sector. On the one hand, there was a proliferation of small masters, most perched on the edge of collapse. In bread and fancy baking, there were 132 such small masters in the period from 1863 to 1900. By contrast, only seven small masters on either side of the industry managed to set up manufactories. Only one of these managed to attain the status of a factory. The stages of industrial capitalism coexisted over an extended period. At the base one had craftsmen who would have felt at home in the medieval city; at the top was one firm that exploited the national market and anticipated the emergence of monopoly capital. It is within the determinant context of this complex portrait of the mode of production that the working-class struggles in the industry must be seen.

Workers and Working Conditions

Stratification within the mode of production produced stratification within the work force. Moirs employed skilled journeymen, unskilled women, and children in the factory; the manufactories gradually expanded from their basic work force of journeymen to incorporate women employees; and the small masters generally employed at the most one or two journeymen or children. As the manufactories and factory expanded, the effect on the labour force was profound. The largest change, as Table 5 indicates, was in the 1870's: child employees, who had comprised 8.9 per cent of the labour force in 1871, made up 21.6 per cent of the workers in 1881. The number of women employees also increased, from 11.2 per cent of the labour force in 1871 to 16.2 per cent in 1881. This figure dropped to 14.2 per cent in 1891. If the statistics for 1901 were available, they would probably indicate a far higher proportion of female labour.

Table 5
The Labour Force, 1871-1901

| | Over 16 | | Under 16 | | Total |
	Men	Women	Boys	Girls	
1871	71	10	6	2	89
1881	127	33	44	—	204
1891: Bakeries	46	7	7	1	61
1891: Confectionery	138	30	19	12	199
1891: Totals	184	37	26	13	260
1901*	Wage earners: 273, Salaried: 41				

*1901 statistics for firms of five employees and more.

SOURCE: *Census of Canada,* 1871, 1901, Table III.

These aggregate statistics do not allow us to assess the impact on the work force of various phases of industrial capitalism. Unfortunately, only two sources will shed further light on this critical question. The evidence of the manuscript census in 1871 (presented in Table 6) suggests that the bakeries of 1871 were the bastions of the adult journeyman, but that there was an even balance of men and women in confectionery.

Table 6
The Labour Force, 1871

	Over 16		Under 16	
	Men	Women	Boys	Girls
Confectionery				
Allen Bros.	5	4	2	2
Henry Wilson	1	2	—	—
Jane Robinson	2	—	—	—
Maria Crook	—	3	—	—
F.M. Phelan	2	1	—	—
Bakeries				
Moir & Co. Flour Mill	9	—	2	—
Moir & Co. Bakeries	25	—	3	—
John Scriven Biscuit Manufactory	14	—	—	—
Mary Scott	3	—	—	—
James Mitchell	2	—	—	—
J.R. Wilson	2	—	—	—
Thomas Kent	6	—	1	—
James Ellis	4	—	—	—
William Smith	3	—	—	—
Patrick Joyce	2	—	—	—
Thomas Gentles	3	—	—	—

SOURCE: 1871 Manuscript Census, Halifax West and Halifax East, Schedule No. 6, Return of Industrial Establishments.

A published list of the employees of Moirs in 1891 confirms the impression that women were more extensively employed in confectionery than in baking. It lists thirty "girls" working in the factory, out of a work force of 143 people. The factory therefore had a higher percentage of female employees (21 per cent) than the work force as a whole, and employed three-fifths of the female labour force. Out of nineteen divisions, women or "girls" were the majority in the syrups department (five out of seven), the lozenges department (six out of seven), and the box factory (six out of six), and were a sizable minority in the retail store (five or six out of eleven). Women did not work in the factory's soft-bread, hard-bread, or fancy bakery departments. Women, then, were largely concentrated in confectionery.[42]

This concentration of women in confectionery did not mean complete segregation from other parts of the work force. Moirs did not provide separate washroom facilities for women. On the other hand, a woman was appointed as head of the new chocolate-rolling department established in the 1890's, and some evidence of segregation emerges from Moirs' practice of allowing females employed in the candy-wrapping department to leave a few minutes before the men.[43] In general, then, the impact of the factory on the work force was not as one might have expected. Far from being a "massifying" experience, factory labour entailed groups of no more than twelve workers in each department.

The effects of industry on industrial health and safety were far greater. Mixing machines reduced the problem of dust in the air, so potent a factor in the respiratory ailments of bakers. Chronic overwork also contributed to such occupational diseases as consumption. Fumes from the ovens could overpower bakers, and complaints in the factory about ventilation were so many that even Moir felt he had to do something about them. Of the primary hazards in the industry, biscuit-making machinery was the greatest: there is documentation of scores of amputations and lacerations from this machinery. Some of the more persistent workers might obtain some compensation, but most were forced out of productive life.[44]

The primary issue in the baking trade, however, was low pay combined with long hours. Throughout the nineteenth century bakers compared their lot unfavourably with other trades. Few bakers' campaigns did not involve the slogan "White Slavery."[45] In truth the craft was rapidly becoming a forerunner of sweated labour. The contradiction posed in this situation was that the journeymen saw themselves as the equals of other craftsmen and compared themselves to other trades incessantly. "Why do bakers lay behind/ In Labor's ranks, can we not find/ An opening to advance?" asked Peter Connolly, in a poem on the bakers. The answer would appear to have been "No," because of the inability of the bakers to enforce a standard rate. Not only were there differences among the wages of the foreman, first, and second hands, but there were discrepancies among shops. The evidence of the Royal Commission gathered in 1888 suggests that the average pay of a journeyman was $8 per week, and lower in winter. Wage rates at Moirs varied from a high of $12 to $6 for journeyman. A new male child employee earned $1 to $1.50 per week until he gained experience, and young girls earned from $1.25 to $4 per week.[46]

Long hours worked at night were the biggest thing that set bakers apart from their fellow workers. When the free market in labour was allowed to run its course, bakers worked fifteen and sixteen hours a day. Halifax bakers were said to work from eleven and a half to sixteen hours a day, according to various witnesses at the hearings in 1888; the lower figure was the one provided by J.W. Moir. One shop was reported by the leader of the union to have effected a 4 a.m. to 4 p.m. day; all the rest were said to vary.[47] What made matters worse was the fact that bakers had to work at night. This was a general problem in the international trade and became a recurring theme of the deliberations of the International Labour Organization. Night work was necessary because of the need for hot bread in the morning, both to meet consumer tastes and to overcome the problem of perishability. Because of the night work, the bakers were regarded as a special case and came to enjoy the minimal protection of bakehouse laws in Britain and in parts of the United States and Canada. Although there was general support for the bakers in their struggle to end night work (which was regarded as an unnatural thing), the problem lay in trying to achieve the abolition of night work in the context of a highly competitive trade. As the *Canadian Baker and Confectioner* argued, after generally condemning night work as a "menace, not merely to health but bodily and mental development," the one thing standing in the way of the end of night work was the lack of an understanding among master bakers.[48]

The problem of industrial discipline must be posed in terms of the collapse of almost all trade-union controls on the level of exploitation. The most serious aspect presented by the issue of discipline was the difficulty involved in inculcating industrial habits in the minds of children. Within the candy departments of Moirs, children stole nuts and bread.[49] They also entangled themselves in the machinery. J.C. Moir was apt to place the blame for this vexing inconvenience on the moral failings of the children themselves. (In speaking of an accident to a child in 1888, for example, he used the phrase "wholly due to carelessness.") Union members stressed the absence of any protection from the moving parts of the machines and the lack of any system of industrial training in lieu of the defunct apprenticeship system. The real problem lay in teaching children the rudiments of industrial discipline, namely curbing their natural playfulness and replacing it with those qualities of attentiveness and concentration so important for detailed manual labour.[50]

One of the more interesting accounts comes from the earliest stage of the mechanization of Moirs. Charles Brunt was a fourteen-year-old boy hired by Moir to pick up biscuits after they had been cut, pack cakes, and cut a little firewood. At an inquest into his death the theme of natural playfulness emerged directly.

Henry Grace, sworn, said – I have been with . . . Mr. Moir about 5 weeks – I was at work in the upstairs room . . . I was not busy some time before breakfast. – I was some distance from the deceased[.] I saw him playing with a bit of doc [*sic*] at the rollers – I saw him pick up a bit of doc [*sic*] into the rollers; it struck on the side of the hopper; and fell over on the cog wheels, he reached over to get it out [.] I then heard him call out, his face being from me – I run out of the room, as I passed him I saw his arm in the cogwheel. . . .

Christopher McQuinn, sworn, said – I am forman [*sic*] to the department where the deceased worked – I was at the oven on Tuesday morning about eight o'clock, when I heard the deceased call out. . . . I got up and stopped the belt on the down pulley[.] I then saw the arms of the boy in the cog wheel – We had to take one of the cogs off before we got the arms off. . . .

The child died, according to the doctor, from the shock to the nervous system caused by the injury. The jury asked Moir to cover the wheel with a box.[51]

In the case of Joseph Larkins, the difficulty of employing child labour was more an aspect of inexperience than playfulness.

Q. How old are you? *A*. I am 11 years.
Q. What is the matter with your hand? *A*. It got hurt in the machinery.
Q. How? *A*. It got caught in the rollers.
Q. What rollers? *A*. The rollers of a cracker machine – a biscuit machine.
Q. How long were you working in the biscuit factory? *A*. About seven weeks.
Q. Was it part of your work to look after the machinery? *A*. No; I was taken in as a packer and was then put to work on the machinery . . . .
Q. Did you lose any fingers? *A*. I lost one.
Q. Did you lose any of the joints of the others? *A*. I think I will lose a second finger.

The *Morning Chronicle* reported that "The commissioners were so affected by the recital of this story that they immediately made up a subscription for him which he received with tears of gratitude."[52]

Working-class Struggle

This variety of working-class experiences within one industry suggests that the responses of workers would be similarly diverse. There were two systems of stratification at work, one that divided workers vertically by differential pay and authority (typified by the distance between male journeyman and female factory worker), and one that divided workers according to their specialty (bread bakers, biscuit bakers, confectionery workers). Out of this dual system of stratification only the journeymen bread bakers were able to sustain an organization and fight for reforms – reforms that applied only to themselves.

The border between journeymen and small masters was permeable, and this may have had an impact on the ideology of the labour struggles in the industry. There is no great body of union records on which to draw, but newspaper lists of executive members of the union indicate that of forty-nine known executive members from 1868 to 1894, at least fifteen became small masters after holding a union executive post, and an additional four journeymen had been small masters before joining the union executive. There is good reason to suppose (although no direct evidence to prove) that two executive members were small masters while still in the union.[53] Thus, throughout the nineteenth century there existed a feasible alternative to wage labour for the most articulate and active journeymen bakers.

This theme of petty proprietorship was important in each of the three periods of trade unionism in the industry. From 1868 to 1879 the first Journeymen Bakers' Friendly Society established itself in the industry, waged a struggle against the master bakers in 1868, and revealed itself to be a union of craftsmen in battle against the emergent factory. From 1882 to 1888, following the collapse of the union in the recession, the bakers reorganized, fought a remarkable boycott campaign in 1884, and were defeated in their attempt to reform the long hours of the factory. This was again a union of craftsmen, whose battle was now confined exclusively to Moirs and the damaging impact the firm had on the solidarity of trade. In this period there is some evidence to indicate a merging of the interests of journeymen and small masters, as well as a growing gulf between factory workers and the journeymen bakers. From 1889 to 1896, the bakers formed the first Canadian local of the Journeymen Bakers' and Confectioners' International Union of America. This local won a great victory against the employers in 1890, but this was reversed by Moirs' actions in 1891, and the union dwindled to nothing. This was not a step to an expanded militancy of the Halifax bakers, but their final defeat. The pattern throughout demonstrates the divisiveness engendered by capitalist development, and the extraordinary tenacity of craft consciousness.

The First Period, 1868-1879. The emergence of the factory and manufactory in the baking trade in the 1860's meant that class polarization, the basis of all trade unionism, was the inevitable by-product of expanding fixed capital and larger numbers of employees. The institution of the Journeymen Bakers' Friendly Society of Halifax and Vicinity on January 1, 1868, indicated that the industry had developed sufficiently to create a pool of journeymen. Our earlier analyses of the labour force and of the means of production also suggested this. This process of *class articulation* was an important aspect of the history of Halifax and marked the emergence of the manufactory in many sectors.[54]

The founding document of the trade union is the most impressive of any of the constitutions left by the Halifax crafts. The purposes of the society were said to include enabling the journeymen bakers "to increase their wages to a reasonable rate, and to limit their hours of labour to twelve per day; likewise to assist each other in sickness and distress, to defray funeral expenses at death, to promote brotherly affection and fellowship, and to elevate themselves socially and morally among the trades of the city." Both the name of the society and its elaborate provisions for auditing of accounts and payment of dues might lead to the conclusion that it was a mere coffin club, but such was not the case. From the constitution emerges an impression of sophistication and careful thought on the subjects of craft defence against employers and craft discipline within the union. An extraordinary seven-man committee, for instance, was deputed to "decide in all cases of dispute between members, or in any case of ambiguity or oversight in the Rules, or any subject to which the existing Rules do not apply." The union was to maintain a list of out-of-work members and strict rules governed both those members who wished to vacate positions and those who wished to fill them. While the society was composed of journeymen bakers who could afford the membership fee of $4 and could secure the support of two-thirds of the members, "boys" were admitted half-price, although they were without vote until they were eighteen years old.

The constitution not only elaborated a sophisticated set of mechanisms for dealing with conflicts within the trade but also a strategy for its reform. Implicit in Rule XIX of the constitution, for example, was the notion of the closed shop:

> . . . no member of this society [may] work beside a non-member, without the consent of the Committee; and any member employing non-members to work, while a member is unemployed capable of filling the place, or giving information to a non-member where he can find employment, or recommending a non-member to an employer, shall be dealt with as the Committee shall determine.

Members were also to be disciplined if they took employment on terms unsatisfactory to other union members. Together with the internal structure of the society, such regulations for the discipline of members suggest that under the benign title of "friendly society" lurked a fully operational craft union.[55]

The first strike was launched three months after the birth of the union. The demands were for a slight increase of wages and a reduction of hours from fifteen-sixteen to twelve, to start at 5 or 6 a.m. and to go until 5 or 6 p.m., inclusive of meal and sponge time. The journeymen bakers issued a manifesto outlining their grievances in language that was clearly intended to appeal to the widest possible base of support. Claiming that the present system of early and long hours had been the cause of "untold suffering, ill-health, premature old age, and death," the bakers went beyond specific results of overwork to a discussion of its moral and social ramifications.

> In a moral and intellectual point of view it is nearly as bad, as we have no time for recreation, no moral improvement; no time to spend in the social or family circle. We have no time for the public meeting, lecture, concert or religious duty; the Sun shines in vain for us, the trees and plants may grow, and the flowers may bloom, but not for us. To us the delights of the country are a sealed book; to prepare for our early toil we have to go to bed, (those that have one), while the rest of the world is awake, and work while the rest of the world asleep, thus reversing the laws of nature. No wonder that some of us have recourse to stimulants in order to give a spur to our overworked and failing nature, and for the time to bury in oblivion our degraded position.

While no doubt a sincere statement of the craftsmen's dilemma, this was also a shrewd bid for support from the temperance and Early

Closing advocates. To further broaden the appeal, the journeymen bakers went on to argue that the demanded reforms were neither harmful to the trade nor (and this was a piece of inspired inaccuracy) inconsistent with British experience.

> It is not our wish to reduce your [the masters'] Trade or profits, as you will find that when all adopt day work, it will meet all the requirements of the Trade. It has been adopted, and proved a perfect success, in all the large cities of England, Ireland and Scotland. . . .

The only slip the bakers made in this document was to suggest that the slight increase in wages demanded could easily be passed on to the consumer with a price hike of 1¢ per loaf. Apart from this, the document was a perfect appeal to the public conscience in the age of earnest self-improvement.[56]

Because of the importance of the trade to working-class life, newspapers were quick to point out the implications of the strike. The *British Colonist* noted that the marked fluctuations in the price of flour made for "great caution on the part of proprietors of baking establishments to protect themselves from loss, and at the same time give to the public bread at the lowest figure." The demand for the abolition of night-work rested on the public giving up fresh rolls for breakfast, but the newspaper thought that this was a matter that could be amicably negotiated between the parties. The most important response came from the master bakers themselves, who claimed that the demands would lead to increased expenditure in oven accommodation and higher prices. They went on to reject the very idea that journeymen should have a say in setting wages.

> . . . we consider their demands too unreasonable to comply with, nor are we disposed to allow any association to force upon us any positive scale of wages, believing that we are able to discriminate the value of labour we employ, fully as well, if not better than they are enabled to do.

Not only did the master bakers reject the journeymen's demands, but they vowed that in the event of a dispute they would not employ any members of the association "as it at present exists, in any way whatever."[57]

The intransigence of the master bakers lends weight to the thesis that the 1860's saw a widening gulf between employer and employee. The strike became a test of power between two rights, the right of journeymen to improve their position in a collective struggle and the right of masters to hire workers at whatever price suited them. Yet it is apparent that the master bakers did not form a monolithic bloc. The larger manufacturers became the backbone of resistance to the strike; in the end, W.C. Moir was its most hardened opponent. He ran his bakery with strikebreakers imported from the country, as well as a "number of strong, able women and boys," and perhaps even with inmates from the Deaf and Dumb asylum. While small masters all conceded the journeymen's demands, Moir held firm.[58]

The journeymen advanced the debate about the respective rights of employee and employer by setting up a co-operative bakery in premises previously occupied by a small master baker. By mid-April they were reported to have gained a considerable patronage from the public. Other craft societies helped found the co-operative, and there is strong circumstantial evidence to link it with the Halifax Co-operative Society. This co-operative bakery absorbed the trade unionists dismissed by Moir.[59]

Most employers were reported to have taken back their employees by April 23, and by May 2 the strike was counted as over. The outcome was revealing. The bakers had won a clear victory over the small masters and many of these had indeed given in almost immediately; the factory, reinforced by the need for production for the military and high expenditure on fixed capital, held out. The bakers would long remember Moirs' intransigence.

The union stayed alive for eleven years, organized social activities for its members, and maintained a certain rate in the bakeries apart from Moirs. Faced with the long recession, the union collapsed in 1879; many of its leaders had become petty proprietors themselves. One analysis that remains of the union's collapse claimed that the union failed

> not from outside influences but from the men's carelessness, and what is now the consequence; why, instead of men working from 10 to 12 hours per day, as they should, in five of our six bakehouses in the City they [work] from 15 to 18. And there is no remedy [but] of Union, for the deplorable state of affairs, for the Masters know, that we have no sufficient backbone to demand the hours of labour should be curtailed.[60]

The gains of the 1860's were thus wiped out by the collapse of the union in 1879, which brought back the problem of overwork in its rawest form.

What can we infer about the consciousness of the journeymen who organized the union of 1868-1879 and the strike of 1868? It is here that we must be prepared to create "tissues of inference" and presume to go beyond a strictly empirical analysis. It is possible to advance three claims: first, that the bakers were preoccupied with becoming fully identified with other craftsmen and saw their role as being the elevation of their craft to the level of other crafts; second, that inherent in this concept of the elevation of the craft was the adoption of the values of respectability and independence; and third, this adoption of the values and language of respectability was a matter of advancing a claim for general recognition of status and involved the elaboration within the working class of a "negotiated version" of ruling-class values. Each of these claims depends, of course, on inferences from the documents and actions of the journey-men bakers.

The claim that bakers identified themselves with other craftsmen is of great moment, for in their objective conditions of exploitation the journeymen bakers were not like other craftsmen (especially in regard to the problems of a residual craft tradition, overwork, and job control). This difference between journeymen bakers and their fellow craftsmen did not create a separate articulation of ideals and values, but rather drove the bakers to announce their intentions again and again of becoming craftsmen as others were.

The constitution of the union announced that the intention of the bakers was to elevate themselves "socially and morally among the trades of the city." Further, the constitution argued that the rules would "prove to the world that the Baker it not inferior to his fellow working-men of the province, in point of intelligence and true manly worth." Lest members think this road an easy one, the constitution reminded them that "To gain success we must deserve it." The constitution also specified that only the baker who was capable of "discharging his duty in his *profession*" was to be admitted. A final note of craft-consciousness is struck in the provision of the constitution that no member of the union be allowed "to boast of his own, or depreciate the workmanship of another member in the Club room," under a penalty of 25¢.[61] In the strike of 1868 the bakers were aided by other craft societies, and they toasted "Our Sister Societies" at their annual banquets.[62]

It would appear legitimate to infer from these bits of evidence that the bakers saw themselves as craftsmen fighting against the degrada-tion of their craft. The 1868 debate was sharpened by this tension between the self-ascription of craftsmen status by the journeymen bakers, and the difficulty of obtaining general recognition of this status.

If it was indeed the case that bakers identified themselves as craftsmen, it is not surprising to find a heavy emphasis in all their documents on respectability. The document issued in the 1868 strike was, of course, for public consumption and is therefore somewhat suspect as a genuine reflection of the journeymen's thoughts, although the expression of anguish at missing the whole range of voluntary activities of mid-Victorian Halifax may have been genuine. More striking is the extent of the emphasis on respectability in the union's constitution and social activities. The constitution lays down that only journeymen of "good moral character" were to be admitted. The by-laws of the union were particularly adamant on the subject of respectable behaviour. Members who entered the club room in a state of intoxication were to be fined, and further fines were imposed on those making use of profane or obscene language. Any member found guilty of a felony before a Magistrate was to be expelled from the society, although should he "regain his character," he might be readmitted by the consent of two-thirds of the members.[63] The social activities of the union also reflect a concern for respectability. The bakers organized a series of balls and the union even offered instruction for journeymen in ballroom dancing. John Kew and his wife entertained the assembled guests with their singing. The bakers' taste for respectable entertainment recalls the similar activities of the Halifax printers, whose suppers contained the same series of toasts and speeches about the elevation of the mechanic.[64]

Third, the bakers' search for parity with other crafts and their respectable behaviour were unified phenomena and did not merely represent the absorption of "middle-class" values by mechanics. The issue was never the individual advancement of bakers from the ranks of journeymen (although this was an important objective factor) but the collective advancement of the craft and the trade generally. If we identify respectability with mid-Victorian bourgeois preoccupations, it is clear that the journeymen offer evidence of a "negotiated version" of hegemonic ideology, one which could be used as a weapon in trade disputes as well as a demand for the recognition of status and position.

The Second Period, 1882-1888. The leading feature of the first period of the collective struggles of the journeymen baker was the emergence of the factory as their most determined opponent. In the 1880's this theme became more evident with the growth of Moirs as a major industry and the drift of many former journeymen into petty proprietorship.

Like its predecessor of the 1860's, the new journeymen bakers' union (often referred to as the Journeymen Bakers' Friendly Union) was organized in a period of substantial working-class agitation in the province. Both the Halifax unions and the PWA became stable and important organizations; the bakers were clearly inspired by the success of the Provincial Miners' Association and it was a Halifax baker who suggested that the miners' union change its name to the Provincial Workmen's Association to signify its intention of broadening its base.[65] The bakers organized their union in 1882 and affiliated with the Amalgamated Trades Union, the labour council of Halifax.[66] Many new names were on the executive of the reorganized union, but there was some measure of continuity as well. Lewis Archibald, for example, had such vivid memories of 1868 that it appears likely he was involved in the strike. Archibald, a vigorous man and one of the key founders of the revived Halifax labour movement, had worked in Boston and Green Bay, and quite possibly his experiences in such cities had brought him new ideas on organizing.[67] The union also was awake to events in the United States, where throughout the 1880's the boycott became an increasingly popular method of collective struggle.[68] Halifax workingmen had learned from P.J. McGuire that the boycott could be an effective weapon.[69] Whatever the direct impact of such developments, the boycott idea was clearly in the air, and in 1884 the bakers brought the idea into practice by organizing the first province-wide labour boycott in Nova Scotia.

In August, 1884, the journeymen bakers appealed to the Amalgamated Trades Union for support in a united action against Moirs. The bakers (rather surprisingly) reported that a 4 a.m. starting time was general in the city, except at Moirs, where the firm kept bakers at work "just as long as they please, not infrequently until eleven o'clock at night, and always until long after the men in other shops are away from their work." The officers of the ATU waited on Moir, who told them that he declined "to be dictated to by any one."[70]

On September 12, 1884, at a well-attended meeting, the ATU resolved to boycott Moirs and "vowed a vow that every man of them will prefer to walk a mile to buy a loaf of bread or a pound of flour or the staff of life in any other form from any other bakery than patronize Moir." Included in the boycott were any parties who might have business connections with Moirs or purchased from the firm.[71]

This quickly became the one Halifax trade-union struggle to have an impact across the province. The alliance with the miners, established in 1880, blossomed forth in an editorial by Grand Secretary

Robert Drummond, who urged PWA locals not to allow their members to buy candies, crackers, or other products from Moirs. This must have had some impact, for Moirs took the trouble of circulating counter-propaganda among the merchants of Stellarton who had been asked to boycott the company. The struggle was also discussed widely across the province: the editor of a Hants County paper was taken severely to task by Drummond for his attitude to the boycott.[72]

Equally important were the signs that this was a turning point for Halifax labour in terms of the bitterness of the conflict and the wide range of support given to the bakers. There were claims of union intimidation of soft-bread bakers at Moirs unsympathetic to the boycott, and the union put up inflammatory posters near the factory.[73] The support given to the bakers by other craftsmen may be inferred from the sorts of workers who were invited to the September 25 boycott meeting: masons, bricklayers, carpenters and joiners, bakers, printers, painters, plasterers, truckmen, labourers, caulkers, shipwrights, shoemakers, and coopers.[74] There is good reason to suppose that this labour unity made Moirs pay a heavy price for its intransigence.

The best evidence of this comes from the action of the company itself. On October 16 the company's bookkeeper, W.J. Richardson, assembled the employees of the factory in the soft-bread department, appropriately bedecked with flags, and presented an address from the workmen to W.C. Moir. Signed by ninety-one employees (out of a reported work force of 112), the address denied the legitimacy of the boycott movement.

We feel the time has now arrived when we should place ourselves right before the public and would say we have no sympathy with the few irresponsible parties who are vainly endeavoring to inflict injury on a private firm where the number employed and amount disbursed in wages are second to none in this city. . . . We would say the onus of this movement should not be laid at the door of the few working men who have lent their aid in this [farce?], but to a certain combination of men who, ashamed to openly appear and take part in this movement, vainly endeavor to shield themselves behind the trades union, and who in legitimate competition have neither the experience or the business ability therefor.

This display of loyalty was capped with the presentation of a silver epergne to Moir, who replied to the address by noting that the dissatisfaction in the trade had evidently not emanated from his establishment.[75]

We are immediately presented with an insoluble problem: did this document reflect the employees' sentiments? The *Trades Journal* promptly termed it a bogus presentation, and given the financial state of Moirs one can well imagine the sort of threats that might have been brought to bear on employees.[76] Lewis Archibald's reply to the address, however, was not primarily an attack on the way it had been drawn up, although he certainly alluded to this, but to its substance. Indeed he implicitly accepted it as a genuine demonstration of the spinelessness of the factory workers.

> Of the weight to be attached to the address we have this to say, that it is entitled to as much consideration as would be due to anything said by men who are willing to work 16 to 18 hours per day, for, in some cases, less than 10 hours' pay, rather than assert their rights and insist upon fair remuneration for their labours.[77]

Archibald denied vigorously the allegation that the boycott was a movement of small masters.

It is quite suggestive that the Moirs workers did not go on strike to back up the boycott. And it is equally suggestive that their address killed the boycott movement. There was one last great public meeting on November 13, which drew close to 200 workingmen to the Lyceum and gave the boycott's leaders one final opportunity to denounce Moirs, but after this the movement disappeared.[78]

This defeat apparently did not dislodge the union from the other bakeries of the city, but it did drive it to seek alternatives, first in the Knights of Labor,[79] and next in the fledgling Journeymen Bakers' and Confectioners' International Union of America, whose first Canadian local was founded in Halifax in 1889.[80] This was hardly a case of "labour imperialism," for the new union was dominated by the same men who had led the old. Although the bakers saw the new union as a great source of strength, it was probably more important for moral support and as a source of ideas. The period of the greatest conflict in the trade thus ended with the establishment of a new and quite different union.[81]

What conceptions of themselves and society did the 1884 boycotters have? The question is immensely complex, but three points may be established. The first is that the bakers saw the factory as *the* enemy, not only in immediate terms, but as a danger to the independence and respectability of the craftsman. A second point is that the journeymen bakers were separated by a wide gulf from the factory workers, including the journeymen bakers in the soft-bread bakery of Moirs, whose hours they sought to reduce. Finally, it may be claimed that the journeymen were influenced by the petty proprietors, and it was the question of their continued existence that provided much of the fire of the debate. In short, the bakers built on the earlier impulse to parity with other crafts to incorporate the interests of the threatened trade as a whole.

This dispute was the crystallizing moment of opposition to the factory. It was somewhat accidental that the factory emerged as the prime enemy, for the key issue was not the displacement of craftsmen by technology but the continued reliance of the firm on sweated manual labour. Moirs' financial crisis and its military connections were greater factors than a displacement of traditional privileges and controls.

In the bakers' analysis, the factory's policies were "degrading to honest labour," "destroying the independence of the working man."[82] These themes were brought out by Archibald in a speech at the November 13 meeting. In a play on the phrase "arts and mysteries" associated with medieval apprenticeship, Archibald indicted not just Moirs but the large bakery:

He believed that Moir didn't recognize journeymen bakers as whitemen. He wasn't gentleman enough to answer the letter of the committee. Moir told them that he would not be dictated to. . . . The speaker gave his experiences of learning the arts and mysteries of baking. He learned the 'arts' all right in a small shop, but the 'mysteries' were all confined to the large establishments – and they were 'mysteries' that the men had not yet been able to solve.

The system of Moirs, Archibald continued, was a species of "white slavery," "a crime against the man, the family, the home, the state, and nature." And what could become of boys who worked in such a factory? "They could not develop. They could not improve. They could not become good citizens in the highest meaning of that word."[83]

Such comments have obvious links to respectability, and the involvement of leading figures of other Halifax crafts (particularly the painters, printers, masons, and plasterers) indicated the general craft orientation of the struggle. But the specificity of the Moirs' boycott meant that in it the factory, for the first time in the Halifax labour movement, was made the general symbol of exploitation.

Distinctly related to this issue was the highly ambivalent tone of the boycott movement toward the factory workers. This was the response of craftsmen toward an external force, not a movement generated from within the factory.

From Archibald, a former employee of Moirs, one heard general statements of concern about the welfare of juvenile workers, echoed in his testimony before the Royal Commission in 1888.[84] But toward his fellow journeymen bakers at Moirs, Archibald voiced a certain impatience, if not contempt. Speaking of the address of the employees, he suggested that it was "entitled to the weight to be given to the utterances of men who in private curse their employers, not only deeply but loudly, but before them fawn and cringe and lick the hand that smites them."[85] This may have been the outraged response of a man let down by those who had encouraged him, yet the pattern of events in 1884 clearly shows a work force split along the lines of factory and non-factory. It was revealing and significant that one of the speakers at the November meeting was P.F. Martin, who related at great length the painters' experience in fighting the incursions of the unskilled into the trade.[86] The issue in baking and confectionery was more complex than this, for it was not yet a matter of replacing journeymen with unskilled workers. But it nonetheless involved the same split in the consciousness of the work force, between those who, with Archibald, defined themselves in terms of independence and those who had signed the address and had not protested with the journeymen.

Our third point emerges from the first two. The unstated theme of the boycott was the role of the petty proprietors. It is brought out in the presence of Hugh Montgomerie as secretary of the union – the same man whose little bakery is recorded in the probate records, and who either in 1884 or 1885 established himself as a petty proprietor (Table 4). It was also brought out in the address to Moir from his employees, who thought that the movement had originated among the petty proprietors. It is impossible to say whether or not the small handicraft masters had a role in the movement. The most one can say is that the absence of any collective defence of Moirs by other master bakers is suggestive. When Moirs burned down in 1891, the master bakers' organization passed a resolution of condolence and Moirs had the use of his competitors' ovens. Employers also took a collective position in negotiations in 1890, and their organization had a role in recreational activities. It is not impossible that other small masters, recovering from a destructive price war earlier in the year, may have given their support to an action against an undercutting competitor, although no evidence can be brought to bear directly on this point.

What is certain is that the journeymen took the needs of the small masters into account and made them a major focus of their agitation. The edifice that was founded on the slogan "respectability" now incorporated the phrase "legitimate trade": Moir was said to be "gradually but surely sapping the foundation of legitimate trade" when the bakers presented their case to the ATU.[87] In another account of the same presentation (it is not clear if the wording is that used by the bakers themselves) the theme of legitimate trade was sounded again when it was pointed out that "all the other bakehouses have to follow their [Moirs'] lead in getting the most labor possible from their workmen in order to compete with the larger establishments, the action of one firm injuring all the bakers in the city."[88] Archibald, in his reply to the Moirs' address, also focused on the theme of unfair competition: "Our action was taken to prevent others from following in the footsteps of the heartless and mercenary proprietors whose unfair manner of doing business we have opposed and have not dared to come before the public and deny any one of the charges preferred."[89]

Again in his November speech, Archibald pointed out that Moir had monopolized "all the fat contracts ... because other bakers can't begin to compete with him. They haven't the conscience to ask their men to work 18 hours a day." At the thought of Moirs becoming the city's sole bakery, which Moir was reported to have advocated, Archibald cried out, "God help Halifax when Moirs shall be the only bakery in it!"[90] Rather than the domination of the market by one factory, Archibald held out the alternative of price regulation by masters and journeymen: "I would think," he told the Royal Commission in 1888, "if the employers formed an association, if they all agreed to that, that the journeymen and the employers could regulate the price if they could only come together and do it. They are acting independently on their own resources, and one man comes out with cheap bread and of course the other man has to compete with that cheap bread or else the cheap labor and long hours makes [sic] him handicapped."[91]

These indications that journeymen shared the small masters' interest in restraining competition, and hence in restraining the factory, must be located within the economy of the trade. As we have seen, the analysis was an entirely logical and correct appraisal of the balance of productive forces. But the consequences of such analysis were that the journeymen in the agitation of 1884 obviously did not marshall the support of the factory work force, nor even the soft-bread bakers on whose interest they fought, while they often spoke in support of the small masters being threatened by the factory. Indeed, they often spoke on behalf of the petty proprietorship that many of them would one day achieve.

The consciousness of the journeymen in the 1880's was complex, but it would not be entirely wrong to say that the lines of cleavage within the industry had shifted. In the 1860's the journeymen and masters were polarized; in the 1880's, the journeymen approximated the outlook of the small proprietors on the question of competition and unfair practice but were far distant from the outlook of the factory workers.

The Third Period, 1890-1896. The formation of the first Canadian local of the Journeymen Bakers' and Confectioners' International Union of America at Halifax in 1889 was a step of major importance for the bakers. It coincided with a period of rapid expansion in the union, which was quite characteristic of Halifax labour from 1889-1891.

Rumours that the bakers were going to participate in the city's nine-hour movement were afloat in April, 1890, but only in early May did the bakers issue a set of demands. Gone were the rhetorical flourishes and appeals for support. Numbers of men in the union had surged; sixty men marched in the bakers contingent to the 1890 Labour Day Parade, which (if we assume that women and children were largely excluded) was roughly a third of the total work force. If, however, we make the assumption that organization was centred on the bread-baking, then we may conclude that bread-bakers were almost entirely organized.[92] The union was acting with confidence and put forth demands for a complete reform of the trade:

That the hours be 10 per day to commence at 6 A.M., and end at 6 P.M., with two meal hours for breakfast and dinner.

That the wages for a journeyman be $10 per week, for foremen $12 per week.

That the pay for overtime be 25 cents per hour, overtime to be allowed only when no men are idle, or in case of emergency.

We also claim pay for holidays and for time employed in setting sponge.

That the pay for a jobber be $2 per day except in case he should work a full week, then he is to receive the same as a steady hand.[93]

All but three of the master bakers capitulated immediately – Moirs included – and another gave in after a few days. This was a major victory, both in the reforms it had achieved in working conditions and in the very fact that at long last a standard rate had been established. Part of the explanation of the success may lie in the masters' organization, for in this case collective organization on the employers' side was far tighter than it had been before.[94]

The victory was short-lived. Moir, notwithstanding his agreement to the conditions imposed by the union in May, fired all his unionized employees in January, 1891.[95] No sources explain this precipitate action, although the choice of January as a month for such a mass lockout suggests a well-conceived, anti-union drive. Boys and drivers replaced the journeymen in the bakehouse. Although various craft societies pledged not to buy Moirs' products, and the printers even gave the bakers' union $30 for support of the discharged men, it was all to no avail.[96] Moirs had triumphed after all. Soon the local was failing, losing both members and its good reputation in the international union.[97] The union's listing in the trade-union newspaper was dropped in 1896, probably two years after the local had become defunct.

Our notions of consciousness of the bakers in this period of decline and defeat are far more tentative than the earlier discussion because of the paucity of sources. Certainly the communications from Local 89, which often began "Dear comrades," and contained references to "scab shops," indicate a certain evolution on the part of the language of trade unionism. There is no evidence, however, to suggest that the bakers became socialists or made any impact on local politics. The international union was largely peripheral to the history of the industry.

From 1896 to 1920, the industry was not disturbed by agitations, and when in 1920 a strike was organized, it was by those who saw themselves as factory labourers, not craftsmen. The effects of disorganization were felt throughout the industry; in 1904 the *Herald* reported that long hours and low pay were again the leading features of the Halifax trade.[98] In 1896 ended a long history that was formed in the matrix of the evolution of the factory; and it was the lesson of this history that, in the long term, the factory could always defeat craftsmen who confronted it as an external threat to their livelihood.

Conclusion

The factory produced a stratified labour force whose unity both within and outside its walls was highly vulnerable. Because handicraft bakeries persisted alongside the factory, the option of petty proprietorship remained open to journeymen throughout our period. While this did not create a passive work force – indeed the theme of petty proprietorship inflamed the boycott movement of 1884 – it limited the wider resonance of the journeymen's struggle. This is not a question of skilled workers rejecting factory workers because of selfishness, craft narrowness, or moral failing. It was rather a case of cleavages within the work force following the boundaries dictated by production itself.

How typical was this case? If outright proletarianization of the craftsman was an unusual event, as it would appear to have been in Halifax, and if the formulation of "concurrent phases" accurately captures the general evolution of capitalist production, the case of the Halifax bakers may be taken as a moment of a far more general phenomenon of division within the working class. British historians, for example, have developed the theory of the labour aristocracy to account for a persistent tendency for workers to divide on lines of skill. The labour aristocracy, it is argued, embodied highly ambivalent values, incorporating both accommodative and radical elements; such a stratum could not identify fully with the entire working class.[99] American theorists have approached the question of division within the working class by analysing the process of segmentation within the labour market, which they see as a process initiated by large corporations in the 1920's and 1930's.[100]

The case of the Halifax baker seems to indicate a process of segmentation within the working class of the city. The journeymen bakers developed a strong sense of unity with other craftsmen and a strong hostility to men outside their craft tradition who worked in the manufactories. Although the bakers can hardly be considered highly privileged, they did identify with the small masters of the trade. The organization of the mode of production precluded any effective class alliance with the unskilled factory workers. Could one not therefore argue that implicit in the uneasy coexistence of the handicraft, manufactory, and factory was the development of working-class strata whose defensive struggles unified craftsmen but not the working class as a whole? Perhaps it is by exploring cases such as this one that we will begin to understand the strange stability of nineteenth-century Canadian capitalism.

4

The "Nationalization" of the Bank of Nova Scotia, 1880-1910

James D. Frost

Surprisingly little attention has been paid to the role of capital in the economic history of the Maritimes. Some general information may be gleaned from the official histories of the Bank of Nova Scotia, the Royal Bank of Canada, and the Canadian Bank of Commerce,[1] and several recent studies have provided insight into the fortunes of some of the region's smaller banks.[2] The significance of finance capital in regional development has been most forcefully underlined by T.W. Acheson and R.T. Naylor, who have advanced some provocative generalizations about the role of the banks in the industrialization of the Maritimes. Acheson has argued that the Maritimes lacked institutions prepared to finance large-scale industrialization, and as a result the responsibility for undertaking industrial investment was thrown largely on the shoulders of individual entrepreneurs. Industrialization therefore took place in the smaller towns of the region, with only limited involvement by Halifax and Saint John businessmen and banks.[3] Similarly, Naylor has argued that the larger banks retained a "commercial" orientation and that while the financing of industrialization was undertaken by smaller local banks, the major banks promoted the flow of capital out of the Maritimes and into the Canadian West and the Caribbean, thereby starving local industry of needed capital.[4]

For most of the critical years in the industrialization of the Maritimes, the three decades from 1880 to 1910, the Bank of Nova

Reprinted with permission from *Acadiensis*, XII, 1 (Autumn, 1982), pp. 3-38.

Scotia was the largest and most influential banking institution in the region. A close examination of the bank's lending practices during this period casts doubt on the conclusion that the large Maritime banks failed to support industrial enterprises in the region. The Bank of Nova Scotia had no special hostility toward industrial investments. In the 1880's the Bank of Nova Scotia was a significant participant in attempts to industrialize the Maritimes and appeared to support the grand design aiming to make Nova Scotia one of Canada's industrial heartlands. Nevertheless, it is also clear that the Bank of Nova Scotia became increasingly interested in exploring business opportunities beyond the region. By the end of the 1890's the shift of attention away from the Maritimes was reflected in the opening of new branches outside the region and in the flow of funds out of the region. In 1900 the general manager's office was removed to Toronto, and by 1910 the Bank of Nova Scotia had been effectively transformed from a regional bank into a national financial institution.[5]

The decision to concentrate on building up business outside of the Maritimes was based on a variety of considerations. A little-examined commercial depression during the mid-1880's had a large impact on the thinking of the bank's general manager and board of directors, who began to look for more stable investments than could be found in the Maritimes. At first, the forays beyond the region were experimental in nature, and the bank continued to make large sums of capital available to borrowers in the booming industrial and resource districts of the Maritimes. However, the opening of branches in the American Midwest and in central Canada quickly began to have substantial effects on the bank's profitability, and after 1900 every effort was made to expand the bank's branch system in Ontario and the Canadian West. While new branches were opened in the Maritimes after 1900, they were primarily intended to gather deposits to support expansion elsewhere. For the Bank of Nova Scotia the Maritimes became an area of "surplus savings," where deposits exceeded loans, and in the years after 1897 enormous sums of money were drained away from the region.

Formed in 1832 as part of a challenge to the monopoly position of the Halifax Banking Company, the Bank of Nova Scotia enjoyed slow growth and modest success in its early years. Branches were established in Windsor, Pictou, Yarmouth, Annapolis Royal, and Liverpool in the 1830's, but from 1842 to 1870 the bank's paid-up capital remained stable at $560,000 and total assets grew slowly from $1.2 million to $2 million. Fortunes fluctuated with the business cycle, but the bank's financial statements suggest that the Golden Age, Reciprocity, and the U.S. Civil War brought no great prosperity to the bank, a result that may be attributed in part to the rise of rival banks and in part to poor management (including fraudulent book-keeping) on the part of the bank's chief official. The discovery of the cashier's defalcation in 1870 marked a turning point in the history of the bank, and after changes in the board of directors and the appointment of a new cashier, a flurry of expansionary activity followed. By 1880 the bank's paid-up capital was increased to $1 million and total assets had reached more than $4.3 million. In addition to the older branches (two of which had closed and then reopened), new branches had been opened in New Glasgow (1866), North Sydney (1867), Kentville (1870), Amherst (1871), Saint John (1874), Bridgetown (1877), Digby (1877), Moncton (1880), and Woodstock (1880).[6]

Figure 1
Comparison of Maritime and Non-Maritime
Loans and Deposits

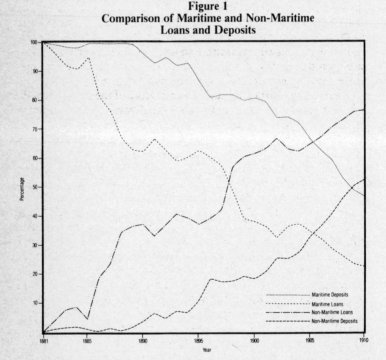

While the directors maintained tight control over the bank's affairs in these years, the bank's operations were increasingly influenced by Thomas Fyshe, who was appointed to the position of cashier, or general manager, in 1877. A native of Haddingtonshire, Scotland, Fyshe had received his training as a banker from the Bank of Scotland in the town of Leith. When Fyshe arrived in Halifax, the Bank of Nova Scotia had no systematic lending policy, but under his tutelage the bank gradually acquired an extremely efficient and highly coherent lending policy. The philosophy Fyshe brought from Scotland was beautifully simple: "the main consideration of success in banking is not large profits but small losses."[7] Under Fyshe's regime agents, or branch managers, were encouraged to avoid accommodation paper, renewals, past due bills, and unsecured overdrafts. Loans were extended for terms of thirty, sixty, or ninety days. But while the bank was not prepared to provide financing for longer terms than this, it is important to note that as long as the loan was paid back as it fell due, the bank was prepared to renew as desired. Nevertheless, the Bank of Nova Scotia was by no means prejudiced in favour of mercantile investments. Under Fyshe's direction, the bank was prepared to supply short-term working capital to any customer, whether dry goods merchant, factory owner, West Indies trader, or coal mine operator. Lending decisions depended exclusively on the quality of endorsements, the amount of security provided, and the prospect of success in each venture.[8]

It is also significant to note that although all of the members of the bank's board of directors in the 1880's had begun business as merchants of one kind or another, the directors were also themselves active participants in the industrialization of the Maritimes in the 1880's. Three of the bank's directors were directors of the Nova Scotia Cotton Company in Halifax, and two directors sat on the board of the Nova Scotia Steel Company of New Glasgow. The bank's directors were sizable shareholders in a variety of Maritime businesses. At his death in 1889 J.S. MacLean held shares in the Nova Scotia Sugar Refinery ($12,000), Nova Scotia Cotton ($2,500), and Scotia Steel ($2,200). S.A. White had invested in the Nova Scotia Cotton Company ($1,250), Moncton Sugar Refinery ($250), and Truro Consolidated Milk Company ($1,050). Daniel Cronan's investments were mostly in municipal bonds, banks, and insurance companies, but also included a $5,000 subscription of Halifax Cotton Company stock. John Doull's investments included Dominion Coal Company ($5,650), Eastern Trust Company, Halifax Tramway Company, Commercial Cable Company ($6,460), and National Salt Company ($7,400). Adam Burns, who joined the board in 1883, was a Halifax dry goods merchant, but he had extensive investments in Nova Scotia Cotton, Eastern Trust, Scotia Steel ($25,000), and Dominion

Coal ($9,000). Jairus Hart was another West Indies trader, whose holdings included Scotia Steel ($10,000) and Dominion Coal ($7,000).[9]

Fyshe's policy toward industrial investments and the directors' own interests were reflected in the expansion of the bank's branch system. Between December, 1880, and October, 1883, new branches were added in fourteen locations: Moncton, Woodstock, Newcastle, Winnipeg (closed 1885), Chatham, St. Stephen, Charlottetown, Richibucto (closed 1889), Campbellton, Sussex, Fredericton, Canning (closed 1886), Summerside, and Montague (closed 1885). Far from being reluctant to support the region's industrial aspirations, the Bank of Nova Scotia willingly endorsed such plans by advancing necessary capital. Drawing on the capital that came to it in the form of deposits, the Bank of Nova Scotia through its branch system advanced loans for investments in areas undergoing industrial expansion. While the bank did not play the role of the individual entrepreneur or direct investor, its role in mobilizing the capital resources of the region for the use of the business community was a significant contribution to the industrialization of the Maritimes.

In Halifax, where the bank's directors were closely linked to the Nova Scotia Cotton Company, the bank provided the company's working capital, which amounted to more than $80,000 by August, 1883.[10] In Saint John the principal account was that of William Parks and Son's cotton mill.[11] The opening of a Bank of Nova Scotia agency in Moncton in 1880 coincided with the construction of a sugar refinery, a cotton mill, and a gas light and power plant. While these were largely financed by the Harris family and by a prominent local private banker, Josiah Woods, the Bank of Nova Scotia supplied working capital of $62,000 for the Moncton Sugar Refining Company and more than $30,000 for the Moncton Cotton Company.[12] Before opening at Fredericton, the bank's agent was instructed to solicit the lumber and cotton business of Alexander Gibson and the lumber and rolling mill accounts of Isaac Burpee.[13] Similarly, the bank expanded to St. Stephen in May, 1882, and one year later it was supplying working capital for the St. Croix Cotton Manufacturing Company.[14] In Amherst the bank acquired the accounts of the Amherst Boot and Shoe Company and that of the growing manufacturing concern of Rhodes, Curry and Company.[15] At New Glasgow the bank's accounts included the Nova Scotia Steel Company and the Nova Scotia Glass Company.[16] In areas where industrialization was less extensive, there were other important accounts. In Pictou the bank obtained the accounts of the Pictou

Iron Foundry, the Pictou Boot and Shoe Company, and the Hope-well Woollen Mills, to which $10,000 of working capital was ad-vanced.[17] In Newcastle the most important account was that of J.J. Miller and Company, tanners, who were advanced at least $25,000 for their operations, while at Woodstock another important link with the region's tanning industry was formed with the acquisition of the account of a hemlock bark extract plant.[18]

The demand for capital in the industrializing towns of the Mari-times in the early 1880's had a major impact on the flow of funds through the branches of the Bank of Nova Scotia. By 1884 the group of branches in the eight principal industrializing towns amounted to $3.1 million per annum and accounted for almost 70 per cent of the bank's lending activity in the Maritimes. While most of these funds were generated from local deposits, more than $550,000 of "surplus" savings were marshalled from elsewhere.[19] The most active lending areas were Halifax and Saint John. In 1884 average loans at Halifax were more than $1.3 million, while deposits amounted to only $861,358. At Saint John loans averaged more than $800,000 in 1882 and 1883 and more than $750,000 in 1884; in all of these years loans exceeded deposits. The Bank of Nova Scotia was perhaps most optimistic about sugar, cotton, and railways-related industrial activ-ities in Moncton, where loans in 1884 amounted to $462,889 against deposits of only $54,461. While not extensive, the Bank of Nova Scotia also played a significant role in the industrialization of St. Stephen, Amherst, New Glasgow, and, to a lesser extent, Yarmouth and Fredericton. At St. Stephen, the St. Croix Cotton Manufactur-ing Company accounted for about 40 per cent of the loans; the branch's lending amounted to almost $150,000 in 1884, against deposits of only $37,751. In Amherst, where industrial activity was only beginning to make an impact, loans had exceeded deposits by about $50,000 during the three years 1881-83, though in 1884 the situation was reversed and deposits amounted to almost $160,000, against loans of about $150,000. The situation at New Glasgow was similar: in 1884 loans amounted to $114,261, while deposits exceeded $150,000. At Yarmouth the lending activity had increased from $35,088 to $208,991. At Fredericton the amount of activity was minimal, but in 1884 loans amounted to $43,663 against deposits of only $20,168.[20]

A critical turning point in the attitude of the bank to the indus-trialization of the Maritimes came during the economic crisis of 1882-84.[21] As early as February, 1883, Thomas Fyshe began to predict that the next three to four years would be difficult. He was worried by the lack of liquidity or ready cash, which resulted from the enormous amounts of money tied up in "permanent investment," the growing number of commercial failures, and the lack of protection under the Insolvency Act of 1875, which had been repealed in 1880.[22] By the end of 1883 the amount of "undesirable" paper in the Bank of Nova Scotia's books had reached epidemic proportions. "Notes and Bills Overdue" had increased by 383 per cent over the previous year and "Authorized Overdrafts not Specially Secured" were up 158 per cent. In 1882 Fyshe had listed seven major business failures in his records but at the end of 1883 his list had grown to more than 130.[23] Probably the worst single failure affecting the bank's business in the Maritimes in 1883 was the collapse of F. Shaw and Brothers of Boston, reputed to have been the largest tanners in the world. This failure affected a wide range of tanneries and boot and shoe makers scattered throughout Maine, New Brunswick, Nova Scotia, and Newfoundland, and also affected the St. Stephen Bank, the Bank of New Brunswick, and the Bank of Nova Scotia, all creditors to the Boston firm. The failure involved the Bank of Nova Scotia in several ways. The bark extract plant in Woodstock, New Brunswick, the bank's main customer in the town, was a creditor for a substantial amount. The bank also had a claim of many sixty- and ninety-day drafts drawn by the various tanneries on the firm in Boston, amounting to about $200,000.[24]

During 1884, as the depression in the Maritimes worsened, Fyshe instructed his agents not to discount accommodation paper without head office approval, to avoid renewing loans without a substantial reduction, and to get all paper strengthened with additional collateral if there was the slightest doubt about it. A week after these instructions were issued, Fyshe declared his willingness "to cut business down by one third, if necessary, in order to get it into a strictly legitimate shape."[25] By July, 1884, Fyshe expected the year to be the worst in the bank's history because of a list of failures that included such important firms as the Halifax West Indies trading company, the firm of J.J. Bremmer, one of the bank's directors.[26] The bank's annual statement for 1884 showed a loss of $460,000; $130,000 was taken out of the reserve fund, and total assets declined from $6.7 million to $5.6 million.[27]

This crisis had a profound material and psychological effect on the Bank of Nova Scotia. One of the first steps taken by Fyshe was to attempt to systematize the bank's lending policy in order to minimize the possibility of future losses. In a circular containing "Special Instructions to Agents in lending the Bank's Money and Getting it

Back Again," Fyshe required that loans must be secured by at least two good endorsements or one endorsement with approved collateral. Customers who did not punctually meet their notes or acceptances as they fell due were to be avoided in the future and no renewals were to be made without getting a substantial reduction on the paper. All loans or discounts that were expected to be paid out of profits rather than revenue were to be avoided "as you would the plague" and no transactions were to be entered into on a promise that the required security would be furnished later. "The Banker as a rule trusts too much to his Customer," wrote Fyshe in his circular to branch members. "There are really very few men anywhere who can be trusted to handle prudently and safely unstinted loans of money. The proverb 'give him rope enough and he will hang himself' fully illustrates the tendency of the average trader to get into difficulty when he is provided with unlimited supplies of money."[28]

By mid-1886 Fyshe had pulled the Bank of Nova Scotia out of the crisis, but he remained extremely pessimistic about the general business climate of the Maritimes. He did not blame the poor economic outlook on entrepreneurial failure, transportation rates, or a lack of resources, but, at least initially, pointed his finger at the Government Savings Banks. Forty-five out of fifty of these banks were located in the Maritime Provinces, with deposits amounting to more than $15 million. Fyshe contended that these banks drained the Maritimes of banking capital, since per capita deposits in chartered banks in the region were only $12, compared to $35 in Ontario and Quebec, while deposits in Government Savings Banks were $19 per capita in the Maritimes compared to $6 in the upper provinces. Fyshe called for the abolition of Government Savings Banks or at least a marked reduction in the amount of interest paid out by them, which was 4 per cent compared to the chartered banks' 3.5 per cent.[29] The Minister of Finance responded with an Order-in-Council reducing the limit of deposits in the banks to a maximum of $300 in one year, up to a total of $1,000, although the interest rate remained at 4 per cent.[30]

Ironically, despite Fyshe's attack on the Government Savings Banks, he had already begun looking for safer uses for the Bank of Nova Scotia's "idle" money and had begun to explore the idea of investing in United States railroad bonds. His idea was to invest in safe railroad bonds yielding 5.5 to 6 per cent interest. To guard against possible failures he proposed to limit each investment to $10,000. By March, 1885, the Bank of Nova Scotia had invested at least $289,000 in these bonds.[31] As Maritime business continued to slump, this activity was expanded, and by December 31, 1885, the bank's investment amounted to more than $600,000. This represented 11.35 per cent of the bank's total assets, and based on an average yield of 5 per cent, accounted for about 40 per cent of the bank's profits.[32]

A not unrelated development was the Bank of Nova Scotia's foray into the American Midwest. An ill-fated attempt to establish a branch in Winnipeg accidentally led the bank's full-time inspector, James B. Forgan, to scout the business climate in neighbouring Minneapolis,[33] which was booming in 1885 but lacked the short-term credit required in the lumber and milling industries. To avoid the mistakes made in Winnipeg it was decided "not to do a general banking business . . . but to make loans to the best houses on good collateral security."[34] The Bank of Nova Scotia's Minneapolis business soon consisted of making collaterally secured loans, bank rediscounts, and foreign exchange transactions. The exchange business, which was extended to include supplying the smaller local banks with New York exchange at a small profit, soon became a significant part of the operation and arrangements were made with a Chicago broker to supply daily quotations on foreign and New York exchange. One of the bank's customers was the Washburn Mill Company. On May 2, 1886, the bank loaned the company $150,000 at 6 per cent for thirty days. On June 1, 1886, the company applied for an extension on the loan plus an additional $26,000, in effect agreeing to pay 12 per cent interest for a sixty-day loan.[35] Before long Forgan had built up quite a substantial lending business in Minneapolis. By 1886 these loans averaged $872,474, or 18.6 per cent of all the bank's lending activity, while deposits amounted to just $3,266. The demand for money was so great that Forgan frequently requested additional funds from Fyshe.[36]

Before the end of the decade, the Bank of Nova Scotia also extended its operations to Montreal and to Kingston, Jamaica. As early as 1883 Fyshe had seen Montreal as a possible outlet for surplus funds. In 1887 Fyshe and the bank's directors were embarrassed when their rivals, the Merchants' Bank of Halifax, preceded them to Montreal and in 1889 they opened a branch of their own in Montreal. This new branch was not intended as another outlet for surplus funds but to negate the effects of having the bank's notes discounted at less than par value in Montreal. Prior to 1888, the Merchants' Bank of Canada had collected Bank of Nova Scotia notes in Montreal at a ⅛ per cent discount, but the increase of trade between the Maritimes and the rest of Canada had begun to make this arrangement very costly.[37] Fyshe also hoped to cultivate a good proportion of the sterling exchange business of Montreal by taking advantage of the bank's connections with Kidder, Peabody and Company of Boston, John Paton and Company of New York, and the Royal Bank of Scotland, all of whom were among the bank's correspondents. While the bank's comparatively late arrival in Montreal made it difficult for the inexperienced agent to get "in touch with the real exchange business of the place," by the end of the decade this branch was also becoming an important outlet for surplus funds, with more than $500,000 in loans against only $90,000 in deposits.[38]

The move to Jamaica arose out of the suggestion from an American stock broker that the Bank of Nova Scotia might take advantage of the potential exchange business arising from the construction of a railway on the island. Aside from this exchange business the Bank of Nova Scotia was soon handling Canadian government business in Jamaica as well as providing the mercantile houses with short-term capital to finance their sugar, rum, cocoa, and coffee exports.[39]

Fyshe's strategy for the recovery of the Bank of Nova Scotia had important implications for the Maritimes. The branches most seriously affected by the depression were those closely linked to the Maritimes cotton industry, which was beset by problems of over-capacity and American dumping. Late in 1883, the Saint John Cotton Company, headed by William Parks, was denied further credit after some of its notes fell past due, and the company was told to seek financing elsewhere. Between 1884 and 1885, the bank's loans in Saint John dropped from more than $750,000 to about $450,000, and by 1888 they had plummeted to $185,000.[40] Similarly in St. Stephen, when the St. Croix Cotton Company got into difficulties, in January, 1884, Fyshe instructed his agent to collect all of the company's paper as it fell due. While this episode did not in itself lead to a severance of the account, Fyshe was not anxious to extend the bank's services to the company. When the company presented some improperly endorsed notes it wanted to have discounted at 6 per cent without providing any collateral security, the request was refused and the company took its business elsewhere. Between 1884 and 1886 loans in St. Stephen declined from almost $150,000 to only $57,820, although a substantial recovery was made to $147,000 by 1890.[41] In Moncton, Fyshe had no quarrel with the management at the local cotton company, but his confidence in the industry had been badly shaken and he refused to make any new advances except for the purposes of selling existing stock. All past due bills were called in by December, 1884. Loans at Moncton declined from a high of $465,000 in 1884 to slightly more than $200,000 in 1887. A partial recovery was made by 1890, to about $300,000, but at no time in the next twenty years did lending activity in Moncton reach its former level.[42]

In 1888 Fyshe was appointed one of the auditors for the Nova Scotia Cotton Company in Halifax, which had paid dividends of only 3 per cent in the six years of its existence, a record that caused widespread dissatisfaction among the shareholders. After looking over the company's books, Fyshe became convinced that "it had never earned any money." Because it had been spending money on its capital account without first consulting the bank, which was supplying the working capital, Fyshe began a general agitation for a change in management, and the bank's vice-president, John Doull, and director Adam Burns were ousted from their positions as president and director of the cotton company.[43] Fyshe's ability to bring about these changes without putting his own job in jeopardy says a great deal about the power he wielded after pulling the bank out of the depression. Moreover, while the bank continued to support the cotton company with working capital, it did not do so "unhesitatingly," as one director suggested it should, and the company continued to experience problems related to the depressed conditions of the industry. In 1889 it had its "worst year ever" and in 1890 it cut production to three days a week from mid-June to mid-September. The company's directors became convinced that "the only hope of improving the existing conditions of the mills is to place them under one management" and six months later the company's stock was transferred to the Dominion Cotton Mills Company headed by David Morrice and A.T. Gault.[44]

Despite the problems experienced at Saint John, Moncton, St. Stephen, and Halifax, the Bank of Nova Scotia continued to show an interest in developments in Amherst and New Glasgow. In Amherst, capital investment in manufacturing increased from $81,000 in 1881 to $457,040 in 1891; the number of industrial employees jumped from 283 to 683; and the value of the town's output increased from $283,000 to $724,312. After the depression, the bank's loans increased rapidly, from $150,000 in 1884 to $480,836 in 1890. Because deposits grew more slowly, from $159,000 in 1884 to $344,842 in 1890, the branch had to borrow funds from the head office to support this loan activity. By 1890 the branch at Amherst was doing the second largest lending business of all the Maritime branches.[45]

New Glasgow experienced even greater industrial expansion. As capital investment in manufacturing increased from $160,000 in 1881 to over $1 million in 1891, the number of employees in industry grew from 360 to more than 1,000, and the value of the town's output increased from $313,000 to more than $1.5 million. The bank's loans in this area also increased rapidly from less than $100,000 in 1884 to almost $310,000 in 1888, and because local deposits were insufficient to meet local needs, from 1885 until 1889 this branch also had to borrow from the head office.[46] Unfortunately, in June, 1886, the bank's agent, J.W. Carmichael, granted the Nova Scotia Steel Company a $25,000 unsecured overdraft. Mindful of what had happened in 1883-84, Fyshe wrote: "I do not expect anything but disaster to follow concessions of this kind." When Graham Fraser, the head of the steel company, insisted in November, 1887, on a *carte blanche* – unlimited overdrafts without collateral security – Fyshe declared: "I have done all I could for your company consistent with the safety of the Bank . . . I think we have some reason to complain of the grasping and exacting disposition of some of our New Glasgow friends considering how we have endeavoured to serve them." The account was lost, and by 1890 the bank's loans in New Glasgow had dropped to $150,000.[47]

While the Bank of Nova Scotia continued to show an interest in regional development, Fyshe's policies did lead to a change in emphasis. Between 1886 and 1888 deposits in Maritime branches grew by $1.2 million, but loans in the Maritimes increased by only $200,000. Part of the rationalization of lending policy was undoubtedly designed to serve the agency in Minneapolis, where loans grew from $872,000 in 1886 to more than $1.6 million in 1888, with deposits of only $3,200 and $24,000 in these two years. Only Halifax and Amherst absorbed more of the bank's funds than Minneapolis. While the eight industralizing towns in the Maritimes accounted for almost 76 per cent of the Bank of Nova Scotia's Maritime loans in 1890, more than 50 per cent of the Maritime loans went to Halifax and Amherst. Clearly, the regional leadership the Bank of Nova Scotia had provided during the early 1880's had been severely compromised both by the depression and by the prospect of enormous profits to be made elsewhere.

The pattern established during the 1880's continued in the following decade. By the end of the century the flow of funds within the branch system of the Bank of Nova Scotia had begun to drain money out of the Maritimes. In 1891 the bank's Maritime branches accounted for 95.2 per cent of all deposits and 66.6 per cent of all loans; by 1900 almost 50 per cent of deposits still came from the

Maritimes, but only 32.5 per cent of all lending activity took place in the Maritimes and more than $5.3 million of "surplus" capital was leaving the region for employment elsewhere.[48] While the demand for money was cyclical, the bank's records suggest that there was distinct reluctance to build up the lending aspect of its Maritime business. In a circular in 1893, for instance, Fyshe admonished his agents thus: "The bank's loans in the lower provinces have increased nearly $400,000 since May 25. All this money has had to be brought here from Chicago where it might have been getting 10 per cent or more." And in 1896 Fyshe offered his branch managers similar counsel: "Judging from our own experience there has been a large expansion of loans in the Maritime Provinces during the last two years, an expansion altogether out of proportion to the healthy growth of trade."[49]

A number of problems continued to undermine the bank's confidence in the region. One of these was the gradual collapse of a once thriving industrial and financial community in Yarmouth. The Bank of Nova Scotia attempted to assist in efforts to make the transition from the old sea-faring economy to the new industrialism by lending working capital to the Yarmouth Cotton Duck and Yarn Company and the Burrill and Johnson Iron Company. But while the cotton company accounted for almost 45 per cent of the bank's loans in 1892, a large proportion of its remaining business was with companies or individuals who had not made the transition. By 1895 a dozen companies were listed as "bad accounts" with "excessive liabilities." The Cape Sable Packing Company, with $7,800 capital, had bills payable of $5,800 on their books in Sepember, 1897.[50] E.K. Spinney, a local hardware merchant and entrepreneur, had liabilities owing to the Bank of Nova Scotia amounting to $73,500 and about $40,000 to the Exchange Bank of Yarmouth–altogether about $113,000 of bank accommodation on a business aggregating total sales of about $200,000 yearly.[51] Another customer, Jacob Sweeney, a furniture manufacturer, had $9,060 overdrawn on an average current account of $69 and had to renew his bills payable of $25 and up. "What a commentary on banking in Nova Scotia!" exclaimed H.C. McLeod, who succeeded Fyshe as general manager in 1897.[52]

More serious was the situation in Saint John. Although average loans increased from almost $250,000 in 1891 to more than $850,000 in 1899, McLeod felt that many of the loans had been made at the expense of sound business practice, ignoring the dictum that "our sole desire . . . is to have you build up a good, safe business, the first consideration being safety, magnitude and profits being secondary."

In 1898 McLeod initiated a general house-cleaning of the branch's bad accounts. They included the account of Blair and Company, bankers and relatives of the branch manager, who owed more than $90,000 against collateral security of less than $70,000; Whittaker and Company, who had failed in 1887 but for whom the manager was still discounting paper; and Rankin and Moulson, grocers, who kept an average current account of $1 and to whom the manager had loaned $2,409. The clamp-down involved at least twenty-seven firms, some of which had widespread influence in Saint John's business community.[53] To offset any illwill, McLeod proposed to offer a seat on the bank's board to one of the partners of Manchester, Robertson and Allison, wholesale and retail dry goods, carpets, and furniture dealers, whose business was "the most important in New Brunswick."[54] Nonetheless, by 1900 lending activity by the Bank of Nova Scotia had been severely curtailed in Saint John. Loans dropped by $150,000 between 1900 and 1901, and by another $200,000 the following year. Saint John became an area of "surplus savings," by 1900 exporting almost $350,000 for employment elsewhere.[55]

Similar conditions prevailed in New Glasgow, St. Stephen, Moncton, and Halifax. In New Glasgow, industrial capital investment declined by almost 60 per cent from slightly over $1 million to about $440,000, the number of industrial employees dropped from 1,117 to just 430, and the value of the town's output fell from $1.5 million to $438,767. These figures are difficult to explain, since New Glasgow was the centre of significant development in the coal, iron, and steel industries, culminating in the formation of the Nova Scotia Steel and Coal Company in 1900. Yet the Bank of Nova Scotia's lending figures reflect the census data. Loans averaged $185,000 per annum for the whole decade, rising as high as $239,534 in 1897 and as low as $143,488 in 1900. Contrary to what might be expected, New Glasgow was actually sending more than $700,000 of "surplus" to the head office for employment elsewhere in 1900 and only 16.9 per cent of the funds deposited there were going back into the community.[56]

The only bright spot among the eight towns that had attempted industrialization in the 1880's was "Busy Amherst," which experienced remarkable growth throughout the 1890's. Industrial capital investment more than tripled, from $457,040 in 1890 to more than $1.4 million in 1900, the number of persons employed in industry almost doubled, from 683 to 1,299, and the value of the town's output more than doubled, from $724,312 to $1.5 million. The bank's lending pattern reflected a great deal of confidence in the town, and its accounts included the Hewson Woollen Mills, Amherst

Table 1
Loans and Deposits, Maritimes Branches,
Bank of Nova Scotia, 1881-1910

Year	Loans ($)	Average Rate of Interest on Loans (%)	Deposits ($)	Ratio Loans/Deposits
1881	3,473,981	6.82	2,132,406	1.629
1882	4,251,802	6.74	2,769,408	1.535
1883	4,357,909	6.63	3,021,982	1.442
1884	4,571,670	6.56	3,275,416	1.395
1885	3,818,938	6.84	2,737,087	1.395
1886	3,737,437	6.91	2,837,864	1.317
1887	4,030,314	6.86	3,289,581	1.225
1888	3,937,310	6.97	4,655,745	.971
1889	4,310,288	7.18	4,610,545	.934
1890	4,545,940	6.93	4,934,039	.931
1891	5,323,962	7.00	5,156,692	1.032
1892	5,281,662	7.22	5,241,811	1.006
1893	5,062,173	7.32	6,201,596	.973
1894	5,654,287	7.22	5,464,430	1.035
1895	6,412,012	7.12	6,342,651	1.054
1896	5,658,204	7.07	6,594,592	1.046
1897	6,838,160	7.02	7,119,857	.952
1898	4,858,481	6.90	8,149,338	.572
1899	4,963,760	6.79	9,194,293	.540
1900	5,459,952	6.41	10,770,234	.506
1901	5,741,979	6.24	12,491,658	.460
1902	5,637,779	6.43	13,924,245	.398
1903	5,718,153	6.74	14,908,843	.454
1904	7,641,391	6.64	16,247,624	.462
1905	7,663,753	6.60	19,972,131	.472
1906	7,377,877	6.49	15,364,399	.450
1907	7,354,411	6.74	15,684,543	.469
1908	6,351,099	6.96	15,635,772	.406
1909	6,619,966	6.73	16,351,431	.405
1910	7,717,729	6.78	17,635,452	.438

SOURCE: Compiled from Statistical Records, 1881-1914, Bank of Nova Scotia Archives.

Boot and Shoe Company, Cumberland Packing Company, Amherst Lumbering Company, Amherst Foundry Company, and Amherst Malleable Iron Company. Between 1891 and 1900, loans averaged $472,623, ranging from $368,000 in 1892 to $548,000 in 1895. The branch was a net borrower of funds from the head office throughout the period, since the amount on deposit was insufficient to meet local needs. But Amherst was very much the exception among the Maritime branches during the 1890's.[57]

The drain of funds away from the industrializing towns was offset to a certain degree by a sharp increase in lending activity in areas associated with staples-related industries. The best example of this phenomenon was the branch at Sussex, New Brunswick. Located on the Kennebecasis River in an agricultural and lumbering district, the village's hinterland of Kings and Albert Counties in 1901 accounted for industrial investments of $754,986, mostly in log products, butter and cheese, mineral waters, flour and grist mills, and two foundries. There was also a very active merchant class in the village, headed by the White family who owned the Sussex Mercantile Company and whose influence in the surrounding area was actively cultivated by the Bank of Nova Scotia. Between 1891 and 1900, loans at Sussex increased from $115,047 to $412,231. Because deposits grew at a slower rate, from $62,190 to $247,904, the branch had to borrow funds from the head office. By 1900 the bank's business at Sussex had grown to such an extent that it was doing the fifth largest lending business of all the Maritime branches, behind only Halifax, Amherst, Saint John, and Charlottetown.[58]

At the same time, the bank's expansion beyond the Maritimes continued unabated. In 1892 the agency at Minneapolis was moved to Chicago to take advantage of foreign exchange business created by the Chicago Exhibition of 1893. As a financial and industrial centre, Minneapolis was rapidly losing ground to Chicago. By 1892 the Minneapolis-based industries required smaller amounts of local funds, for as consolidations took place in the lumber and milling industries, the new conglomerates sought financing in national money markets where credit could be obtained at cheaper rates. It is perhaps not a coincidence that when the newly created Pillsbury-Washburn Flour Mills Company moved its headquarters to Chicago, the Bank of Nova Scotia, one of the company's bankers, followed shortly after. The bank's activities in Chicago were extremely profitable. By 1900 annual loans at that branch amounted to more than $3.7 million, or about 22 per cent of the bank's total lending activity.

While there was a significant growth in deposits, from $47,102 in 1892 to $480,402 in 1900, about $3.6 million had to be transferred to meet the lending requirements of the Chicago branch.[59]

The Montreal branch was also doing well by the end of the decade. Loans increased from about $500,000 in 1890 to over $2.1 million in 1900, while deposits increased from $95,000 to $375,000.[60] In Jamaica, however, the bank's deposit and lending activity remained very modest. Deposits grew from $56,302 in 1890 to $376,742 in 1900, while loans grew from $41,940 to $155,040. The ratio of loans to deposits averaged .66, which means that 66 per cent of all money deposited was finding its way back into the community. Since the interest rate for loans averaged 4.72 per cent, the rates prevailing in Jamaica made it relatively inexpensive to borrow money. Over the whole decade "only" $424,407 was exported as "surplus," which means that on the whole Jamaica's interests were better served than those of many towns in the Maritimes. But the bank's Jamaican business up to 1900 was a disappointment to the directors and management, and further opportunities to expand in the West Indies were postponed.[61]

On the other hand, the Bank of Nova Scotia did expand into Newfoundland during this period. In 1892 both the Commercial Bank of Newfoundland and the Union Bank of Newfoundland collapsed. In the wake of this crisis, a scandal broke; it was discovered that the five directors of the Commercial Bank were in debt to that bank for $1.8 million. Further enquiries revealed that the premier of the colony had been closely associated with the Commercial Bank, and that the government's borrowings for public expenditures had been so great that the bank had been left in a terminally weak position.[62] Under these circumstances, the Newfoundlanders looked to the Canadian banks for assistance, and the Bank of Nova Scotia, the Merchants' Bank of Halifax, and the Bank of Montreal obliged. In fact, the Bank of Nova Scotia would have gone to the island without an invitation, for the directors had already decided to "send two officers to that place to look after the interests of the bank, and to give what assistance we could to the banks and mercantile houses there."[63] While the Canadian banks may appear to have been merciless predators in this crisis, the resources of the Bank of Nova Scotia were severely strained by this decision, since, unlike the Merchants' Bank of Halifax, it did not increase its capital to underwrite this expansion. Contrary to what one writer has suggested, Newfoundland was not an area where "surplus" funds were gleaned, at least not for the Bank of Nova Scotia. In 1900 loans at St. John's were

$658,155 against $437,814 on deposit, and the agency borrowed $398,331 from the head office. These figures were offset, however, by another agency that was opened in Harbour Grace, Newfoundland, in 1895. This branch was devoted mainly to gathering deposits, which amounted to $168,683 in 1900, of which $131,485 was transferred to the head office account.[64]

Between 1900 and 1910 the Bank of Nova Scotia moved most dramatically to become a national financial institution. Sixty-two branches were added; these included nineteen in the Maritimes, twenty-eight elsewhere in the rest of Canada, nine in the Caribbean, five in Newfoundland, and one in the United States. By 1910 the bank was operating a total of ninety-eight branches: forty-four in the Maritimes, thirty-four in other parts of Canada, and twenty branches outside Canada. Though the bank's head office remained nominally in Halifax, in March, 1900, the general office was moved to Toronto, apparently in order to bring its administration closer to developments taking place in Ontario, the American Midwest, and the Canadian West.[65] Ontario quickly became the main focus of the bank's activity, with nineteen new branches being added after the general office was moved, eleven in the Toronto area alone. During that decade total loans for all of Ontario increased from $1.4 million to $9.1 million, or from about 10 per cent of all lending activity to 28 per cent. This expansion was initially financed by savings from either the Maritimes or the West Indies, although Ontario began to supply some of its own "surplus" from outside Toronto and Hamilton. Total Ontario deposits grew from $270,134 in 1900 to more than $5.3 million in 1910, and by the end of the decade over $1.4 million of "surplus" was being generated in Ontario.[66]

In Montreal the bank also expanded its activities after 1900. It acquired such important accounts as the Wire and Cable Company, controlled by Bell Telephone, and A.E. Rea and Company, the second largest retail dry goods business in Canada. Overall, the bank's lending activity in Montreal fluctuated considerably from as low as $1.7 million in 1905 to as high as $3.6 million in 1910, but as in Ontario considerable growth in deposits took place, from $371,452 in 1900 to more than $1.7 million in 1910.[67] Elsewhere in Quebec, a branch was planned at Shawinigan Falls after an agreement was reached with the Belgo-Canadian Pulp Company to take on their account. While the deal collapsed, this example illustrated the type of account the Bank of Nova Scotia was interested in securing.[68]

Additional branches were also added in western Canada after 1900. The board decided to open branches in Vancouver, Calgary,

Table 2
Loans and Deposits, Non-Maritimes Branches,
Bank of Nova Scotia, 1882-1910

Year	Loans ($)	Average Rate of Interest on Loans (%)	Deposits ($)	Ratio Loans/Deposits
1882	165,068	9.27	34,264	4.818
1883	377,502	8.54	54,143	6.972
1884	432,798	6.58	63,423	6.824
1885	173,378	5.27	27,335	5,906
1886	872,474	6.03	3,266	267.138
1887	1,245,237	6.98	55,774	25.211
1888	1,847,327	5.69	49,331	38.456
1889	2,456,277	5.91	44,785	28.971
1890	2,708,111	5.71	201,325	13.477
1891	2,656,676	5.85	259,668	10.255
1892	2,126,058	5.07	266,610	11.814
1893	3,511,446	6.63	418,690	8.391
1894	3,727,579	4.95	400,808	9.300
1895	3,827,240	5.53	906,044	4.224
1896	4,500,199	5.83	1,465,847	3.070
1897	4,957,126	5.54	1,535,408	3.235
1898	6,219,664	4.80	1,774,650	3.505
1899	7,636,064	5.84	2,121,351	3.434
1900	8,857,392	5.94	2,444,732	3.636
1901	10,040,819	5.49	3,316,756	3.027
1902	11,569,243	5.78	4,846,316	2.387
1903	11,678,673	6.90	5,187,686	2.276
1904	11,662,266	6.23	5,845,724	1.995
1905	13,160,139	6.32	7,334,880	1.782
1906	15,344,418	6.17	8,739,549	1.756
1907	17,990,339	6.65	10,818,095	1.649
1908	17,710,223	6.53	13,533,681	1.309
1909	21,098,330	6.14	16,909,643	1.248
1910	25,039,285	6.40	19,852,645	1.291

SOURCE: Compiled from Statistical Records, 1881-1914, Bank of Nova Scotia Archives.

Edmonton, Fort Saskatchewan, Strathcona, and Wetaskiwin, Alberta.[69] While these branches lost about $10,000 in their first year of operation, by early 1905 the branch at Calgary was considered to be "self-sustaining." In Winnipeg there was also a growth in activity. For the first six years after reopening the branch in 1899, the bank concentrated on building up a good deposit business before committing itself to any commercial or industrial accounts. Between 1899 and 1905 loans increased from $39,491 to $271,762, while deposits grew from $37,583 to $441,461 to more than $1.7 million, against a corresponding increase in deposits from $441,409 to $717,030.[70]

The Bank of Nova Scotia's good business connections in Chicago led to an agreement with the newly formed International Harvester Company to do its collections in western Canada, Ontario, and, when an office was opened in Saint John, the Maritime Provinces. International Harvester expanded rapidly and by 1901 the Bank of Nova Scotia was discounting more than $325,000 of the company's paper in Saint John alone.[71] This account provided a clear indication of the bank's emerging national and international stature. Indeed, despite some losses incurred by the failure of the Chicago National Bank and other companies controlled by A.G. Becker, as well as some worry caused by the suspension and reorganization of the Pillsbury-Washburn Flour Mills, business in Chicago grew steadily. Annual loans fluctuated between $2.9 million and $4.3 million, while deposits grew from $480,402 to more than $1 million, and this branch boasted the second highest volume of loans in the whole bank in 1910.[72]

In the Caribbean, nine new branches were added, six in Jamaica, two in Cuba, one in Puerto Rico, and an ill-fated one in Trinidad. A hurricane in 1903 and an earthquake in 1907 resulted in disappointing profits in Jamaica, but the prospect of competition from the Bank of Montreal in 1906 led to a very aggressive policy through which the Bank of Nova Scotia hoped to become "The Bank" of Jamaica. The Jamaican government's account gave the bank a firm foundation on the island, and deposits increased from $376,742 in 1900 to more than $5.2 million in 1910. Lending activity was mainly confined to the United Fruit Company and loans did not keep pace with deposits, increasing from $155,040 to $865,277. As a result Jamaica became an area of surplus savings.[73] In Cuba, the Bank of Nova Scotia purchased $16,000 of Havana Central Railroad bonds in 1901, but a branch was not opened there until 1906. For the very short period until 1910, loans at the two Cuban branches exceeded the amount on deposit, and Cuban borrowers benefited from imported funds.[74]

Changes in the membership of the bank's board of directors also reflected the bank's growing interest in developments outside the Maritimes. Between 1900 and 1910 eight new directors joined the board, and although most of them were Maritimers and all of them had strong interests in Maritime businesses, their other interests and holdings also indicated that they were alert to investment opportunities outside the region as well.[75]

After 1900 the Bank of Nova Scotia continued to maintain an interest in the industrialization of the Maritimes, especially in the expansion of the coal and steel industries of northeastern Nova Scotia. Two rival industrial complexes had emerged in this field: the Montreal and Toronto dominated Dominion Iron and Steel Company and the Nova Scotia Steel and Coal Company, which was the long-awaited marriage of New Glasgow industrial capitalists and Halifax finance capitalists.[76] Bank directors J. Walter Allison and George S. Campbell, who were also directors of Scotia Steel, proposed to H.C. McLeod that the Bank of Nova Scotia make a large investment in an issue of Scotia bonds. But mindful of other failed ventures in the Maritimes and doubtful of the company's prospects, McLeod demurred at the suggestion and the rest of the board accepted his view, at least temporarily.[77] However, McLeod soon agreed to allow the bank to act as agents for issuing the bonds, and as Scotia became increasingly successful Allison and Campbell gained influence and their views began to prevail.[78] A token investment of $10,000 was made around 1906, and in 1909 $500,000 of the bonds were purchased, which easily made Scotia Steel the largest single investment in the bank's portfolio. When Rodolphe Forget and Max Aitken attempted to merge Scotia Steel with the newly formed Dominion Steel Company in 1910, the Bank of Nova Scotia made direct advances to the directors of Scotia so that they could buy back shares from Forget. By July 30, 1910, these direct advances amounted to $825,000 and the attempted merger had been thwarted.[79]

The connection with Scotia also made the branch at New Glasgow an important location for lending activity, though not to the extent that might be expected. Although loans increased from $143,588 in 1900 to almost $450,000 in 1910, deposits increased from $851,913 to $1.1 million and for this whole period New Glasgow was a net exporter of funds to the head office. In 1902 New Glasgow sent as much as $1.03 million, but as the views of Allison and Campbell began to prevail this trend was reversed, so that by 1910 the branch's "surplus" was reduced to $672,227.[80] The branch at Stellarton also expanded during this period as it acquired the account of the Acadia Coal Company. At first, McLeod was reluctant to supply the company with capital but good markets, including a contract with the Grand Trunk Railway, pushed its credit limit up from $100,000 to $450,000. By 1910, however, the company had secured about $600,000 of English capital and therefore was able to minimize its banking requirements.[81] At North Sydney the flurry of activity associated with the expansion of the Nova Scotia Steel and Coal Company made for a veritable boom town. In 1900 loans were $93,995 and in 1903 they amounted to $380,596, but after 1905 they had dropped to about $198,000. This suggests that the Bank of Nova Scotia provided short-term loans for material required during the construction phase of Scotia's expansion there. Deposits grew steadily, but not spectacularly, increasing from $202,079 to $322,065 by 1905 and tailing off to about $300,000 by 1901.[82]

The same pattern was also at work in Amherst. By 1910, more than $15 million was invested in manufacturing in Amherst, more than in any other town in the Maritimes except Sydney. The most dramatic growth took place between 1900 and 1906, and the Bank of Nova Scotia's activity in Amherst matched this growth, as loans increased from $515,620 to almost $800,000.[83] But in 1907 the town was afflicted by the general economic recession of that year and Amherst's industries never fully recovered. Local industries, such as the Amherst Boot and Shoe Company and Hewson Woollen Mills, began to experience difficulty and others, such as Rhodes, Curry, the town's largest employer, merged with Canada Car and Foundry, which subsequently began to reduce production in Amherst. The Bank of Nova Scotia was also adversely affected when the Royal Bank unilaterally broke a *modus vivendi* that had existed between the two banks and opened a rival branch that captured the accounts of Cumberland Packing Company, Amherst Lumbering Company, Amherst Foundry Company, Dunlop Cook and Company, and the Amherst Malleable Iron Company. Loans at Amherst dropped off by almost 50 per cent between 1907 and 1910.[84]

The other Maritime towns that had attempted to industrialize in the late 1880's also became increasingly important as sources of "surplus" funds for the Bank of Nova Scotia. The branch at Saint John continued to be plagued by its borrowers' poor management and entrepreneurial ineptitude. In 1901 the account of the Cushing Sulphite Fibre Company went sour. Cushing appears to have been an innovator in the pulp and paper industry of New Brunswick but his company underestimated the cost of producing pulp by about $250,000. As a result, McLeod began to doubt the company's potential profitability. When Cushing began to dishonour some of his bills, the Bank of Nova Scotia demanded the immediate payment of $10,000. The company countered by issuing $280,000 in bonds, but one of its directors, instead of paying off part of the company's bank debt with the proceeds of two pulp shipments, applied the money to meet some of the company's obligations to himself. In response the Bank of Nova Scotia launched a suit to have the company wound up. Subsequently, the bank's lending business in Saint John began to improve. Although the reason for this is not very clear, the limited evidence available suggests that the city became less important as an industrial and manufacturing centre than as a "transit warehouse and regional service centre."[85] However, the census data show an increase in industrial investment and in manufacturing output, and the fact that the Bank of Nova Scotia coveted the highly lucrative account of the Maritime Nail Works in 1910 undermines this interpretation. The statistical data is also inconclusive. While in mid-decade average loans were only about $400,000 and the branch was sending more than $600,000 of "surplus" funds to the head office, by 1910 average loans had increased to $952,912 and only $294,802 was leaving as "surplus."[86]

The branch at Yarmouth also experienced a modest increase in lending activity in the decade after 1900, but the nature of these loans changed substantially. McLeod relentlessly insisted upon avoiding small operators and sought out the accounts of companies that would likely be less dependent on local business conditions. One example was the acquisition of the account of the Yarmouth Cotton Duck Company. In 1901 the bank agreed to underwrite, to the extent of $152,000, C.T. Grantham's purchase of this company from the Lovitt family. Another novel account was that of the Yarmouth Cycle Company. Although the account was small ($5,000) and this type of business was a radical departure for Yarmouth, McLeod was eager to strengthen the bank's presence in Yarmouth, as several "Upper Canadian" banks were casting eyes on the town.[87]

Even an industrializing centre like Halifax, which did experience considerable growth after 1900, became an exporter of surplus funds for the Bank of Nova Scotia. Capital investment in manufacturing in Halifax rose from $6.6 million in 1900 to $14.1 million in 1910, as the city acquired some heavy industry in the form of the Silliker Car

Works and the federal government committed itself to spending $35 million in waterfront redevelopment. But the bank's statistical data indicate minimal participation in this expansion. While loans fluctuated throughout the decade – $1.1 million in 1900, $1.3 million in 1906, $752,921 in 1909, $1.3 million in 1910 – Halifax was sending its surplus elsewhere in this period, with as much as $1.3 million leaving in 1905.[88]

While the Bank of Nova Scotia gradually curtailed its lending activity in the towns industrialized during the 1880's, the bank did increase loans in staples-producing areas. The branch at Campbellton experienced the most remarkable growth, and by 1906 it had the third highest volume of loans of all Maritime branches. New capital investment in the town increased from $210,560 in 1900 to $1.1 million in 1910 and the value of its manufacturing output increased from $322,233 to $1.2 million. The lumber industry accounted for 96 per cent of all capital investment in Restigouche County and the Bank of Nova Scotia's lending activity was concentrated in this industry. The bank's major customer in Campbellton was the Shive Lumber Company, which had $350,000 in advances or 55 per cent of the branch's total loans in 1905. The result of this expansion was that loans at Campbellton increased from $177,295 in 1900 to $756,169 in 1907, then held steady at about $680,000 until 1910 when they plummeted to $364,209.[89] The branch at Fredericton was also involved in the lumber industry. Its main creditor was the Scott Lumber Company, which had total liabilities to the Bank of Nova Scotia of $185,000 in 1904, or about 56 per cent of the branch's loans. Although there was a substantial decline to as low as $85,000 in 1902, loans averaged about $300,000 annually until the end of the decade. Sussex also remained an important centre for lending activity. Although capital investment in manufacturing amounted to only $223,259 in the town itself, the immediate hinterland enjoyed a considerable increase from $754,986 to $1.7 million between 1900 and 1910. Most of this investment was also in the lumber industry. Loans at Sussex increased from $412,331 to $594,178 between 1900 and 1904, remained at more than $400,000 until 1906, and then dropped to $275,865 in 1910. Until the end of the decade, however, Sussex was a net borrower of funds.[90]

Despite the Bank of Nova Scotia's continuing interest in some parts of the regional economy after 1900, there could be no doubt that the Bank of Nova Scotia had become a national financial institution. The flow of funds within the bank's branch system revealed an accelerating shift toward the national market. In 1900 total deposits in the Maritimes amounted to $10.7 million, or 79.05 per cent of the total, while loan activity in the Maritimes accounted for $5.4 million, or 32.5 per cent of the bank's total loans. By 1910 total Maritime deposits had increased to $17.6 million but represented only 46.7 per cent of the total deposits, and while the bank's loan activity in the Maritimes had increased slightly, it now represented only 19.3 per cent of the loans extended by the bank. Between 1900 and 1910 the total amount "due by Head Office" to Maritime branches had increased from $5.9 million to almost $10 million.[91]

By 1910 an enormous sum of capital was being drained away from the Maritimes by the Bank of Nova Scotia, and thus Naylor's assertion that the major banks promoted the drain of capital out of the Maritimes is supported by the evidence in the case of the Bank of Nova Scotia. However, it would be misleading to attribute this development to the existence of a "commercial" or "mercantile" bias on the part of the Bank of Nova Scotia, or to conclude that the Bank of Nova Scotia had no interest in supporting long-term industrial investments. Instead, the explanation for the bank's shift away from the Maritimes must rest with the economic recession of the mid-1880's, which shattered the bank's faith in the region. The lessons Thomas Fyshe had drawn from that crisis were also taken up and applied by his successor, H.C. McLeod. After successfully weathering the stormy crisis of the 1880's, the Bank of Nova Scotia became at once reluctant to expand its Maritime business and also eager to explore the unparalleled opportunities for expansion beyond the region.

While the nationalization of the Bank of Nova Scotia was obviously the outcome of an accumulation of decisions made by the directors and general managers of the bank, this development was also part of a larger process at work in the growth of Canadian capitalism. The creation of a national financial market was one key feature of the concentration and centralization of capital and industry in the central parts of the country. As late as 1900 there had been thirteen banks in the Maritimes, but by 1910 only three were left.[92] Apart from the Bank of New Brunswick, which would be absorbed in 1913 by the Bank of Nova Scotia, the only survivors were the Royal Bank of Canada (formerly the Merchants' Bank of Halifax) and the Bank of Nova Scotia, both of which had shifted their attention from the Maritimes to national and international financial markets. Between 1880 and 1910 every Maritime bank that had failed to expand

beyond the Maritimes disappeared either through failure or amal-
gamation. The virtual disappearance of regional banking in the
Maritimes suggests that in order to survive and prosper it was
necessary for the Bank of Nova Scotia to expand beyond its native
region.

5

The Administrative Revolution in the Canadian Office: An Overview*

Graham S. Lowe

> The construction of the modern office grows constantly more like the construction of the factory. Work has been standardized, long rows of desks of uniform design and equipment now occupy the offices of our large commercial and financial institutions. With the increasing division of labour each operation becomes more simple. The field in which each member of the staff operates is narrower. (*Monetary Times*, 1 October 1920, p. 10.)

The turn of the century marked a watershed in Canada's socio-economic development. The forces of industrialization and urbanization propelled the country into the twentieth century. By the onset of the Depression, corporate capitalism was well entrenched, as evidenced by the presence of large corporations and factories that employed thousands of workers in growing urban centres. While the factory and the joint-stock corporation are widely recognized as the hallmarks of this emerging industrial era, equally important was the development of the modern office with its expanding corps of clerical workers. As the above editorial from the *Monetary Times* attests, by 1920 a transformation was underway in many major Canadian offices. Today it is obvious that capitalism could not function without huge office bureaucracies staffed by an army of

*This paper is based on the author's doctoral dissertation. Financial support provided by the Canada Council is gratefully acknowledged.

From *Work in the Canadian Context*, edited by K. Lundy and B. Warme (Toronto: Butterworths, 1981). Reprinted by permission of the publisher.

subordinate clerical workers. But how and why did this form of administration originate? What brought about the proliferation of clerical jobs? More fundamentally, how was this combination of changes – which we shall refer to as the administrative revolution – shaped by the development of corporate capitalism in Canada after 1900? The intent of this paper is to examine these questions in detail.

There was no sharp dividing line between the old-style office of the nineteenth century and the modern twentieth-century office.[1] Yet we can locate the origins of the administrative revolution roughly between 1911 and 1931. We will argue that during these years, leading corporate and government offices underwent far-reaching changes that established the framework for the modern office and created a new stratum of subordinate clerical workers. Documentary evidence presented below will show how the administrative revolution was a direct result of the organizational and economic forces of corporate capitalism. We will first trace the growth and development of clerical occupations and corresponding changes in office organization and the clerical labour process. The second part of the paper will offer a theoretical discussion of how the rise of corporate capitalism precipitated the transformation of administration so graphically described above by the *Monetary Times*. The concept of administrative control will be used to help us explain both the expanding administrative functions of the office, as the scope of managerial powers increased, and the subsequent rationalization of the clerical labour process.

The Administrative Revolution: Major Occupational and Organizational Dimensions

The rise of corporate capitalism pushed the office into the centre of the economic stage. The small, informal office of the nineteenth century was characterized by unsystematic administrative procedures. At the hub of the old counting house was the bookkeeper. A generalist, he learned his craft through apprenticeship and carried the office systems in his head. In sharp contrast, the modern office that emerged during the early decades of the twentieth century was a large bureaucratic organization, staffed by countless rows of clerks who performed specialized tasks with mechanistic routine. The mass of low-level clerical jobs necessitated by economic progress resembled in many respects jobs found in factory work.[2] Jobs within the expanding office bureaucracies became increasingly standardized and specialized, subjected to the constraints of rigid hierarchy and formalized work relations. The implications of these changes for clerks were severe, for as Dreyfuss observes, "the bookkeeper in a large firm is no longer in a position to know whether 'the books are in good shape.'"[3]

A persistent metaphor in social science is Adam Smith's notion of an "invisible hand" regulating the capitalist marketplace. However, in the era of corporate capitalism, hidden market mechanisms were replaced by elaborate administrative systems devised by managers whose newly acquired expertise emphasized organizational efficiency and the regimentation of labour as the route to higher profits.[4] Administrative co-ordination through the modern business enterprise became the most effective means of regulating economic activities. New technologies, expanding markets, increased competition, and the greater production, marketing, and consumption of goods and services created the economic environment in which these changes in the office took place. Paper work became the lifeblood of administration. And as Simon suggests, the actual job of carrying out the objectives of an organization is delegated to those workers at the bottom of the administrative hierarchy.[5] Clerical employment soared, leading Mills to refer to the twentieth-century office as "the 'Unseen Hand' made visible as a row of clerks."[6]

With this background, we can now itemize the main features of the administrative revolution in Canadian offices.[7] The organizational and occupational changes occurred gradually. Moreover, their development was uneven in the sense that not all offices, even within large organizations, experienced the full impact of the administrative revolution. We can nonetheless assert that by the Depression five characteristics could be found in central offices of leading firms and major government departments across the country. Here, then, is what gave shape to the administrative revolution between 1911 and 1931: (a) a huge increase in the clerical sector of the labour force; (b) a dramatic shift in the clerical sex ratio toward female employees; (c) a concentration of new clerical jobs in the leading industries of corporate capitalism; (d) a relative decline in the socio-economic position of the clerk; and (e) the rationalization of office work by an emergent group of "scientifically oriented," efficiency-conscious office managers.

The Growth of Clerical Occupations. The proportion of clerical workers in a country's labour force is a good index of both the internal bureaucratization of enterprises and the general level of industrialization.[8] It is thus not surprising to find that rapid clerical

Table 1

Total Labour Force, Clerical Workers, and Female Clerical Workers, Canada 1891-1971*

	Total Labour Force	Total Clerical	Clerical Workers as a Percentage of Total Labour Force	Female Clerical	Females as a Percentage of Total Clerical	Female Clerks as a Percentage of Total Female Labour Force
1891	1,659,335	33,017	2.0%	4,710	14.3%	2.3%
1901	1,782,832	57,231	3.2	12,660	22.1	5.3
1911	2,723,634	103,543	3.8	33,723	32.6	9.1
1921	3,164,348	216,691	6.8	90,577	41.8	18.5
1931	3,917,612	260,674	6.7	117,637	45.1	17.7
1941	4,195,951	303,655	7.2	152,216	50.1	18.3
1951	5,214,913	563,083	10.8	319,183	56.7	27.4
1961	6,342,289	818,912	12.9	503,660	61.5	28.6
1971	8,626,930	1,310,910	15.2	903,395	68.9	30.5

*Data adjusted to 1951 census occupation classification.

SOURCES: Dominion Bureau of Statistics, Census Branch, *Occupational Trends in Canada, 1891-1931* (Ottawa, 1939), Table 5; Meltz, *Manpower in Canada* (Ottawa: Queen's Printer, 1969), Section I, Tables A-1, A-2, and A-3; *Census of Canada, 1971*, vol. 3, Part 2, Table 2.

growth paralleled the ascendancy of corporate capitalism in Canada after 1900. Table 1 shows that the number of clerks increased from 33,017 in 1891 to 1,310,910 in 1971. In other words, the proportion of the total labour force engaged in clerical occupations shot from 2 per cent to 15.2 per cent. Now the largest single occupational group in Canada, clerks have been at the forefront of the expansion of the white-collar labour force throughout the century.

Table 2
Percentage Increase Each Decade: Population, Labour Force, and Clerical Occupations, Canada, 1891-1971*

	Population	Labour Force	Clerical Occupations
1891-1901	11.1%	10.4%	73.3%
1901-1911	34.2	52.8	80.9
1911-1921	21.9	16.2	109.3
1921-1931	18.1	23.8	20.3
1931-1941	10.9	7.0	16.5
1941-1951	21.8	26.1	85.4
1951-1961	30.2	22.4	45.4
1961-1971	18.3	33.6	60.1

*Data adjusted to 1951 census occupation classification.

SOURCES: Computed from Dominion Bureau of Statistics, Census Branch, *Occupational Trends in Canada, 1891-1931*, Table 5; Meltz, *Manpower in Canada,* Section I, Table A-1; *Census of Canada,* 1971, vol. 3, Part 2, Table 2; *Canada Year Book, 1974* (Ottawa: Information Canada, 1974), Table 4.1, p. 160.

As Table 2 indicates, the clerical growth rate peaked between 1911 and 1921. While this was followed by another decade of intensified expansion between 1941 and 1951, the earlier period is most significant because it demarcates the administrative revolution. The 1911-1921 boom in clerical jobs cannot be attributed to either population or labour force growth, both of which were much more pronounced during the preceding decade. The lag in clerical growth during the 1920's does not mean that the administrative revolution was losing its force. Rather, it was in this decade that the growing army of clerks was moulded into an efficient corps of administrative functionaries. Clerical procedures were increasingly rationalized and mechanized to consolidate and control the burgeoning office staffs. By the 1930's, the foundations of the modern office had thus been laid.

The Feminization of Clerical Work. Nowhere has the feminization trend in the labour force been more pronounced during this century than in clerical occupations. Strictly male-dominated at the turn of the century, by 1941 the majority of clerical jobs were held by women (see Table 1). The rate of feminization in the office was highest from 1891 to 1921. Increases exceeded 166 per cent in each decade, almost ten times that for the total female labour force.[9] There was an absolute increase in the number of female clerks over this period from 4,710 to 90,577, with the female share of clerical jobs reaching 22.1 per cent by 1921 (Table 1). This signals the emergence of a trend that resulted in the concentration of 30.5 per cent of all female workers in clerical occupations by 1971.

The segregation of women into a small number of relatively unrewarding occupations has remained fairly stable since 1900.[10] This is especially true of clerical work, where the share of clerical jobs held by females steadily increased over this century. Segregation characterized certain key office jobs even in the early stages of the administrative revolution. In stenography and typing, for example, the "female" label became firmly affixed as the proportion of jobs held by women rose from 80 per cent to 95 per cent between 1901 and 1931.[11] What this represents is a more basic trend in office employment: the creation of many new specialized, routine jobs in the lower reaches of administrative hierarchies. It was into these jobs that women were increasingly recruited. The multiplication of such tasks brought about a shift in demand from male to female workers. In this way, the feminization trend largely accounts for the remarkable growth of clerical occupations, especially during the 1911 to 1921 period.[12]

The Changing Industrial Distribution of Clerical Workers. There is a direct connection between shifts in the industrial employment patterns of clerks and the advance of corporate capitalism. In brief, clerks became concentrated in manufacturing and in major service industries. As Table 3 reveals, the most rapid expansion of clerical jobs between 1911 and 1931 occurred in manufacturing, the sector most directly connected with the entrenchment of corporate capitalism. Facilitating the creation of a manufacturing base in the economy was the development of a wide range of services, especially in trade, finance, and transportation and communication. By combining these four sectors – manufacturing, transportation and communication, trade, and finance – we can account for over 85 per cent of total

Table 3
Increases in Clerical Occupations by Major Industry Groups, 1911-1931*

	Net Increase, No. of Clerks	%
Manufacturing	51,743	34.5
Transportation and communication	21,165	14.1
Trade	23,412	15.6
Finance	31,333	20.9
Community and business service	12,688	8.5
Government	6,496	4.4
Construction	3,004	2.0
Sum of all increases	149,841	100.0

*Data adjusted to 1951 census industry and occupation classifications.

SOURCES: Computed from *Census of Canada*, 1901, Bulletin I, *Wage-Earners by Occupations* (Ottawa: King's Printer, 1907), Table II; *ibid.*, Bulletin XI, *Occupations of the People* (Ottawa: King's Printer, 1910), Table II; *ibid.*, 1911, vol. VI, Tables I, III, and IV; *ibid.*, vol. IV, Table IV; Dominion Bureau of Statistics, Census Branch, *Occupational Trends in Canada, 1891-1931*, Table 5; Meltz, *Manpower in Canada*, Section II, Tables D-1, D-2, and D-3; unpublished DBS working tables for the censuses of 1901, 1911, and 1921, showing occupations by industries, using 1951 census occupation classification.

clerical growth between 1911 and 1931. It was during this period that the most dramatic shifts in the industrial distribution of clerical employment occurred.

Most of the new clerical jobs created in manufacturing and service industries between 1911 and 1931 were fundamentally different from the craft-like bookkeeping jobs typical of the nineteenth-century office. Traditional clerical tasks were fragmented and routinized. Employers thus offered lower salaries, expecting less job commitment from workers. Women were considered more suitable for this new stratum of clerical jobs than men. Lower female wage rates, the higher career aspirations of male clerks, and stereotypes of women as better able to perform monotonous, routine work underlay this shift in clerical labour demand. Consequently, we find that by 1931, manufacturing, trade, and finance each accounted for over 20 per cent of all female clerical employment.[13] These three sectors had over 40 per cent of their clerical positions occupied by women in

1931.[14] The most dramatic shift in sex composition occurred in the finance industry. Women were a rarity in banks, insurance companies, and other financial institutions in 1900, yet within years they came to occupy almost 50 per cent of the clerical posts in such firms.[15] In short, the industrial concentration pattern of female clerical employment highlights the massive restructuring of administration.

The Relative Decline of Clerical Earnings. Accompanying the rapid growth of clerical jobs was the erosion of the clerk's socioeconomic position. This is to be expected, given the "de-skilling" of the clerical labour process and the influx of lower-paid females into offices. Table 4 traces the earnings pattern for clerical workers, broken down by sex, from 1901 to 1971. Examining the total clerical group, we find that wages entered into a steady decline after 1921, cutting below the labour force average wage by 1951.[16] Influencing this general trend were the rise in blue-collar wages over the century and the expansion of the potential clerical supply through the spread of public education.

The feminization process created two fairly distinct clerical labour pools, one male and the other female. It is noteworthy, then, that the wages for both groups have declined relative to the total labour force

Table 4
Average Clerical Earnings as a Percentage of Average Earnings for the Total Labour Force, 1901-1971*

	1901	1911	1921	1931	1941	1951	1961	1971
Total	116%	113	125	119	106	95	87	77
Male	128%	128	118	125	112	102	92	89
Female	145%	147	137	148	149	127	117	106

*Data adjusted to 1951 census occupation classification.

SOURCES: Computed from *Census of Canada*, 1901, Bulletin I, *Wage-Earners by Occupations*, Table II; *ibid.*, 1911, unpublished working tables for wage-earners, Statistics Canada microfilm roll number 11002; *ibid.*, 1931, vol. 5, Table 33; *ibid.*, 1971, vol. III, Part 6, Table 14; Dominion Bureau of Statistics, *Manufacturing Industries of Canada*, Section A, Summary for Canada, 1961, p. 16; Statistics Canada, *1971 Annual Census of Manufacturers*, Summary Statistics, Preliminary, July, 1973, p. 3; Meltz, *Manpower in Canada*, Section V, Table A-1; M.C. Urquhart and K.A.H. Buckley, *Historical Statistics of Canada* (Toronto, 1965), p. 99.

since 1901. As Table 4 indicates, male clerical wages dropped from 25 per cent above the labour force average in 1931 to 11 per cent below the average by 1971. Likewise, female clerks, while better off than women in other jobs, have been rapidly losing ground. From a wage advantage of between 48 per cent and 49 per cent from 1931 to 1941, female clerical salaries fell to only 6 per cent above the female labour force average by 1971. In making the comparisons between male and female clerical wage trends, we must bear in mind that female clerks earned 53 per cent of their male counterparts in 1901, inching up slightly to 58 per cent by 1971.[17]

To summarize, the decline of clerical wages relative to the rest of the labour force reflects, more than anything, the erosion of skill levels and responsibilities associated with the old-style office and the resulting inundation of clerical ranks by relatively cheaper female workers. The advance of office rationalization, when combined with the general clerical wage trends, provides evidence of gradual clerical proletarianization. Indeed, the women who now operate modern office machines are considered the most proletarianized sector of the white-collar work force.[18] Clearly, the roots of proletarianization can be traced back to the administrative revolution in the early decades of the twentieth century.

The Rationalization of the Office. The transition from nineteenth-century small-scale entrepreneurial capitalism to twentieth-century corporate capitalism involved a number of fundamental organizational changes. Foremost among these was the growing predominance of bureaucracy, for it was the form of work organization best suited to capitalism.[19] As Bendix argues, industrialization is "the process by which large numbers of employees are concentrated in a single enterprise and become dependent upon the directing and co-ordinating activities of entrepreneurs and managers."[20] Accompanying the rise of bureaucracy was the emergence of a new occupational group, the expert salaried manager. The growing size and complexity of enterprises compelled owners to delegate daily operating responsibility to hired managers. Administration thus became a specialized activity after 1900, as managers sought the most efficient ways to achieve organizational goals.[21] The major strategy utilized by managers was organizational rationalization. Consequently, rigid hierarchies with clear lines of authority were developed, new accounting procedures were implemented to control production and labour costs, traditional labour skills were broken down as the division of labour became more specialized, and workers' control over the productive process passed to management with increasing standardization and mechanization of tasks. Braverman claims that the key to all modern management is "the control over work through the control over decisions that are made in the course of work."[22] This principle applied equally to office and factory.

When William H. Leffingwell published the first book on scientific office management in 1917, he found a receptive audience among many American and Canadian office managers. By the early 1920's, there is evidence that large offices were being rationalized according to the dictates of scientific management in order to increase administrative efficiency.[23] In fact, after 1910 major business publications such as the *Monetary Times, Industrial Canada,* and the *Journal of the Canadian Bankers' Association* devoted increasing coverage to a variety of managerial reforms designed to rationalize work procedures. Even as early as 1905, Canadian manufacturers were cautioned to control rising office overhead.[24] In the finance sector, the Bank of Nova Scotia pioneered a system for measuring the efficiency of branch staff.[25] Not until 1910, however, did the new science of management really catch hold in Canadian industry. Canadian businessmen, as well as senior government administrators, were attracted to the ideology of efficiency which, inspired by F.W. Taylor's program of scientific factory management, pervaded the Progressive Era in America.[26] Taylor himself published accounts of his scientific management system in *Industrial Canada* during 1913. It is thus not surprising to find that employers such as the Canadian Pacific Railway, the federal civil service in Ottawa, the government of Quebec, Massey-Harris, and Canadian Cereal and Flour Mills Ltd. rationalized their operations by hiring American efficiency experts.

The most advanced scientific office management practices during the 1920's were found in the insurance industry. Sun Life Assurance Company led the way when it appointed a personnel manager at its Montreal head office in 1920. Scientific methods of staff recruitment and training were implemented, departmental structures were re-organized to improve internal co-ordination and integration, the latest in office machines were introduced, and standardized job classifications and salary scales were developed.[27] The formation of the Life Office Management Association in 1924 by Canadian and American life insurance companies is a good indication of the advancing administrative revolution in the industry. The aim of the organization was to collectively develop innovative methods of "correct organization and administration of . . . clerical activities."[28]

Mechanized clerical procedures were perhaps the most visible feature of office rationalization. As we have indicated above, tasks such as typing and operating other office machines were defined as "women's work" from their inception. The close interconnection between feminization and the mechanization of office work clearly demonstrates how the rationalization of the clerical labour process was fundamental to the administrative revolution. Interestingly, early stenographers performed craft-like jobs – evidenced by their range of skills, responsibilities, and high level of job control – and consequently attained considerable socio-economic status.[29] However, by World War I, dictation and typing, the two core elements of the job, were being separated. Dictation machines facilitated the organization of central typing pools. Combining technical innovation with organizational rationalization, these pools gave rise to the "office machine age."[30] Many large Canadian offices had typing pools by the mid-1920's. Employees resisted the pool concept, but management found that centralized typing operations were easier to control and more efficient because machines could be kept in continuous use.

The Hollerith punch card system, the forerunner to the electronic computer, fully established the "office machine age." The female operators of these machines performed repetitive, minutely subdivided, and machine-paced tasks. In short, their jobs resembled those found in many mass-production factories.[31] A revolution in office technology was underway, marked by the inclusion of the job title of "office machine operator" in the 1921 census. The application of Hollerith office technology was fairly extensive. International Business Machines, the main supplier, had 105 Canadian offices among its customers by the early 1930's.[32] The new class of office machine operators that emerged in the 1920's is an enduring feature of the administrative revolution, as any observer of the contemporary office will quickly recognize.

To briefly recap, we have documented how specific organizational and occupational changes in the office between 1910 and 1930 represented a transformation in administration. Considering the rapid growth of clerical occupations in key industries, the influx of women into routine office jobs, the deteriorating economic position of the clerk, and the rationalization of office organization and procedures, there can be little doubt that fundamental changes occurred in early twentieth-century Canadian offices. All of these changes are directly related to the process of capitalist development. The exact nature of this link will be the subject of the second part of this paper.

Administrative Control
and the Transformation of the Office

A prominent theme in our discussion thus far has been that the changing nature of administration – and what this entailed for clerical workers – was a result of the development of corporate capitalism. Now we must probe the complexities of this relationship more carefully. Was it simply that a large, rationalized office staff was an inevitable by-product of the logic of capitalist development? Clearly, to argue that economic factors alone were responsible for the transformation in administration would be simplistic, ignoring major organizational variables we have already identified as instrumental in these changes. Certain characteristics of large-scale organizations – such as their intricate division of labour, numerous departmental sub-units, and sheer size – must also be considered as decisive in the growth and transformation of administrative activities. There is no need to engage in debate over whether economic or organizational factors are more critical once we recognize that corporate capitalism provided the environment that nurtured the spread of bureaucracy. We are nonetheless concerned with how organizational and economic forces interacted during the early twentieth-century to precipitate a revolution in the means of administration. In this respect, the concept of administrative control will be used to integrate economic and organizational factors into a comprehensive explanation of this phenomenon.

Briefly, we have argued that the modern office is the administrative centre of corporate capitalism. Through the office, managers attempt to exercise greater control and co-ordination over internal operations and employees as well as larger environmental factors affecting the organization. However, for the office to function effectively in this role, inreasing control had to be exercised over office administration. The notion of administrative control thus has a dual meaning. In the first sense, control can help us explain the growth of clerical occupations. The second can account for the rationalization of the office and the clerical labour process. In short, we are suggesting that for administrative control to be exercised *through* the office, managers also had to apply the same principles of control *over* the office.

Let us set this argument out in more detail before exploring its theoretical underpinnings. The concept of administrative control encompasses the organizational, occupational, and economic dimensions of the administrative revolution. But exactly how did these variables interact to transform the means of administration? On the economic plane, the rise of corporate capitalism after 1900 brought rapid expansion to Canada's manufacturing and service industries. It was in these industries, we have noted, that the escalating demands for the processing, analysis, and storage of information created a boom in clerical employment. The central organizational feature of the administrative revolution was the rise of the office bureaucracy. Driven by the competitive forces of the marketplace, capitalists carried out mergers and consolidations. The resulting corporate entities had their equivalent in the public sector in the form of large government bureaucracies. Whether the organizations were public or private, or engaged in services or manufacturing, the office became the nerve centre of management, for it was through the office that the daily operations of large-scale organizations were run. This brings us to the main occupational dynamic underlying the administrative revolution. The modern corporation – and in a similar fashion, the public bureaucracy – delegates operating authority to expert salaried managers. This new semi-professional group became increasingly concerned over aspects of organizational design, the work process, and other nontechnical factors that may have hindered the achievement of overall goals, be they profit maximization or efficient public service.

As the role of the office became enlarged to include co-ordination of internal activities and regulation of environmental factors impinging upon the organization's future, strains and inefficiencies resulted. In short, the office itself became stricken with bureaucratic maladies. Soaring clerical costs threatened to undermine profits or, in the case of public bureaucracies, cost efficiency. By the First World War, office managers were beginning to recognize the advantages of office rationalization. It was the managerial drive for higher efficiency in clerical operations and greater regimentation of the office labour force that underlay the rationalization of the clerk's job.

Two trends thus converged, precipitating a transformation in office work. First, more clerks were required to process the flood of information. Second, managers increasingly came to rely upon the office as the support system for their power and authority. The office was the key instrument in all managerial decision-making. Together, these factors magnified the scope of office procedures. Inefficiencies in clerical routine – resulting from organizational weaknesses as well as from the underlying tensions of worker resistance to their subordination – were exacerbated. This launched a managerial drive for control over the clerical labour process. The result was a highly rationalized office in which "de-skilled" jobs were defined as suitable women's work. What this suggests is that three factors, linked by the concept of administrative control, underlay the administrative revolution: (a) the rapid growth of manufacturing and service industries; (b) the growing predominance of large-scale bureaucratic work organizations; and (c) the operation of these organizations by a cadre of salaried managers concerned with the efficient co-ordination of work activities and the regulation of workers. It is now useful for us to analyse how each of these factors contributed to the administrative revolution.

The Dynamics of Corporate Capitalism. There can be little doubt that the rise of corporate capitalism paralleled the changes we have already documented in administration between 1911 and 1931. Manufacturing, the cornerstone of an industrial economy, underwent tremendous expansion after 1900. Between 1880 and 1929, the number of manufacturing establishments was reduced from 50,000 to 22,000 through mergers and acquisitions. At the same time, the gross value of production soared from 700 million to 3,116 million (constant) dollars.[33] The wheat boom in western Canada during the first decade of the twentieth century provided the primary stimulus for this rapid industrialization.[34] The First World War also was crucial, precipitating faster, more far-reaching expansion of industry than would have occurred under normal conditions. Much of the new industry established was accounted for by U.S. direct investment. The number of U.S. manufacturing branch plants increased from 100 in 1900 to 1,350 by the end of 1934.[35] By 1918, we find that "the foundation for a modern industrial economy had been laid."[36] In fact, corporate capitalism was so well established by 1929 that, in that year, investment in manufacturing achieved a peak that would not be surpassed until the 1950's.[37]

A direct measure of growing demand for clerical workers in manufacturing is the changing ratio of administrative to production workers. As the economy expanded and factories grew, more office staff was required to administer the rising production. We thus find that the number of administrative employees (mainly clerical, but also including supervisory workers) for every 100 workers in manufacturing increased from 8.6 in 1911 to 16.9 by 1931.[38] What this demonstrates is the direct connection between the advance of industrialization and the development of large central offices.

Service industries also underwent remarkable growth in response to the demands of an emerging industrial economy. Similarly, this sparked an enlargement of office staff. The development of white-collar bureaucracies was, in fact, most apparent in the service sector. For example, the insurance business grew by 850 per cent between 1909 and 1929, yet the number of companies only increased by one, to forty-one.[39] Sun Life Assurance began acquiring other insurance firms in 1890, when its head office staff numbered twenty. Between 1910 and 1930, thirteen acquisitions were made, bringing the number of head office staff to 2,856 employees.[40] Likewise, in transportation we find the same type of concentration of capital and employment. The railways, for instance, became the nation's largest employers, with Canadian National and Canadian Pacific having a combined work force of 129,000 in 1931.[41] Another indicator of economic expansion is the rise of a huge civil service bureaucracy. Total employment – much of it clerical – in all three levels of government soared from 17,000 in 1901 to 108,000 by 1931.[42]

In sum, the rise of manufacturing and service industries established a modern capitalist economy in Canada by the 1930's. Fundamental to this economic development was the concentration of employment into large bureaucracies. It is indeed significant that, during the period we are studying, there were two major waves of corporate mergers and acquisitions, one from 1909 to 1913 and another more pronounced wave from 1925 to 1929.[43] This combination of industrialization and bureaucratization set the stage for the rise of modern administration.

Bureaucracy and the Modern Office

How, though, did the characteristics of bureaucracy influence the evolution of administration? As the office became the administrative centre of the economy, unsystematic, *ad hoc* office procedures were replaced by comprehensive administrative systems designed to provide an orderly flow of information. Only in this way could management exercise control over both external and internal factors affecting the achievement of organizational goals. Clerks became the functionaries of these new administrative systems. The basic function of the office is to facilitate the making and executing of managerial decisions.[44] As Kaufman argues, all administration is designed "to 'carry out,' to 'execute' or 'implement' policy decisions, or to co-ordinate activity in order to accomplish some common purpose, or simply to achieve co-operation in pursuit of shared goals."[45] However, this is a Weberian view of administration and, as such, presents an image of bureaucracy that cannot fully account for the changes encompassed in the administrative revolution.

Weber assumes that bureaucracy is the most efficient form of organization under capitalism.[46] His ideal-typical bureaucracy rests on the notion that all forms of administration tend toward full rationality and efficiency. Although Weber never concisely defines bureaucracy, he stresses that formal rules and regulations are its foundation. Rules inject order and stability into organizational life, specifying the division of labour, the delegation of responsibilities, and the hierarchy of authority. The advantages of this in terms of administration include "precision, speed, unambiguity, knowledge of the files, continuity, discretion, unity, strict subordination, reduction of friction and of material and personal costs."[47]

There are two related problems with the Weberian concept of bureaucracy. In the first place, Weber's critics claim that he avoids the problem of administrative efficiency that underlies the facade of formalized rules and hierarchical structure.[48] Examples of how bureaucracy creates conditions that tend to undermine the achievement of organizational goals are especially found in the subdivision of tasks and the multiplication of departmental sub-units. Administrative theory after Weber focused on how managers could achieve greater co-ordination and integration within large-scale organizations. As Gulick argues, the increasing subdivision and delegation of work tends to create confusion.[49] Even as early as 1900, managers recognized that task specialization was only a cost-saving technique if accompanied by administrative measures that integrated the tasks into an efficient, unified whole.[50]

Secondly, the Weberian concept of bureaucracy posits internal organizational dynamics as determinant in administrative change. For example, office rationalization involving "the development of greater standardization, consistency and co-ordination" is essentially viewed as inherent in the process of bureaucratization.[51] What this overlooks is that rationalization must be consciously planned by management. Furthermore, given the conflict of interests existing between management and workers under capitalism, one can expect that the very fact of the workers' subordination will generate resistance to organizational change. This is especially true with respect to how hierarchy and the division of labour tend to downgrade work by eliminating the control that workers traditionally exercised over their jobs. As such, the bureaucracy is fraught with potential inefficiencies because tactics designed to tighten management's grip over the work process are resisted by workers.

This perspective draws on Marx's insights regarding class relations, viewing the thrust for administrative control as coming not from organizational imperatives but rather from decisions made on behalf of capital. Capitalism's competitive context, its need to grow and survive, and its antagonistic class relations create organizational strains that are remedied through the rationalization of production.[52] This leads Marglin to claim that capital accumulation, not technical efficiency, underlay the origins of hierarchy.[53] Simply put, managers are in a better position to regulate the creation and allocation of profits once they have usurped the control of production from workers.

Yet neither the Marxian nor the Weberian view alone can fully address the question of how and why the administrative revolution took place. It is therefore useful to combine aspects of both. The Marxian perspective helps us to see how modern management largely entails the transfer of control over the productive process from workers to managers. The results, plainly evident in the twentieth-century office and factory, are devastating: job fragmentation, rigid hierarchies, and the coercive discipline and surveillance of workers – what Braverman refers to as the degradation of labour.[54] But it is also reasonable to assert that inefficiency stemming from organizational problems often has sparked rationalization. How else would one explain the dramatic transformations in government offices, executed by foremost American scientific management experts, during the 1920's? The issue of organizational inefficiency suggests, then, that a modified Weberian view is also useful. The problems of large-scale organization reflect the tendency for co-ordination and integration to break down with increased division of labour and structural differentiation. These are organizational problems, although one could argue that the rise of modern bureaucracy was itself fundamentally a by-product of capitalist development. What this misses, however, is that against the background of capitalist development, managerial initiatives were also directed against problems resulting directly from the expansion of bureaucracy.

By combining the economic and class perspectives of Marxism with the organizational emphasis of the Weberian tradition, we can thus account for the growth of clerical jobs and the transformation of office procedures in both public and private bureaucracies. This is achieved by defining administrative control as encompassing strategies to deal with the economic forces of competition and capital accumulation, means of regulating labour and diminishing class conflict, and systems to improve the co-ordination and integration of organizational operations. To more fully understand how administrative control was exercised through the office, and its impact on clerical workers, we must consider the origins and functions of modern management.

Modern Management and the Office. The rise of modern management was a crucial aspect of the administrative revolution, for only through the actions of this new semi-professional group were changes brought about in the office. The office began to assume its contemporary functions in the closing decades of the nineteenth century. Litterer documents how specialized staff functions originated with the advent of cost clerks and production control clerks in factories.[55] Cost accounting – toward which Canadian manufacturers turned their attention after the turn of the century – and other scientific approaches to factory management were the administrative sequel to mechanized production.[56] The office thus began to dominate the factory, becoming the "visible hand" of management. As Braverman notes, management functions themselves became labour processes as administrative tasks were increasingly subdivided and delegated to a growing clerical work force.[57]

The most prominent managerial strategy for dealing with organizational problems and regulating workers' activities was Taylorism. Frederick W. Taylor's science of management, widely disseminated by the start of the First World War, involved three basic axioms: (a) the dissociation of the labour process from the skills of the workers; (b) the separation of the conception and execution of a task; and (c) the application of management's resulting knowledge of the labour process to control each step in production.[58] The cumulative effect of these initiatives leads Rinehart to observe that "today, most workers are locked into jobs that require little knowledge and skill and that are defined and controlled from the upper echelons of complex organizations."[59]

Two points can be made regarding the impact of the managerial thrust for control of the office. First, especially in manufacturing we find a direct link between the extension of managerial control and clerical growth. For example, Rushing and Melman both suggest that the disproportionate increase in administrative staff relative to production workers in U.S. manufacturing reflected the enlargement of management control functions.[60] And second, as the scope of office operations expanded, managers in both manufacturing and service industries found it necessary to apply principles of rationalization, which originated in the factory, to clerical work.

"Management, the brain of the organization," to use a physiological analogy, "conveys its impulses through the clerical systems which constitute the nervous mechanism of the company."[61] This underlines how clerical work furnished the means of integrating the components of an organization. Even in white-collar industries, such as insurance or banking, special departments were established to facilitate managerial control over administrative practices. As one insurance executive asserts, "office administration is not a job by itself. We are in the insurance business, and office administration, scientific office administration, is merely one of the tools to help us carry on the insurance business more efficiently."[62] By the First World War, office managers in both Canada and the U.S., already aware of the importance of systematic administration, were being told that Taylorism and other scientific factory management schemes could be easily adapted to the office.[63] The logic of office rationalization is clearly expressed by the father of scientific management, W.H. Leffingwell:

> Effective management implies control. The terms are in a sense interchangeable, as management without control is inconceivable, and both terms imply the exercise of a directing influence.... The clerical function may then be correctly regarded as the linking or connecting function, which alone makes possible the efficient performance of hundreds of individual operations involved in the "sub-assembly" cycles of the business machine as a whole.... If (management) co-ordination requires clerical mechanisms and cannot function without them, it follows that the problems of management through them constitutes a major function and is unquestionably vital to the conduct of business.[64]

This statement encapsulates the essential nature of the modern office. Without clerical procedures as efficient, predictable, and regimented as the factory assembly line, managerial control over external and internal factors affecting organizational goals would be diminished. An efficient bureaucracy, whether its goals are public service at the lowest cost or capitalist growth and profits, requires systematic administration. The entrenchment of these changes in major Canadian offices is precisely the concern of the editorial in the *Monetary Times* cited at the opening of the paper.

Conclusions

The purpose of this paper has been to analyse the administrative revolution that occurred in major Canadian offices between 1911 and 1931. By the onset of the Depression, the central features of the contemporary office were well in place. Increasingly, the typical clerk was a woman who performed a specialized job, often machine-paced, in a highly regimented bureaucratic setting. As in any kind of large-scale social change, the transition from the old nineteenth-century counting house to the modern twentieth-century office was not a smooth, all-encompassing process. The changes described above in the nature of clerical work as well as in office organization and management took place in a more or less halting, uneven fashion. Evidence suggests, though, that alterations in the means of administration were sufficiently sweeping and well rooted by the 1930's to characterize them as a "revolution."

Theoretically, our task has been to unite into a comprehensive explanation the broad occupational, economic, and organizational forces associated with the rise of modern administration. This has been achieved by using the concept of administrative control. We have shown that control was the central feature in both the growth of the office and its rationalization by management. Yet in drawing on the theories of Marx and Weber to develop this explanation, we have merely glossed over many of the knotty theoretical problems involved in any attempt to merge these contrasting perspectives. Still, the relevance of this approach to explaining changes in the labour process during particular stages of capitalist development is clear. A one-sided theory, whether emphasizing economic forces, as Marxists are wont to do, or positing organizational imperatives as determinate, as do Weberians, cannot possibly account for the intricate causal nexus underlying the rise of the modern office. No doubt the same would be true in studies of the expansion and rationalization of other work settings.

6

The Political Economy
of the Automobile Tariff, 1926-31

Tom Traves

By the 1920's the automobile industry was a creature of the tariff. All the leading Canadian auto companies were subsidiaries of American producers; most had established operations in Canada in order to exploit the price differential created by the tariff on American imports. Although the Canadian industry was in many ways a replica of its American counterpart, it did differ in one important respect: by and large the Canadian branches operated simple assembly plants where American parts were "manufactured" into Canadian cars; these vehicles were then sold for prices far in excess of those prevailing south of the border. In 1926, however, the Canadian government introduced tariff changes designed to force substantial price reductions and encourage a greater degree of indigenous auto production. Naturally these changes severely disrupted the economic environment within which the Canadian auto companies operated. Over the next five years the auto producers struggled to adjust their operations to these changed conditions; when market forces turned against them at the end of the decade they demanded another reform of the tariff schedule.

The 1920's in North America are remembered popularly as the age of the flapper and the flivver. In 1920 one out of every twenty-two Canadians owned a car; by the end of the decade the motor-bound population increased to one in 8.5 Canadians (see Table 1). Most people drove cars produced by either the Ford Motor Company of Canada or the General Motors of Canada Corporation. Between

Reprinted from *The State and Enterprise: Canadian Manufacturers and the Federal Government, 1917-31* (1979), with the permission of the University of Toronto Press.

Table 1
The Canadian Automobile Industry, 1917-31

	Pro- duction	Im- ports	Ex- ports	Re- exports	Apparent consumption	Regis- trations
1917	93,810	16,656	9,492	567	100,407	197,799
1918	82,408	10,812	10,361	322	82,537	275,746
1919	87,835	11,750	22,949	305	76,331	341,316
1920	94,144	9,145	23,012	542	79,735	407,064
1921	66,246	7,270	10,726	254	62,536	465,378
1922	101,007	11,591	37,958	268	74,372	513,821
1923	147,202	11,822	69,920	438	88,666	585,050
1924	132,580	9,301	56,655	326	84,900	652,121
1925	161,970	14,632	74,151	341	102,110	728,005
1926	204,727	28,630	74,324	370	158,577	836,794
1927	179,054	36,630	57,414	438	157,832	945,672
1928	242,054	47,408	79,388	467	209,607	1,010,664
1929	262,625	44,724	101,711	671	204,967	1,888,929
1930	153,372	23,233	44,553	818	131,234	1,232,486
1931	82,559	8,738	13,813	726	76,759	1,200,907

Data on production, imports, exports, and consumption include passenger vehicles and trucks; data on registrations include motorcycles, road tractors, and government vehicles as well as automobiles and trucks.

SOURCE: Dominion Bureau of Statistics, *Automobile Statistics for Canada, 1932.*

them these two firms supplied 61.7 per cent of all Canadian consumption from 1920 to 1930, and their combined output during this period accounted for 77.6 per cent of all Canadian production.[1] Although other firms such as the Willys-Overland Company, the Chrysler Corporation, Durant Motors of Canada, the Studebaker Corporation, and the Dodge Brothers Motor Company of Canada also sold popular cars, they had little choice but to follow the price leadership and sales strategies established by General Motors and Ford.

The auto industry developed in Canada at a time when the protective tariff on completed cars and chassis was 35 per cent. Since the duty on most parts was lower than on the completed automobile, several Canadian carriage makers, including Gordon M. McGregor and R.S. McLaughlin, who founded respectively Ford and General

Motors of Canada, were inspired to secure arrangements with some of the newly established American producers to import most of their parts and assemble them in Canada. In other instances, the American producers themselves established subsidiary branch plants in Canada to serve Canadian and imperial markets. The president of the Studebaker Corporation testified in 1920: "We are merely a subsidiary of the Studebaker Corporation of South Bend, Indiana. We are in Walkerville purely because of the tariff on the completed automobile and because we could assemble the parts in Walkerville, make some purchases in Canada and reduce the cost slightly. If it were not for the present tariff on the completed automobile it would simply be a case of there being no advantage in being over here. That is all there would be to it. We have our plant at South Bend and we would simply ship from there."[2] In time, some parts were manufactured by domestic producers, especially for the Ford company, but progress was slow and in 1926 most of the companies still operated what were little more than assembly plants.

Even the simple assembly of more than 200,000 vehicles a year, however, had a substantial impact on the Canadian economy. In 1926 eleven auto plants were capitalized at $82.8 million and about 12,000 men and women were directly employed by the auto companies. Another 2,750 workers were engaged by the parts producers. Moreover, it was clear that the auto industry exerted a considerable impact on other parts of the economy. *Industrial Canada* noted that "If the production value of the plants producing automobile supplies, tires and refined petroleum be added to that of the automobile industry proper, the total considerably exceeds that of any other industry." The article went on to point out that substantial amounts of iron and steel, brass and bronze, tubes and piping, lead, glass, fasteners, lumber, and upholstery materials were consumed by the auto producers. Even the railroads, which suffered so much from the development of motor transportation, benefited to the extent of over $10 million in freight revenues from automotive products.[3]

Such figures were impressive, but most people outside of the Oshawa-to-Windsor region cared only about the price they had to pay for a Canadian-built car. Everyone knew that automobile prices were much higher in Canada than in the United States. Part of this sacrifice could be rationalized as the cost of supporting a domestic automobile industry. But why was the cost so high? Most industry spokesmen replied with an "economies of scale" argument. A Ford official, for example, contrasted the unit costs of making 55,000 cars in Canada with those arising from the production of a million units in the United States. He concluded that lower American prices were "due entirely to uniform quantity production and merchandising made possible by the more favourable geographical location of the territory served by the American company."[4] While few doubted the obvious advantages of mass production, the question still remained why Canadian prices were so uncomfortably close to the sum of the American price plus the tariff. Canadian prices ranged between 29 and 54 per cent above those prevailing a few hundred miles to the south; the tariff stood at 35 per cent.[5] Were the Canadian producers simply taking advantage of the tariff to secure higher prices and extra profits?

Apparently the government thought they were. On April 15, 1926, the Minister of Finance, James Robb, announced a sharp reduction in the industry's rate of protection. The general tariff, which covered American imports, was slashed from 35 to 20 per cent for all cars valued at not more than $1,200; fully 75 per cent of the Canadian market was covered by this change. More expensive vehicles were reduced from 35 to 27.5 per cent. The general rate on most parts remained fixed between 27.5 and 35 per cent, but a significant new feature appeared in respect to these duties. In order to increase the rate of indigenous production the government announced that those companies that purchased or produced 50 per cent of the value of their finished automobile in Canada henceforth would be eligible for a 25 per cent drawback on all duties paid on parts and materials.[6] These regulations marked the first time that made-in-Canada content requirements had been attached to the tariff schedule, although they were a common feature of the imperial tariff system within which Canada received preferential treatment.

The government's new policy clearly reflected the exigencies of its political position. In April, 1926, the Mackenzie King Liberal administration had two objectives that stood above all others. It had to keep the support of the agrarian Progressive Party in Parliament, and it had to regain an increased measure of public support from an electorate that had only recently voted a plurality to the opposition Conservative Party.[7]

The reduction of the duty on automobiles served both these ends. The Liberals had considered such tariff revisions in 1924 and again in 1925, but were reluctant to proceed. By 1926 these changes became imperative. King's canvass of his supporters following the disastrous 1925 campaign revealed that auto prices were a serious cause of complaint among voters. One defeated MP urged: "Get the support of the Progressives, by a substantial reduction in the Tariff on Automobiles, and some other lines; which will appeal to the rural voter." The mayor of Calgary complained "that the whole of the West are grumbling (and have been for years now) at the prices the motor car manufacturers, with the aid of high protection, have been making them pay."[8]

The made-in-Canada provisions of the new tariff schedule also reflected the temper of the times. During the twenties nationalist sentiment rose sharply. Organizations such as the Canadian Manufacturers' Association supported and encouraged this tendency by massive advertising campaigns urging consumers to purchase Canadian-built products in order to build up the country's manufacturing base. The drawback provision of the new schedule finally provided a mechanism whereby nationalist sentiments could be translated into action. As one manufacturer noted following the announcement of the new budget provisions: "It is a question whether exploitation of Canada by American manufacturers who have no interest in the country except profits for themselves will be of ultimate value."[9] Obviously the government hoped to appeal to these sympathies by promoting what appeared to be a more nationalistic industrial development strategy. Shortly after the 1926 budget debate Mackenzie King observed: "It was evident to me in the Border Cities [Windsor] that the working men had come to see that our budget is a real boon to them in the matter alike of employment and savings."[10] Later, a contemporary student of the auto industry noted that "Mr. Robb, in one of the few comments which he has subsequently made upon his tariff revisions, when approached in connection with this very subject, stated that it was frankly the intention of the government to force plants to produce at least half of the value of their products in Canada or purchase an equivalent amount from other Canadian firms."[11] Even the auto companies responded to the nationalist surge, General Motors adopting the slogan "It's Better Because It's Canadian" in its advertisements.[12]

At the same time, the automobile producers naturally reacted fiercely to the government's initiatives. Reduced protection and increased pressure to expand the degree of Canadian content in their output threatened to alter the terms under which they had traditionally conducted their affairs. Within days of the new budget the auto companies began a massive campaign to preserve their position. On April 21, over 200 manufacturers representing thirty-four cities, towns, and villages in Ontario and Quebec assembled in Toronto to demonstrate their allegiance to the auto producers' cause. Five days later a similar meeting in Montreal attracted another 100 manufacturers. The most massive demonstration against the new tariff, however, occurred in Ottawa on April 23 when some 3,000 auto workers from Oshawa jammed Keith's Theatre to cheer on a series of anti-government speakers. General Motors encouraged its employees' support by publicizing an American head office directive not to release inventory orders beyond August 1, an unsubtle hint that the Oshawa plant might soon be shut down if the new tariff remained unchanged.[13] W.R. Campbell, the president of Ford of Canada, protested that it was now cheaper to import a finished car at a duty rate of 20 per cent than to assemble or manufacture in Canada, since the tariff on parts still ranged from 27.5 to 35 per cent.[14] Such threats naturally received extensive coverage in the nation's press, whose attention was guaranteed by a series of belligerent advertisements paid for by the automobile companies.[15]

In spite of the intensive campaign, the auto manufacturers' power to move the government was limited. For their part, the Liberals were trapped by broader political considerations and consequently had little room to manoeuvre. Sharply focused consumer agitation represented a potent political force. Adept politicians could exploit the mass market just as effectively as businessmen. In this instance the auto makers possessed very little countervailing power. They could shut down their plants, of course, but this involved the potential loss of substantial fixed capital. Moreover, their U.S. parent companies could ill afford to export cars since freight rates were much higher for assembled automobiles than automobile parts. What is more, despite their enormous fortunes, the principal auto manufacturers were isolated from the country's major centres of political power. In Canada the auto industry developed on reinvested profits, not bank loans or stock flotations, and politically powerful financiers, brokers, and bankers had no significant political stake in its fortunes.[16] Thus, excluding the support of some interested manufacturers the car makers were unable to find allies with sufficient political clout with the King government to forestall completely the administration's intended reforms. For example, in February, when the government drafted its new budget, a parade of powerful businessmen trooped in to advise the Prime Minister to sacrifice the auto industry for the good of the party. J.H. Gundy of Wood, Gundy and Company,[17] and later W.E. Rundle of National Trust, Sir Clifford Sifton, and Leighton McCarthy all urged that the auto tariff must be reduced. At the same time they recommended that the government raise the duties on woollens, glass, boots, and shoes. Such increases served to prevent a general uprising by the manufacturers and protected the Liberals' flank if the Progressives decided to desert the government.[18]

Above all, Mackenzie King's personal influence was decisively deployed against the auto industry. The Prime Minister had a very low regard for Canadian car makers. Once, he described them as "the hardest looking lot of manufacturers' promoters I have seen, a genuinely brute force gang from Fords and other concerns."[19] Moreover, it seems clear that the auto tariff revisions greatly appealed to King's imagination; in one stroke he increased jobs and reduced prices for the working man, he strengthened the Liberals' popular political base, and he furthered the Liberal-Progressive party alliance.

Henry Ford did not help matters for the Canadian manufacturers. A committed free-trader, Ford upstaged his Canadian associates' dramatic protests in a devastating interview carried in newspapers across the country. "You people are just waking up," he said. "You ought to rub the other eye, now, too, and clean out the tariff." Ford claimed that it was now possible to produce cars in Canada as cheaply as in Detroit: "Give me that plant at Ford City [Windsor], and I'll compete with the plant here at Highland Park any day. Why shouldn't I? Our unit in Canada can buy as cheaply as we can here. We make every part of the car in the Canadian plant, and 95 per cent, over 85 per cent anyway is supplied right in Canada. We get our steel from Algoma, lumber, everything we need." Economies of scale seemed no longer an issue. Canadian producers would just have to become more efficient. "Free competition brings healthy business," concluded Ford. "I can tell you that those fellows over in our Canadian unit are going to manufacture more efficiently now. They'll have to; it's going to be a better plant over here, better organization. That's another reason why it's a good thing for the manufacturer."[20]

Setting their sails against this ill wind the auto producers launched into a series of negotiations aimed at mitigating the impact of the new tariff schedule. On May 1, the manufacturers and the independent parts producers lobbied the Minister of Customs and Excise, Georges Boivin. The parts makers opposed the government's reforms too: they believed that the auto companies would pass the tariff cuts along to them, and they were already hard-pressed to compete with American exporters. The Canadian content quota offered little promise either, since the auto companies could play off the parts producers against each other by demanding price reductions on parts that apparently were not necessary for the auto producers' qualification for duty drawbacks. Ultimately, all parts producers would suffer since only the auto companies really knew the true state of their Canadian content levels. Accordingly, the parts producers preferred that the government lower the maximum duty on parts from 35 to 25 per cent and drop the drawback provisions and content regulations.[21]

The auto producers merely repeated their previous claims. Naturally they did not object to a reduction on parts duties. However, since imported parts were still subjected to higher duties than fully assembled automobiles, ultimately, they claimed, manufacturing must cease. An article in *Canadian Machinery and Manufacturing News*, however, pointed out that this view was "entirely erroneous, as it would take the parts of two or three cars to equal in value for duty purposes the value of one finished car." In addition, the manufacturers neglected to discuss freight rate differentials on parts and fully assembled frames, which also affected locational decisions in the auto industry.[22]

The Canadian industry's export position also weakened the force of threats to withdraw. As Table 1 indicated, export sales amounted to 36.8 per cent of total Canadian production during the twenties. Under preferential imperial tariff arrangements Canadian exports to imperial markets soared.[23] Apart from increased economies of scale and huge revenues, exports were particularly important to Canadian producers since sales in southern markets such as Australia, New Zealand, and South Africa peaked at precisely the period when the Canadian market sunk into the winter doldrums. Accordingly, export sales made it possible for Canadian producers to smooth out their annual production schedules and to provide year-round employment for both their men and machinery. The Canadian government had long recognized the obvious benefits of exports to both the industry and the country and had sought to encourage such sales. Canadian producers who imported parts for subsequent re-export, either in completed chassis or in pieces, received a 99 per cent drawback on all duties and sales tax paid. The far-reaching 1926 amendments to the tariff schedule did not disrupt this important feature. Canada's preferred access to imperial markets still provided an important locational advantage for American automobile corporations.

Mackenzie King was ill-disposed to accept the industry's prophecies of doom and gloom. When General Motors dramatically shut down its Oshawa plant, turning out 3,000 employees, the Prime Minister calmly noted: "All a bluff and result of threat – good for us, however, as showing tariff changes meant something, also as something to point to later when industry continues to prosper, as was the case with agricultural implements." Four weeks later, on May 14, King still felt that "full consideration is showing that agitation did not have very much ground," but by then he was prepared to admit that "we may consider some minor adjustments in committee." [24]

Several elements combined to force the Prime Minister into a more flexible position. First, although the business community was far from united behind the industry,[25] opposition to the new tariff had spread beyond the auto manufacturers' narrow circle. C.M. Bowman, an insurance company executive, impressed upon King that he was "fully convinced beyond all doubt that unless some solution is found, that the Mutual Life Assurance Company of Canada has very substantial mortgage investments in Oshawa which will not be worth 50 cents on the dollar." Bowman was a life-long Liberal. Other prominent members of the party also opposed the government's position. The Liberal leader of the opposition in Ontario, Oshawa MPP William E.N. Sinclair, wrote: "I think that even yet your government can give certain concessions in the way of certain drawbacks or further relieving of sales tax, or excise, in such a way as not to injure the country. But at the same time to make it possible for the companies to carry on without hardship." [26]

These external pressures reinforced opposition to tariff reforms from within the cabinet. At least two ministers, Robb and Boivin, were reluctant to proceed with drastic changes. Boivin had "become convinced that several firms now manufacturing cars in Canada cannot carry on unless they are given some relief." Robb, the Finance Minister, who was closely connected with St. James Street financial interests, opposed tariff reductions from the start and even went so far as to carry his opposition to the caucus. Later, King noted privately: "I confess I have little confidence in the Finance department so far as tariff changes go. They make little real investigation." [27]

Ultimately these pressures enabled Robb to press his case for relief for the industry to a successful close. Under Schedule 1 of the revised (1926) War Revenue Act, Robb proposed that the government repeal the excise tax of 5 per cent on the retail price up to $1,200, and 10 per cent of the excess over that, on all cars that met the Canadian content regulations. The tax continued to apply to imported vehicles. King and the Progressives finally accepted this amendment when the auto producers publicly promised that consumers would receive the full benefits of this tax cut.[28]

Although the auto producers were not entirely satisfied with this arrangement, they had to accept it. Customs Minister Boivin reported that

> . . . it is bitterly opposed by the Durant people, Dodge Bros., the Studebaker Corporation and the Chrysler automobile manufacturers. They all employ several hundred hands in Canadian assembly plants but the fact that their cars are not 50% Canadian would place them at a disadvantage as compared with Ford, Overland and Chevrolet cars which are slightly more than 50% Canadian made. It appears that Mr. McLaughlin stated before his departure last night, that he had no objection to the plan proposed by Mr. Robb because it would give him some relief in connection with his Chevrolet car, but that it would be no advantage in inducing the General Motors to continue the manufacture and assembling of their higher priced cars in Canada. Mr. Campbell of the Ford Company would welcome the removal of the 5% excise tax . . . .[29]

Since the two largest producers supported the Robb plan, the smaller companies had little choice but to concede agreement. The government subsequently mollified these dissident firms by agreeing to reduce the content regulations to 40 per cent Canadian labour and materials until April 1, 1927, when the 50 per cent content condition became effective. Furthermore, the government also agreed to base drawback qualifications upon total factory output rather than individual models.[30]

These amendments, introduced on June 7, 1926, made the Tory leadership almost apoplectic at what they considered King's duplicity. Arthur Meighen described the events from April through June as "nothing but sham and fraud." The excise tax repeal effectively increased protection to 26 per cent. By this step, Meighen wrote: "the government has put the automobile people back practically where they were so far as protection is concerned, and whatever reduction in price there is already made or yet to be made, is at the expense of the treasury of Canada." It especially irked the Conservative leader that these changes occurred only "after getting many weeks of publicity for what they have done."[31]

The 1926 tariff reforms had a significant impact on the development of the auto industry over the next four years. First, the tariff cuts did produce price reductions. Estimates vary, but one auto official indicated that the range of Canadian prices, which were 29 to 54 per cent above American levels, declined to a range of 23 to 30 per cent higher. A Dominion Bureau of Statistics memorandum in 1928 reported an estimated reduction of 10 per cent from 1926 price levels.[32]

The repeal of the excise tax produced less noticeable results. Ford's new 1928 Model A cost roughly 30 per cent more in Canada than a similar model south of the border. General Motors maintained a 25 per cent price spread, while Willys-Overland's Canadian touring cars were 25.9 per cent and its sedan cars were 28.3 per cent above the price of their American equivalents. Canadian auto manufacturers, however, denied that they were exploiting the extra protection afforded by the excise tax on imports. The general manager of General Motors, for example, explained that "the markup has no relation as far as we are concerned, to duty or excise tax." Cynics scoffed at these claims, however. "The Ford Company seems, on the face of it," noted one journalist, R.J. Deachman, "to be charging American prices plus an allowance for the inconvenience of going over and buying a car in the United States, plus another sum which by strange coincidence, works out at almost exactly five per cent and represents or appears to represent the luxury or excise tax a car would have to pay if it were brought in from the United States."[33]

In contrast to their expectations, the parts makers did not suffer under the new regulations. Total sales by the parts industry climbed from $52.9 million in 1925 to $104.9 million in 1929, an increase of almost 100 per cent.[34] By 1928 all the Canadian auto companies had qualified for duty drawbacks, which meant thay all contained at least 50 per cent Canadian content according to Customs Department regulations. At the end of the decade, one parts producer confessed: "we knew one thing [in 1926], that we were out 25% duty protection, and I think the average parts man felt worse about that than he did about the thought of additional business. But after three years of operation I think every parts man is a unit in feeling that this brought a great deal of business to Canada, and, speaking for our own point of view, we would be loath to see that taken out of the present Act."[35]

Even the auto companies prospered initially under the new tariff. Canadian sales rose steadily between 1926 and 1929 as consumption increased from 102,000 vehicles per annum to 205,000 vehicles. However, imports also increased dramatically. Total imports rose from 14,632 vehicles in 1925 to 44,724 units in 1929;[36] the imports' market share also jumped from 14.3 to 21.8 per cent over the same period.[37] Since the Canadian industry utilized only 66 per cent of its total capacity at this time,[38] these imports represented a serious check on its prosperity.

Ford of Canada was the first company to react to these developments. Although Ford was the leader of the Canadian industry at the start of the decade, in the period following the 1926 tariff reforms its position deteriorated badly. Ford's market share declined from 43.4 per cent over the period 1920-26 to 23.2 per cent during the remaining years of the decade; over the same period, General Motors became the industry leader by increasing its market share from 25.1 to 32.1 per cent.[39] Of course the 1926 tariff reforms did not cause this dramatic shift in market shares. Rather, Canadian developments merely reflected the transformation of the continental industry.[40] Henry Ford's Model T had swept all competition before it during the first two decades of the century when the mass market in automobiles first developed. As early as 1921, however, it became evident that the low-price market, which Ford dominated, was becoming saturated. Many consumers now preferred to trade in their old black Model T, and interest in different or better products mounted.[41] Under these circumstances commercial strategy and organization requirements in the industry changed. Production techniques, at which Ford excelled, became relatively less important, and marketing and management skills soon became the key to industrial success. While Ford resisted change, General Motors' executives took up the challenge of devising an organizational structure necessary to run a corporation dedicated to the market strategy of "a car for every purse and purpose."[42] By 1927 these strategic and structural changes produced a market revolution. The Model T was vanquished and Ford plants throughout the world shut down operations in order to facilitate the costly shift to production of Henry's new Model A. Despite the subsequent success of the Model A, General Motors managed to maintain its new position as market leader in both the United States and Canada.[43]

Ford of Canada attempted to halt the decline of its share of the market by seeking favourable tariff reforms. When the Advisory Board on Tariff and Taxation met to review the auto tariff, Ford of Canada demanded three major amendments to the existing schedule.[44] The first was designed to hamper its foreign competition. Ford proposed that the Customs Department consider retail prices in an import's country of origin rather than wholesale rates when they established the value for duty. Since American auto companies usually granted their distributors a 30 per cent discount on the list price of their cars, Ford's proposal meant that the effective rate of protection would increase by 6 per cent (30 per cent discount times 20 per cent duty rate).

Ford's other proposals struck directly at its domestic competition. "The Drawback and Excise Tax exemption," the company argued, "should operate as an inducement to promote . . . manufacturing in Canada."[45] Since 1927 Canadian producers had qualified for this exemption on the degree of Canadian content in their entire factory output. Diversified producers thus maintained high-volume production runs by assembling some models and manufacturing others. Ford, however, was basically a one-model company. Accordingly, Ford lost little when it proposed that individual models rather than the total factory output qualify for drawbacks and tax exemptions. Moreover, since Ford had long managed to achieve a Canadian content level of about 75 per cent, it had no hesitation in proposing that required content levels must henceforth increase from 50 to 60 per cent. Naturally, some of Ford's more diversified competitors would have had problems complying with either proposed regulation.[46] These companies also objected to Ford's final proposal to abolish duty drawbacks for their more expensive models, which to now had been protected at a general rate of 27.5 per cent.

The entire industry was united in support of Ford's plan to restrict imports. General Motors pointed out that customs valuations based on retail prices would force the Essex, which sold 16,000 units in 1929, out of the Canadian market since its dealers would no longer receive a profit margin sufficient to permit further marketing of this car in Canada. The parts makers also supported Ford's plan, but naturally import dealers and consumer groups opposed it.[47]

Yet the industry could not close ranks against this opposition because Ford's proposals for Canadian content regulation reforms obviously divided them. In 1926 the industry's opposition to content regulations had collapsed when the dominant producers conceded that they could live with the government's proposals. By 1929, the industry was split again because the most "Canadian" of all the producers sought to capitalize on its position by pushing the government to an even tougher stand on content regulations. The chairman of the tariff board probed this split when he noted that Ford was not a member of the industry's Canadian Auto Manufacturers and Exporters Association. W.R. Campbell, Ford's president, reluctantly explained: "Well, if you must have reasons, I think it is because there is not a common interest between ourselves and the others in the industry." A spokesman for the Studebaker Corporation explained the basis of this divergence of interest very clearly:

Our position differs slightly from other Canadian automobile manufacturers in that we offer a larger variety of models through one dealer organization than does any other manufacturer. The same volume included in fewer types of cars would entail less difficulty in meeting the present qualifications requirements for duty refunds, which refunds are essential to our continued manufacturing operation; however, we find in actual experience that we must offer to the Canadian buyer the same advantages and the same choice of models as if the cars were imported. . . . Obviously, any increase in content requirements for duty refunds or any reduction in the duty refund itself, would seem to preclude the possibility of our continuing a manufacturing operation in Canada.[48]

The Great Depression heightened the auto industry's desire to procure tariff reforms at the same time that it produced political circumstances that made such changes possible. On July 28, 1930, the King government fell from power and an avowed protectionist succeeded to the Prime Minister's office.[49] Along with its ideological sympathy, the Bennett government had other reasons for responding to auto industry pressures. First, economic collapse added a bite to the industry's complaints that had been missing in the record years from 1926 to 1929. By 1931, output had fallen by 68 per cent from 1929, and excess capacity in the industry reached 45 per cent. The auto producers also had better political connections to the Bennett government than to King's Liberals. For example, T.A. Russell, the president of the Willys-Overland Company, was a close adviser to Bennett. Also, E.B. Ryckman, the new Minister of National Revenue, who supervised the department responsible for customs valuations, had previously served as president of the Dunlop Rubber and Tire Company and as a director of the Russell Motor Car Company.[50]

Nonetheless, the new government did not move immediately to limit imported automobiles. Dealers in imported and higher-priced cars also had to be considered. By February, 1931, however, the pressure for increased protection via changes in valuation practices became overwhelming. The auto producers organized a campaign of telegrams and petitions from their salesmen across the country, while Conservative MPs from Windsor badgered the Prime Minister with letters on behalf of their leading constituents.[51] A Windsor paper, *The Border Cities Star*, reported on February 20 that "Assurance was given last September that action was to be taken, but consideration for the dealers in high priced cars and other factors intervened to prevent anything being done while the prime minister was in England." At the beginning of February, 1931, "intimation was privately given that the order-in-council was to be passed then. Again the case of the dealers of high priced cars came under review." The dealers, particularly those who carried Packards, argued that if the government forced a reduction in their dealer discount they could not continue their sales operations in Canada at current price levels.

The Minister of National Revenue attempted to promote a compromise solution to these conflicting interests. Ryckman suggested that the government fix dealer discounts at 20 per cent only on cars priced below $1,200. "It will well take care of the low priced field – Essex, Hudson, Nash, Graham-Paige, etc.," he wrote Bennett, "and will not draw general attention to an increased tariff on the poor man's car." Thus, high-priced dealers would be exempt from the proposed changes. This proposal did not upset the Canadian manufacturers since they concentrated their efforts on the production of low- and medium-priced automobiles.[52]

The Prime Minister was more sensitive to the political implications of this proposal than his advisers. "My difficulty, I am sure you appreciate . . ." he wrote his friend T.A. Russell, "is the difficulty of favouring the high priced car against the low priced car. In other words, the city dweller with large means against the rural citizen with limited resources." At the same time, though, Bennett also was convinced that "it is now quite apparent that unless the industry is to be wiped out, something must be done and action will be taken in that direction without delay."[53]

The government finally took action on February 19, 1931. By order-in-council the cabinet fixed a maximum discount for valuation purposes on imported cars of 20 per cent off the list price in the country of origin. The *Border Cities Star* on February 20 estimated this change "to mean increased tariff protection of from 10 to 15 per cent, as wholesale prices on which the customs duties have been levied have been between 25 and 35 per cent below list prices." In return for this arrangement the auto companies delivered their familiar solemn pledge not to take advantage of their increased protection in order to raise prices.

The government's policy seemed vindicated only a few days after it was announced. A General Motors vice-president wrote the Prime Minister: "I am very pleased to advise you that I have just received permission from New York to immediately start operations in our Regina plant which had previously been closed down due to lack of business. This is a direct result of the favourable consideration given by you to our request for increase in value for duty purposes on imported completed automobiles entering Canada."[54]

The long-run impact of the tariff changes is reflected in subsequent import statistics and industry policies. Completely finished imports, which averaged roughly 20 per cent in 1929 and 1930, dropped to a mere 8.1 per cent of Canadian consumption in 1931 and 1932. Moreover, four of the leading American exporters during the 1920's – Nash, Hudson, Graham-Paige, and Packard – all established manufacturing and assembly operations in Canada during the first two years of the Depression.[55] The "Canadianization" program begun in 1926 thus achieved a significant success within just a few years of its adoption.

Government policy alone did not determine the auto industry's development; nor did market forces operate exclusively. Rather, the history of the Canadian industry and the changes in its rate of protection reveal the complexity of the interplay between industrial structure, institutional forces, and the process of economic development. More directly, the history of the automobile tariff casts an interesting light on an important aspect of government industrial development policy during this period, as well as on the complex and often hostile environment within which corporate investment strategies were formulated to deal with specific uncertainties.

The tariff policies adopted by the King and Bennett governments reflected their attitudes toward industrial development in Canada. King's administration appeared to oppose the auto producers while Bennett's seemed to favour them, but such differences do not necessarily reveal different development policies. The circumstances that each government confronted were dissimilar, but the thrust of their policies was much the same. In 1926 the Liberals discerned a need for a greater Canadian manufacturing component in the auto industry's output. Since the majority of firms operated assembly plants rather than manufacturing concerns, the auto companies opposed this policy. By 1929-30, however, the industry had become Canadianized, at least within the terms laid down in the tariff regulations, and the Bennett government agreed to protect it against American competition. In both cases, then, the government of the day agreed to develop and protect domestic production facilities and jobs against foreign competition. Neither government sought to influence or disrupt the pattern of ownership in the industry. The National Policy of 1879, in short, served as the basis of the policy decisions of both governments.[56] In Bennett's case, this is the accepted view of his administration. King's efforts have not been so widely appreciated.[57]

Government policy certainly disrupted the environment within which auto industry planning proceeded. It is clear that after 1926 political and institutional imperatives affected the course of structural change in the Canadian industry at least as much as the changing nature of the market. The Canadian industry owed its existence in large part to Canadian tariff policies. Historic political decisions to differentiate and isolate Canadian demand from American suppliers sustained the domestic market, not any combination of distinctly Canadian demographic or geographic factors. However, once automobile prices became the focus of class and sectional politics in Canada, the industry was especially vulnerable to pressures to change the terms of the tariff schedule under which it operated. After 1926 these forces, together with changing market conditions and altered entrepreneurial capacities, decisively reshaped the environment within which auto producers made their investment decisions.

Ultimately, the auto industry adapted to changed circumstances, but adaptation was slow and hesitant. The industry's response to uncertainty took the form of revised product policies, temporary price cuts, and a long-term campaign to persuade the government to modify its tariff regulations. In Canada the tariff campaign was critical, yet auto producers disagreed on the goals and the methods of tariff reform. Radical changes in market shares produced sharp conflicts of interest among the different automobile companies; unity emerged only in the face of disaster.

Tariff decisions in the automobile industry reflected the delicate balance of political and economic power in Canada. Forced to act by the critical deterioration of its political base, one government struck out against the auto industry and lowered the protective barrier against foreign competition. Another government, forced into action by the critical deterioration of the country's economic base, raised the barrier once again. Throughout, auto manufacturers struggled to gain a new sense of equilibrium, a new sense of stability in the wake of the winds of change. Industrialists alone did not and could not shape their own destiny. The impact of political decisions rebounded throughout their industry and manufacturers had little choice but to throw themselves headlong into the politics of the tariff.

7

Management Relations in a Multinational Enterprise: The Case of Canadian Industries Limited, 1928-1948*

Graham D. Taylor

On March 23, 1944, the Hon. M.J. Coldwell, MP for Rosetown-Biggar, rose in the Canadian House of Commons to denounce the favouritism allegedly practised by his government in awarding war contracts to Defence Industries Ltd. Since 1939, he noted, this company had received almost one-third of all Canadian government assistance to business, an expenditure estimated at $600 million. Mr. Coldwell's objection was, however, only partially directed toward the issue of favouritism. His main argument was that the recipient of this largesse was the wholly-owned subsidiary of Canadian Industries Ltd., which, he maintained, "is not a Canadian enterprise. It is jointly owned and controlled by the du Pont de Nemours company of the United States, and Imperial Chemical Industries Ltd. of the United Kingdom." Far from being an enterprise devoted to developing Canadian resources for the ultimate benefit of the national economy, he added, Canadian Industries Ltd. was nothing more than a unit in the global operations of a cartel established by these

*Financial assistance for the research in preparing this study was provided by the Dalhousie University Research and Development Fund in 1976, and the Centre for International Business Studies at Dalhousie University, Halifax, Nova Scotia, in 1977-78. The author is also indebted to Alfred D. Chandler, Jr., for suggestions relating to research sources and to Richmond Williams and the staff of Eleutherian Mills Historical Library, Greenville, Del., for their assistance.

Reprinted from *Business History Review* LV, 3 (Autumn, 1981). Copyright © The President and Fellows of Harvard College.

two foreign chemical giants, intended to strangle potential competition in Canada, to prevent the entry of Canadian manufacturers into the international chemical and explosives markets, and to exploit the resources of Canada for their exclusive corporate gain.[1]

Mr. Coldwell's observations were based on material presented by the U.S. Justice Department in initiating an antitrust suit two months earlier against Du Pont and Imperial Chemical Industries, naming Canadian Industries Ltd. as "co-conspirator." At that time the U.S. antitrust spokesman, Assistant Attorney General Wendell Berge, characterized the corporate structure of which CIL was a part as an Anglo-American "monopoly . . . throttling the growth of industry within the dominions of the British Empire . . . treating these dominions as economic colonies."[2]

Despite protests by C.D. Howe and other government members in the Canadian Parliament that there were "many Canadian shareholders" in CIL, and that its securities "are quoted on Canadian markets every day," the charge that Du Pont and ICI jointly held overwhelming majority control was verified. The two companies admitted later that each held between 46 per cent and 48 per cent of all the voting shares in CIL, a total of 92 per cent to 94 per cent of all shares between 1927, when the company was established, and 1951. At that time the U.S. court before which the antitrust case was heard upheld the charges that CIL had suppressed competition in Canada and declined to enter the export market to serve the interests of its British and American corporate parents.[3] Subsequently, Du Pont sold its shares in CIL, establishing a new directly owned subsidiary in Canada, while ICI maintained its equity in CIL, now holding approximately 74 per cent of the voting shares in the Canadian company.

From one perspective, then, the experience of CIL appears to provide a forceful illustration of the problems raised by the presence of local subsidiaries of foreign companies, in the view of nationalist opponents of multinational enterprise in Canada and other countries in which substantial foreign direct investment has occurred. In such companies, decisions on policy are made by investors not residing in the host country and without reference to or interest in that country's economic needs.[4] Indeed, CIL's position as an element in an international cartel would seem to strengthen the case made by critics of multinational enterprises. Measures imposed by Du Pont and ICI on CIL, such as restrictions on exports and the denial of funds to move into new domestic markets or develop new technology, could be seen as detrimental to CIL as a company and to the growth of the chemical industry in Canada, given the strong position of CIL in the field at the time.

But there is a different perspective from which CIL may be observed, and from which a less clear-cut picture of the relationship between CIL and its corporate parents emerges. To the American judge examining the evidence and to Canadian critics of CIL, the demonstration of foreign ownership established a presumption of subordination of the local management to the wishes of these foreign investors. An examination of the internal workings of CIL and the relations between the executives of CIL and those of Du Pont and ICI reveals a more complex pattern that, while it may not alter the ultimate circumstance of subordination, introduces an element of bargaining that is not apparent when the end results, the policy decisions and disposition of company earnings, are treated out of this context. This bargaining element was an essential feature of the parent-subsidiary relationship. The multinational aspect of the companies, moreover, enhanced the bargaining element, and must be taken into account when analysing the structure of authority in these organizations.

The Development of CIL

Canadian Industries Ltd. was the final outgrowth of a process of consolidation and diversification in the Canadian explosives and chemical industries, paralleling in many ways the development of these industries in the United States and Great Britain. The company was also the product of the cartel arrangements that had prevailed in these industries since the middle of the nineteenth century and provided the particular framework of relations between the leading American and British companies in the field.[5] CIL was more than a paper organization: it owned plants, produced and marketed goods, carried on extensive research and development in new technology, and otherwise behaved like a conventional industrial firm. At the same time, however, CIL was regarded by its owners, Du Pont and ICI, as primarily a part of their international arrangements, the instrument through which they would jointly exploit the Canadian market and avoid competition with one another. In this sense, CIL differed from other Canadian subsidiaries of foreign owners.

In 1876, the American powder trust, whose dominant member was E.I. du Pont de Nemours Co., purchased shares in several powder companies in Ontario, which later merged under the name of one of the firms, Hamilton Powder Co., established in 1862. During the next two decades, Hamilton Powder Co. bought other properties in Ontario and Quebec, including a liquid nitroglycerine plant and a heavy chemical company. In 1899, the British company, Nobel Explosives Ltd., bought a large block of shares in the Hamilton company to give it a foothold in the Canadian powder market. Between 1899 and 1908, Nobel also bought three other Canadian firms, Victoria Chemical Co., Acadia Powder Co., and Dominion Cartridge Co. Following the death in 1910 of Thomas Brainerd, the Canadian who had managed Hamilton Powder Co. and held the balance of its shares, Nobel induced Du Pont to join with it in merging the four companies into Canadian Explosives Ltd., with Du Pont taking 45 per cent and Nobel 55 per cent of the shares.[6]

Between 1911 and 1927, Canadian Explosives Ltd. (CXL) took over Canadian branch plants of Du Pont manufacturing paints, nitrocellulose plastics, and an artificial leather called Fabrikoid. CXL also acquired the Canadian properties of other American firms, including those of the Giant Powder Co. of San Francisco and the Atlas Powder Co. of Wilmington, Delaware, a company in which the Du Pont family had an interest and which itself had a minority interest in CXL. By the end of 1926, CXL had three major explosives plants, substantial investments in acids and heavy chemicals, and a number of smaller properties producing organic chemical-based products. CXL also held a block of 260,000 shares of General Motors. Nobel and Du Pont shared majority control of the company, valued at about $8 million in 1926, with Atlas Powder Co. and a small Canadian interest holding the balance of shares.[7]

In December, 1926, Nobel merged with Brunner, Mond and Co., Ltd., the large British fertilizer and heavy chemical producer, and two smaller firms, including British Dyestuffs Corporation Ltd., which specialized in organic chemical products, to form Imperial Chemical Industries Ltd. This merger gave the new British company an industrial potential parallel in many product lines to those developed by the Du Pont corporation in the United States since 1917. Even before the formation of ICI, Nobel and Du Pont had been expanding a relationship that went back to the days of the powder trust and the establishment of CXL, to include exclusive patent and licence exchange agreements in 1920 and 1925 in explosives and related products, and joint ownership of subsidiary companies to manufacture and sell Duco paints and Fabrikoid in the British Empire outside Canada, participation in the establishment of a company to market tetraethyl gasoline, and the separate purchases of shares in two German competitors in the powder industry, Köln-Rottwiler and Dynamit AG.[8] The predilection on both sides was thus for an extension of their relationship into the chemicals field and a pooling of their interests in regions of potentially damaging competition, such as Canada.

As early as June, 1919, Lammot du Pont had proposed using CXL as the vehicle for manufacturing and marketing in Canada the new chemical products that the Du Pont company was developing. Later that year, he and Sir Harry McGowan of Nobel agreed to divide CXL common stock on an equal basis and agreed that the partners should provide CXL with patents, licences, and other technical assistance to enable that company to diversify in selected fields exclusively for the Canadian market. In 1920 the authorized common stock of the company was increased to $22.5 million and new shares were distributed to permit Du Pont to acquire an equality with Nobel. Five years later, when Du Pont and Nobel renegotiated their general agreements, they arranged that when "exploiting any new products not covered by this agreement," CXL would be given "preference" in acquiring rights to develop these products for the Canadian market.[9] The establishment of CIL in 1927 thus did not represent a major change in policies or corporate relationships but rather a recognition on both sides, though promoted most strongly by McGowan, of the need to reorganize the Canadian operation to expand its industrial activities following the creation of ICI.[10]

Canadian Industries Ltd. was incorporated in June, 1927, with a new share issue of which Du Pont and ICI took 46 per cent each and the understanding that if either party increased its equity in CIL the other would be entitled to acquire an equal amount through a new stock issue. The remainder was held by Atlas Powder Co. and the Canadian investors in CXL. The company was initially set up as a holding company with the largest operating subsidiary, Canadian Explosives, being chartered separately. During the next year, CIL bought the Canadian properties of the National Ammonia Co. and the Grasselli Chemical Co. The Grasselli purchase, part of a larger acquisition by Du Pont of Grasselli in the United States, gave CIL a foothold in the synthetic fertilizer field, and CIL's purchase of Canadian Salt Co. Ltd. in 1928 gave it effective control of the salt industry and its derivatives, chlorine and caustic soda, in Canada. In that same year, CIL was reorganized into an operating company. The various subsidiaries were consolidated into eight divisions, along the lines of the Du Pont corporation, and subsequently reassembled into three broad "groups": the Cellulose Group, including paints and plastics; the Chemical Group, including dyestuffs and alkalis; and the Explosives Group.[11]

Over the next twenty years, CIL continued to expand and diversify its activities within the Canadian chemical industry, largely with technical assistance and some financial help from Du Pont and ICI. Despite an overly ambitious move into the fertilizer business at a time when agricultural commodity prices were collapsing, the company weathered the worst of the Depression with only one year of declining sales and earnings, as CIL opened relatively untapped markets for new chemical products through its access to the Canadian rights to many Du Pont patents. In 1933, CIL opened a plant to produce cellophane, and in 1936 began to produce trichlorethylene, a metal solvent. In 1938, CIL was the Canadian sales agent for Du Pont nylon products, and in 1940 it established a plant to manufacture nylon yarn. These innovations gave CIL a substantial advantage in exploiting the Canadian market for new chemical products.

Balanced against this advantage were the restrictions placed on CIL in the export market, restrictions of no little consequence in the Depression when the relatively small Canadian market shrank even more in the older fields of fertilizers and explosives. Furthermore, the managers of CIL later maintained that on at least two occasions in this period the Canadian government pressured the company to venture into the international market to boost Canadian exports. In 1932, the Canadian company sought to export explosives to the British West Indies as the Canadian government was subsidizing steamship operations to that region and was encouraging Canadian manufacturers to use the facilities. Again, in 1935, the government pressed CIL to enter the export market to increase employment, a point of some delicacy since the president of the firm was at that time head of a national commission on unemployment in Canada. In both cases, Du Pont and ICI vetoed any departure from earlier agreements restricting CIL to Canada.[12]

Despite these rebuffs, CIL seems to have been able to develop a profitable mixture of traditional and new markets in Canada between 1928 and 1942. Company assets trebled in value in this period while earnings per share of common stock rose from $.43 in 1927 to $.72 in 1941, and sales and income rose steadily except for the year 1932.[13] To critics of the cartel and CIL's foreign ownership, the achievement of this growth and generally profitable performance was largely the result of the technical advantages conferred by the Du Pont-ICI connection and did not involve any substantial transfer of management skills to Canada. But while the managers of CIL did not become "Canadianized" in a conventional sense during this period, they did develop a strong proprietary attitude toward the company and deployed bargaining skills that helped ensure that CIL would take full advantage of the opportunities provided by its association with Du Pont and ICI.

The Role of CIL Management

Executives of CIL's parent corporations in London and Wilmington, Delaware, were at least sporadically aware of the local antagonism that their Canadian operations aroused, although they did little to respond to critics' demands before 1948. Du Pont defence attorneys in the U.S. antitrust suit maintained that one of the underlying factors in the establishment of CIL in 1927 was the "widespread local prejudice among Canadians" against foreign, especially American, companies. Even before this point, there were gestures toward recognizing the nationalist issue. In 1924, when Du Pont and Nobel chiefs met in London to select a new president for CXL to succeed William McMaster, "it was unanimously agreed that the CXL president should be a Canadian if at all possible."[14] The man chosen, however, was Arthur B. Purvis, a Scot who had worked for Nobel in South Africa and South America for twenty years, primarily because of his performance in merging Northern Giant Powder Co. with CXL in 1925. After Purvis left to work for the British government in 1939, the subject recurred when Lord Melchett of ICI noted "dissatisfaction . . . expressed by certain representatives of Canadian universities, with CIL's tendencies to draw its senior staff from England and the United States rather than developing such talent among Canadians." Nobody else felt strongly enough about this matter to suggest a Canadian successor to Purvis. Instead, the board confirmed George Huggett, an English-born veteran of various ICI subsidiaries, who had served as Purvis's vice-president since 1927. Melchett, however, did propose that CIL should exhibit its interest in developing Canadian talent by "the creation of scientific scholarships at the principal Universities and technical schools."[15] Some Du Pont executives felt that CIL ought to find Canadians qualified to fill top management positions, but Du Pont president Walter S. Carpenter, Jr., in 1942 indicated an equally strong desire to build a CIL staff with an "American background."[16]

The board of directors of CIL included an equal number of Du Pont and ICI directors, with Purvis as president and managing director. Four of the twelve directors were prominent Canadian businessmen: Ross McMaster, son of William McMaster, Purvis's predecessor, and himself a vice-president of the Steel Company of Canada; Lt. Col. Herbert Molson of the Molson brewing company; Sir Charles Gordon, president of Dominion Textile Co. and the Bank of Montreal; and Charles C. Ballantyne, managing director of Sherwin-Williams Co. of Canada. None of these directors held any significant block of shares in CIL, and except for McMaster they played only a minor role in the deliberations of the board.[17]

Between 1930 and 1944, virtually all the top management group directly beneath Purvis and the board was composed of Du Pont and Nobel veterans, some of whom moved between CIL and the parent companies.[18] By any objective standards, CIL's management was extremely inbred during this period; and, despite periodic twinges of regret, the owners took a resolutely indifferent attitude toward demands for greater Canadian participation.

But while the management of CIL was not Canadian, the executives, particularly Purvis, found it advantageous to emphasize the position of CIL as a Canadian enterprise as well as, or instead of, a branch of two foreign corporations. After taking over CIL in 1927, Purvis involved himself in affairs well beyond those of his company. In 1935-36, he served as a member of the national commission on unemployment, and in 1939 he became a member, and later head, of the Anglo-French Purchasing Board in the United States until his untimely death in an airplane crash in 1941. Purvis was a director of a number of other Canadian corporations and a governor of McGill University in Montreal. Some business associates felt that Purvis was "aiming to become Prime Minister of Canada," and however improbable that may have been, his view of CIL was suitably expansive.[19] He communicated his viewpoint down the line in his organization. At one point, when Purvis and Du Pont chiefs were at loggerheads, George Huggett wrote to J. Thompson Brown of the Du Pont executive committee that "Purvis was an idol both within the CIL organization and outside in Canada," a factor that the Americans were obliged to take into account in their dealings with him and the Canadian company. As Wendell Swint, a member of the Du Pont foreign relations committee, remarked later, "Mr. Purvis was a pretty tough customer," adding, "We preferred to have CIL a well run company and make money for us rather than continue to press him and probably even then not be successful at it."[20]

Purvis also demonstrated considerable political skill in playing his corporate masters off against one another, alternately posing as a true organization man and as a spokesman for a growing Canadian

role in the chemical industry. This attitude proved irritating, especially to Du Pont managers who had to deal with CIL below the
policy level. As one exasperated Du Pont official acidly observed,
after CIL refused to buy from a key Du Pont supplier: "Mr. Purvis
very often talks of the 'family' viewpoint in these matters ... but the
trouble with all these CIL discussions is that they generally wind up in
one direction." [21]

Although on better terms with his old employers at ICI, particularly
McGowan, Purvis did irritate with his persistent efforts to circum-
vent restrictions placed on CIL by a very narrow reading of the
clauses of various agreements between the companies, and by his
expansion of CIL's capacity in fields such as fertilizers, where the
Canadian market was limited. Purvis's response to criticism in this
area was attuned to the conservative, anti-competitive attitude prev-
alent in ICI, arguing that CIL had to develop unprofitable fields to
keep out potential rivals who might then proceed to move into more
profitable areas.[22] Through variations on these different themes,
Purvis successfully promoted CIL's interests through a decade of
constant haggling with Du Pont and ICI.

Purvis also figured prominently in a confrontation with Du Pont
over the shares held by Atlas Powder Co. in Canadian Explosives
and CIL. Soon after the formation of CIL the Canadian company
sought to have the major shareholders buy out Atlas, but Du Pont
objected on the ground that Atlas was asking too high a price for its
shares. Writing to McGowan in October, 1928, Purvis discerned that
the real reason for Du Pont's reluctance was that Atlas was controlled
by "certain Du Pont individuals through the Christiana Securities
Company," giving Du Pont interests a 52 per cent share in the
Canadian companies, contrary to the agreements between Du Pont
and ICI on stock distribution, not to mention "undesirable ... from
the standpoint of a Canadian concern being controlled by U.S.
interests." Under this pressure, Lammot du Pont agreed to pay the
Atlas asking price for CIL shares. Although Alfred D. Chandler, Jr.,
in his biography of Pierre du Pont, has noted that Purvis's view of
the Du Pont-Atlas connection was "exaggerated," there seems to be
little doubt that Purvis played a pivotal role, characteristically combining appeals to one company head against another with rhetoric
about Canadian interests.[23]

In 1939, when Purvis accepted appointment to the Anglo-French
Purchasing Board, Du Pont insisted that he resign as president of
CIL and sell all his shares in the company to avoid conflict of interest
charges. Although Du Pont executives could point to the unfortunate

experience of their own company before U.S. congressional investigating committees in 1934-35 as justification for recommending this step, Purvis regarded the proposal as an effort to purge him because of his independence. Typically, he carried the matter to the executive committee of Du Pont, accusing them of bad faith, while other CIL executives warned Du Pont of the wide repercussions Purvis's peremptory removal would have on CIL's public image in Canada. Ultimately, Purvis called on McGowan to mediate in the dispute, and in the end Du Pont backed down. Purvis remained as president of CIL on extended "leave," retaining his shares in the company as well.[24]

Purvis's successor, George Huggett, proved to be less outspoken and more amenable to the non-Canadian interests, but by this time the parent companies were preoccupied with war production at home and the growing threat of antitrust prosecution, which induced them to undertake substantial changes in inter-company relationships after 1948. Even before that time, CIL, prompted by the Canadian government and critics in Parliament and the press, had embarked on an export drive in the Caribbean, and the 1948 agreement simply recognized an accomplished fact, arranging at the same time for CIL to pay for non-exclusive patents and licences by sharing its royalties on sales for fifteen years.[25]

Symptomatic of CIL's growing independence was its changing policy toward distribution of profits. Up to 1939, an average of 90 per cent of net earnings was distributed as dividends to shareholders, with the result that CIL was tied to its foreign sponsors for any decisions involving substantial outlays of money. As a Du Pont memorandum noted, the Du Pont interest derived a relatively small gain from this policy after tax deductions and exchange rate differences were taken into account, indicating that the main purpose was control. Wartime demands for capital to expand production and retained earnings to cover increased taxes forced a change in this arrangement as CIL kept more of its net profits for re-investment. The practice continued after the war, the percentage of profits distributed as dividends declining from 78 per cent to 72 per cent between 1945 and 1948.[26]

Another development contributing to its independent posture was the increase in stock ownership by CIL management, the outgrowth of a policy to provide stock as a bonus incentive to managers initiated in the early 1930's with Du Pont's blessing. By the end of the decade, CIL internal equity had risen to the point that some Du Pont executives feared a dilution of control by the majority shareholders, with the CIL management interest being in a position to play a balancing role between them.[27] Although this situation never developed, the Americans' concern was not misplaced. While the initiative for the changing relations between the companies came from such external pressures as wartime demands on resources and the U.S. antitrust suit, CIL managers proved to be quite prepared to take advantage of the circumstances, just as Purvis had sought to exploit the more limited opportunities available in his tenure.

Bargaining: Patents and Markets

The essence of the bargaining relationship between CIL and its corporate parents involved a trade-off between the transfer of technology and restrictions on export markets. In principle, Du Pont and ICI had agreed to use CIL as their vehicle for exploiting present and future markets in Canada in all products; in practice, the parent companies, for various reasons, sought to retain Canadian rights over particular products. Under agreements made in 1928 and 1936, CIL was in effect barred from exporting a range of products. Reading the provisions of those agreements as narrowly as possible, the Canadian company continually sought to develop exports in products and regions not specifically identified in the agreements. From these sets of circumstances the bargaining proceeded.

In 1928, the newly established CIL was expected to expand by purchase or merger with Canadian competitors in the chemical industry in Canada, a policy leading to the absorption of such companies as Grasselli and Canadian Salt. The expansionist strategy was stymied, however, by the refusal of Allied Chemical Co., one of Du Pont's major competitors in the United States, to sell a large synthetic ammonia plant at Amherstburg, Ontario, to CIL. Imperial Chemical Industries then agreed to provide capital and technical assistance to enable CIL to expand its production in fertilizers and heavy chemicals; but Du Pont objected to CIL's entering the Canadian dyestuffs market in which the American company was entrenched. As a general principle, Du Pont agreed to give CIL an opportunity to propose to undertake production of any new Du Pont ventures in Canada, but was not bound to do so.[28] Over the next four years, these issues were to reappear in discussions among the companies.

Du Pont had made agreements with American producers of waterproof loading shells not to enter their market. CIL, which held its own patents on waterproof shells, announced in October, 1928, its intention to enter the American market, as this was not a product scheduled for restriction in the Du Pont-ICI agreements. The proposal naturally aroused resentment among American competitors who regarded the CIL move as a Du Pont manoeuvre. To head this off, Du Pont agreed to buy the CIL patents. At the same time, Du Pont finally agreed to share the Canadian dyestuffs market with CIL, which in effect meant with ICI, which supplied most of the CIL product.[29]

In 1931, CIL resurrected the proposal to buy and consolidate Canadian properties of Allied Chemical Co. Du Pont's foreign relations committee was skeptical about this idea since CIL already seemed to have more than sufficient capacity in synthetic ammonia production in a period of agricultural distress. More alarming, however, was the intimation that CIL intended to acquire Sherwin-Williams paint manufacturing and sales properties in Canada, or a share of them. The Du Pont paint division objected to this proposal since it had its own competitive line, and also warned of the possible leaking of technical information to Sherwin-Williams through CIL. In the end, CIL backed down on the Sherwin-Williams deal, but Du Pont was obliged to give ground on the Allied Chemical proposal, although ultimately nothing definite came from discussions with Allied because of the stiff terms offered CIL.[30]

Although the clear implication of the 1928 Du Pont-ICI agreement was that CIL should keep out of foreign markets altogether, the Canadian company was always probing the outer limits of the provisions, seeking markets that neither of the owners would find objectionable. In 1934, H.J. Mitchell of ICI noted that CIL had been selling sporting equipment and ammunition in South America for more than six years, and the Canadian company argued that this market must be retained by them in order to keep manufacturing operations in the field going. At this same time, CIL was demanding the right to sell ammunitiion in the West Indies to alleviate pressures from the Canadian government.[31]

By this time, even McGowan of ICI, who normally supported Purvis's expansive ambitions, was concerned that CIL's interpretation of the general patent and process agreements was placing undue strain on Du Pont-ICI relations at a time when the British company was particularly anxious to maintain the cartel. In a confidential letter to Lammot du Pont, he agreed that a complete review of "the whole situation opposite CIL" was necessary and that "we shall have to call upon CIL to forgo what may be claimed as existing legal rights if we are to get back to the original . . . intention of the parties."[32]

Over the following year and a half, a new agreement was prepared, and after much dickering, it went into effect in December, 1936. In the initial drafts of the agreement, Du Pont had introduced certain new restrictions on CIL: the Canadian firm would be bound to pass on any new inventions or patents to Du Pont and ICI even in non-scheduled product lines, while ICI and Du Pont could continue to withhold patents from CIL if they chose. Du Pont and ICI could also establish manufacturing facilities in Canada independent of CIL for the production of items for export from Canada. Purvis naturally opposed these innovations since CIL was now definitely to be excluded from the export business, and ICI backed his position on the issue of surrendering new patents without reciprocation. Purvis also tried to avoid having the new arrangements drawn up formally, but had to concede that point.[33]

Nevertheless, the final agreement did include some important concessions to the CIL viewpoint. All products were itemized, and the right of CIL to participate in, or be excluded from, manufacture of these items was explicitly noted, in place of the vague general statement Du Pont had proposed. Furthermore, CIL was given the right to request disclosure of new patents and processes developed by ICI or Du Pont, and the reasons for exclusion in any given case should be open for discussion among the three parties. Finally, the right of Du Pont and ICI to establish manufacturing facilities in Canada independent of CIL was restricted to the processing of raw materials or semi-finished products for supplying other subdivisions or subsidiaries of Du Pont or ICI in non-scheduled items.[34]

The years 1937-39 were less troubled, as Purvis concentrated on developing CIL's manufacturing operations and Du Pont arranged for CIL to handle nylon product sales in Canada. But tension persisted beneath the surface. In 1939, CIL proposed to expand its production of synthetic ammonia through a joint undertaking with Shawinigan Chemical Co. Du Pont officials worried that arrangements with a potential rival might result in leaks concerning new Du Pont processes using "water gas" (carbon monoxide and hydrogen), which were applicable to a range of chemical products. Both Du Pont and ICI were also concerned over CIL's heavy investment in the fertilizer business. Despite Purvis's argument that this move was basically pre-emptive, to stymie future competition, the suspicion lingered that CIL was building a case for expanding in product lines and markets when the general agreement came up for renewal in 1940.[35]

The onset of war raised new problems. In 1939, Purvis arranged to take over some of ICI's South American markets for the duration of the war without consulting Du Pont, and also laid plans for a vast expansion of CIL's synthetic ammonia and explosives manufacturing capacity through the establishment of a subsidiary, Defense Industries Ltd. After protracted debate, Du Pont vetoed CIL's entry into South America, where it planned to absorb the entire chemical market hitherto shared with ICI and the German chemical trust, I.G. Farben, at least for the duration of the war. At the same time, Du Pont accepted the plans for Defense Industries Ltd., but made the grudging comment that "C.I.L. had gone a little too far in their proposals for utilizing their own money."[36]

Purvis's departure at the end of the year eased tension somewhat, particularly between CIL and Du Pont, as the new acting president, Huggett, was on close terms with J. Thompson Brown, a Du Pont representative on the CIL board. But the bargaining advantages began to shift more favourably to CIL after 1942. When CIL moved into the West Indies market after the war, it did so on its own initiative after Du Pont and ICI announced that products manufactured by these companies under patents not licensed to CIL would enter Canada on a competitive basis, a measure probably taken to alleviate antitrust pressures.[37]

Bargaining: Intercompany Pricing

Another area of contention and manoeuvring in the CIL-ICI-Du Pont relationship involved inter-company price arrangements for products sold to the Canadian company by divisions of the parent firms. These arrangements were deceptively simple in principle, but immensely complicated in practice, and produced continuous infighting, primarily between CIL and division heads at Du Pont. Du Pont president Walter S. Carpenter, Jr., noted later: "Mr. Purvis was . . . a very astute and aggressive negotiator, and . . . he met men of somewhat similar calibre in some of our general managers . . . [T]he result of those negotiations . . . would be this constant bickering and trading and so on [which produced] a rather unfortunate feeling on the part of both parties."[38] Top management for both Du Pont and ICI at times intervened in these conflicts and sought to work out general formulas to resolve the differences, but their measures were usually only palliatives. In this chronic haggling, CIL often had to give way, particularly if its demands jeopardized the broader ICI-Du Pont arrangements, but CIL negotiators proved no less adept at extracting concessions in this area than they were in discussions concerning patents and markets.

The subject first arose as a matter of controversy between Canadian Explosives Ltd. and Du Pont before the establishment of CIL. Under general agreements between Du Pont and Nobel in 1920 and 1925, CXL was to be given prices on raw materials and semi-finished and finished products equivalent to the lowest market price quoted for American and Canadian customers. In 1927 Purvis, as president of CXL, complained that Du Pont divisions "had taken something of a trading attitude in dealing with C.X.L.," charging higher prices than those given other Canadian buyers. After some discussions Du Pont agreed to have its divisions treat CXL as if it were an 85 per cent subsidiary of Du Pont, "enjoying as low a price as any other subsidiary . . . as would be consistent with Du Pont's costs," except when the product was scarce or difficult to replace.[39]

This agreement did not end the problem, however, since each division had its own special price arrangements with CXL, and when CIL was created, the general principle established was that CIL should be supplied "at mill replacement cost (including factory cost and factory overhead) plus 10 per cent, or the best price allowed to any U.S. customers, whichever is lower." This arrangement was not reached without much manoeuvring for better terms: Purvis had proposed that Du Pont supply certain products at cost on the ground that in the end the Du Pont corporation would benefit from CIL's general return on investment. Carpenter of Du Pont countered with a proposal of cost plus 15 per cent on a long-term contract basis that would operate regardless of market price. Mill cost plus 10 per cent thus represented a compromise. ICI subsequently made a similar agreement with CIL.[40]

Still matters were not settled. In 1932, Du Pont discovered that CIL in its purchases from one or the other of its parent companies had been "playing the two partners against each other to get a percentage lower than 10 per cent over cost," the difference arising from the fact that some divisions included cost of research in the calculation of "factory overhead" while others did not.[41] Steps were taken to bring about better co-ordination, if not uniformity, among divisions and companies.

CIL also asserted its right to go outside Du Pont and ICI if the prices quoted seemed unsatisfactory. In 1932, CIL cancelled an order for ethylene glycol, a synthetic glycerine, from British Dyestuffs, an ICI subsidiary, on the ground that the price was too high, and proceeded to build its own equipment for polymerized glycerine rather than accept the price, a decision G.W. White of ICI (New York) characterized as "relatively disastrous."[42]

Du Pont engaged CIL in an extended controversy over the price of isobutanol, a solvent used in producing paints. In 1936, CIL charged that Du Pont was charging it a higher price than Du Pont's own paint division. The general manager of the Du Pont ammonia division countered that the special internal price was given because of the high demand for butanol by the Du Pont paint division, which might otherwise go outside the company to fill its needs, and because the Canadian butanol price would be higher in any case, and the price offered was below mill cost plus 10 per cent. H. Greville-Smith, of CIL rejected these arguments as specious since the calculation of the Canadian price included duties on imported butanol. At this point Du Pont's foreign relations committee intervened in a vain attempt to demonstrate to CIL that the price offered was the best market price. Rather than accept the Du Pont price, CIL changed its formula for paint solvents from isobutanol to ethyl acetate and pentasol. In 1938, when Canadian duties on isobutanol were lifted temporarily, Du Pont again sought to get CIL's business, but the Canadian company now argued that it had established relations with Shawinigan Chemical Co. for the supply of ethyl acetate and did not wish to endanger a growing connection with Shawinigan in other joint endeavours. Despite the fact that Du Pont's ammonia division was now eager to get CIL's business, the Canadian company maintained its relations with Shawinigan.[43]

Although Greville-Smith later maintained that his company made no effort to keep track of relative purchases from ICI and Du Pont, documents compiled in 1940 and 1948 indicated that a generally equal division was maintained up to 1939. On balance, however, purchases from Du Pont exceeded those from ICI by about $200,000 per year except in the field of dyestuffs in which ICI actively promoted buying by CIL. Outside of this area, CIL seems to have been allowed to follow its own course in seeking the best price between the two parent companies.[44]

The cost plus 10 per cent formula remained in effect until 1946, but in practice it was abandoned after 1940 as individual Du Pont divisions worked out their own sales arrangements with CIL; ICI, with its domestic wartime demand, was practically out of the picture. The Canadian company's growth as a major industry during the war gave it a better bargaining position, and its corporate parents were not necessarily shown favouritism. Between 1941 and 1948, Du Pont's share of CIL's total purchases of raw materials and resale products declined from 25 per cent to 21 per cent and ICI's from 14 per cent to 3 per cent. By contrast, the share of Canadian suppliers rose from 35 per cent to 55 per cent.[45]

Conclusion

This study has emphasized the independence exercised by the management of CIL in their relations with the parent companies between 1928 and 1948. The purpose has not been to argue that this situation was typical of management relations in multinational enterprises even during this period when instruments of communication and financial control were less sophisticated and far-reaching than today. Nor could it be said that CIL operated even in its home market with few restraints. On the contrary, the interesting aspect of this case is that CIL's management possessed any autonomy at all given the preponderance of foreign ownership in the company and the subordinate role that Du Pont and ICI expected it to play in the functioning of the international chemical cartel. Yet from the time of its establishment, the executives of CIL did assert the right to make their own decisions on a range of matters, and continually pressed for a larger role in the international market, while bypassing contractual restrictions placed on them wherever possible. That such a situation should develop within an international corporate system so apparently monolithic to outside observers highlights the need to analyse the actual process of decision-making in these organizations as well as the structure of financial control when seeking to determine the distribution of power within multinational enterprises.

There were a number of factors that helped CIL pursue an independent course in its relations with Du Pont and ICI. After 1942, of course, the growing criticism in Canada and antitrust prosecution in the United States pressured the parent companies to provide CIL with more freedom to enter export markets. But even before that point, such issues as CIL's investment policies, inter-company price policies, and sharing of technology had been settled by bargaining among the companies, not by commands from the parent firms, and in these negotiations CIL's representatives had taken an active part.

In large measure, CIL's autonomy derived from the fact that it was a jointly owned enterprise, and that the two major shareholders were sufficiently different that they could be played off against one another. Despite a tradition of co-operation reaching back to the nineteenth century, Du Pont and ICI were companies run by men of different nationalities, with divergent experiences and objectives;

and, as William J. Reader, the historian of ICI has noted, their alliance was subject to growing strains even before the American antitrust action forced changes in their relationship.[46] Furthermore, CIL had a natural inclination to rely on ICI for support in many situations, since both were tied to the British imperial system, and since Nobel had been the senior partner in control of CIL's predecessor companies before the 1920's. Purvis was particularly skilled at manipulating this connection to CIL's advantage, and the Canadian company fared poorly only when it had managed to antagonize both Du Pont and ICI, as was the case in 1934-35 when CIL pressed too hard for export markets. Du Pont does not seem to have regarded CIL's tactics as evidence of a conspiracy with ICI, although Walter Carpenter, Jr., noted the relatively small number of Du Pont men in CIL management. Nevertheless, it is difficult to avoid the conclusion that Purvis and other CIL executives saw ICI as temperamentally the more sympathetic of the two owners and relied on these ties of personal sympathy in their manoeuvres.

Another contributing factor was the attitude of both Du Pont and ICI toward management autonomy in principle. Both were large multi-divisional companies that had reorganized their own operations at home in the 1920's to promote decentralization at the operating level.[47] A divisional general manager or head of a domestic subsidiary who performed well and ran a profitable operation would not be likely to meet with much interference from above unless his activities adversely affected broader policies. This attitude was exemplified by Wendell Swint's remark about Purvis that "we preferred to have CIL a well run company and make money" even if this meant tolerating a rather outspoken independence of viewpoint. At the same time, the element of individual personality must be given its due: Purvis was by all accounts a skilled and persuasive negotiator, and he was largely responsible for ensuring that CIL's interests were advanced in the early years of the company when he had few resources with which to bargain.

One final element contributing to management autonomy was, ironically, Canadian nationalism. While Du Pont and ICI chiefs were generally unresponsive to direct criticisms of their control of CIL, they could not disregard the nationalist sentiment altogether. Should they have been tempted to do so, Purvis constantly reminded them that CIL was a Canadian company, subject to the laws and pressures that the government and public opinion of that country could bring to bear upon them, and that CIL by right deserved every opportunity to build up its productive capacity, even though in the long run this might require Du Pont and ICI to give it a larger international role than was originally contemplated. In large measure, of course, this kind of argument when made by Purvis was intended to serve his tactical purposes. But the American and British businessmen were made uncomfortably aware that the points he raised had a substantial basis in fact and had to be dealt with diplomatically. To say that concern for Canadian public repercussions conditioned Du Pont's and ICI's relations with CIL in this period would be an exaggeration; but it was a factor of some consequence, and one that could only be of importance in a multinational enterprise.

Bibliographical Essay

Tom Traves

It is almost impossible to provide a bibliography of Canadian business history that does not draw within its purview a wide range of studies also normally cited in references to other fields. Certainly the distinction between economic and business history, especially when the former is written from an institutional perspective, is blurred. The challenge of writing a short bibliographical essay of this sort, then, threatens to get out of hand. Fortunately, the task is eased somewhat by the numerous other bibliographical sources readily available to students and scholars alike. A list of such aids to further study follows. In addition, a short list of important studies, arranged topically and with an emphasis on more recent scholarship, is also offered.

Bibliographies

Previous collections of articles dealing with business and economic history themes have featured excellent bibliographies that should be consulted. Among them the most useful are W.T. Easterbrook, "Recent Contributions to Economic History: Canada," in Easterbrook and M.H. Watkins, eds., *Approaches to Canadian Economic History* (1967); F.H. Armstrong, "Canadian Business History: Approaches and Publications to 1970," in D.S. Macmillan, ed., *Canadian Business History: Selected Studies, 1497-1971* (1972); Glenn Porter, "Recent Trends in Canadian Business and Economic History," in Porter and R. Cuff, eds., *Enterprise and National Development: Essays in Canadian Business and Economic History* (1972). The standard textbook introductions to Canada's economic history also contain helpful guides to further reading, as well, obviously, as insights into the development of the Canadian business system. In particular, see W.T. Easterbrook and H.G.J. Aitken, *Canadian Economic History* (1956); W.L. Marr and D.G. Paterson, *Canada: An Economic History* (1980); and R. Pomfret, *The Economic Devel-*

opment of Canada (1981). More specialized bibliographies for readers interested in a narrower time frame can be found in the multi-volume Centenary History of Canada published by McClelland and Stewart under the general editorship of W.L. Morton and D.G. Creighton. See also W. Clement and D. Drache, *A Practical Guide to Canadian Political Economy: Bibliography* (1981). Finally, see the useful essays in D.A. Muise, ed., *A Reader's Guide to Canadian History: Beginnings to Confederation* (1982) and J.L. Granatstein and P. Stevens, *A Reader's Guide to Canadian History: Confederation to the Present* (1982).

A number of other more specialized bibliographical aides focus more directly on the problems of studying business history. In particular, see P. Craven, A. Forrest, and T. Traves, "Canadian Company Histories: A Checklist," which appears as part of a special bibliographical issue devoted to Canadian business in *Communique*, 4, 3 (1981). See also R. Rice and B. Young, eds., *A Guide to the History and Records of Selected Montreal Businesses before 1947* (1974). John Archer surveys the archival holdings available in Canada in "Business Records: The Canadian Scene," in D.S. Macmillan, ed., *Canadian Business History* (1972). Finally, in a separate category altogether, the numerous entries in the *Dictionary of Canadian Biography* (University of Toronto Press, various dates) devoted to businessmen constitute perhaps the most useful introduction to the study of the business system yet published.

Colonial Commerce

There is no single overview of the development of the pre-industrial commercial system. Surveys such as Easterbrook and Aitken, *Canadian Economic History*, provide a wealth of information on the development of the staple trades and the elaboration of the transportation system, but curiously they neglect to provide a comprehensive analysis of the business system itself. Numerous specialized studies have appeared in recent years, however, which help to fill this gap. For New France, see: John Bosher, "A Quebec Merchant's Trading Circle in France and Canada: Jean-André Lamaltie before 1763," *HS* (1977); Louise Dechêne, *Habitants et marchands de Montréal au XVIIe siècle* (1974); W.J. Eccles, "The Social, Economic, and Political Significance of the Military Establishment in New France," *CHR*, (1971); Michael Gaumond, *Les forges du Saint-Maurice* (1968); J.P. Hardy and D.T. Ruddel, *Les apprentis artisans à Québec, 1660-1815* (1977); José Igartua, "The Merchants of Montreal at the

Conquest: Socio-Economic Profile," *HS* (1977), as well as his "The Merchants and Négociants of Montreal, 1750-1775: A Study in Socio-Economic History" (Ph.D. thesis, University of Wisconsin, 1971); Jacques Mathieu, *La construction navale royale à Québec, 1739-1759* (1971) and "Le Commerce Nouvelle-France/Antilles au XVIIIe siècle" (Ph.D. thesis, Université Laval, 1975); Dale Miquelon, "The Baby Family and the Trade of Canada, 1750-1820" (M.A. thesis, Carleton University, 1966) and *Dugard of Rouen: French Trade to Canada and the West Indies, 1729-1770* (1978); Peter Moogk, *Building a House in New France: An Account of the Perplexities of Client and Craftsmen in Early Canada* (1977); C. Moore, "The Other Louisbourg: Trade and Merchant Enterprise in Ile Royale, 1713-58," *HS* (1979); Cameron Nish, *Les bourgeois-gentilshommes de la Nouvelle-France, 1729-1748* (1968) and *François-Etienne Cugnet, 1719-1751: entrepreneurs et entreprises en Nouvelle-France* (1975); Y.F. Zoltvany, "Some Aspects of the Business Career of Charles Aubert de la Chesnaye (1632-1702)," *CHAR* (1968).

The history of the fur trade overlaps the transition from New France to Quebec, as does the extensive debate on the significance of the Conquest. The best summary of the latter is to be found in Dale Miquelon, ed., *Society and Conquest: The Debate on the Bourgeoisie and Social Change in French Canada, 1700-1850* (1977), which introduces selections by the major historians of this issue and provides a supplementary bibliography. See also Cameron Nish, ed., *The French-Canadians, 1759-1766: Conquered? Half-Conquered? Liberated?* (1966). The fur trade receives extended bibliographical treatment in David Richeson, "The north, the western interior, and the Pacific Coast," in D.A. Muise, ed., *A Reader's Guide to Canadian History: Beginnings to Confederation* (1982) and in L.G. Thomas, "Historiography of the Fur Trade Era," in R. Allen, ed., *A Region of the Mind: Interpreting the Western Canadian Plains* (1973).

Aspects of colonial commerce during the British era have been examined in the following studies: T.W. Acheson, "The Great Merchant and Economic Development in St. John, 1820-1850," *Acadiensis* (1979), and "The Nature and Structure of York Commerce in the 1820s," *CHR* (1969); H.G. Aitken, *The Welland Canal Co: A Study in Canadian Enterprise* (1954); D. Alexander and R. Ommer, eds., *Volumes not Values: Canadian Sailing Ships and World Trades* (1979); D. Alexander and G. Panting, "The Mercantile Fleet and its Owners: Yarmouth, Nova Scotia, 1840-1889," *Acadiensis* (1979); P. Baskerville, "Donald Bethune's Steamship Business: A Study of

Upper Canadian Commercial and Financial Enterprise," *OH* (1975), "The Entrepreneur and the Metropolitan Impulse: James Grey Bethune and Cobourg, 1825-1836," in J. Petryshyn, ed., *Victorian Cobourg: A Nineteenth-Century Profile* (1976), and "Entrepreneurship and the Family Compact: York-Toronto, 1822-1855," *Urban History Review* (1981); D.D. Calvin, *Saga of the St. Lawrence* (1945); J. Cameron, *The Pictonian Colliers* (1974); J.M.S. Careless, "The Lowe Brothers, 1852-1870: A Study in Business Relations on the North Pacific Coast," *BCS* (1969); G.T. Cell, *English Enterprise in Newfoundland, 1577-1660* (1970); D.C. Creighton, *The Commercial Empire of the St. Lawrence, 1760-1850* (1937); L. Dechêne, "William Price, 1810-1850," *HS* (1968); W.S. Dunn, "Western Commerce, 1760-1774" (Ph.D. thesis, University of Wisconsin, 1971); A. Faucher, *Québec en Amérique au XIXe siècle* (1973); L.R. Fischer and E.W. Sager, eds., *The Enterprising Canadians: Entrepreneurs and Economic Development in Eastern Canada: 1820-1914* (1979); H.A. Innis, *The Cod Fisheries: The History of an International Economy* (1940); P.A. Linteau and J.-C. Robert, "Land Ownership and Society in Montreal: an Hypothesis," in G. Stelter and A. Artibise, eds., *The Canadian City: Essays in Urban History* (1979); A.R.M. Lower, *Great Britain's Woodyard: British America and the Timber Trade, 1763-1867* (1973); D. Macmillan, "The 'New Men' in Action: Mercantile and Shipping Operations in the North American Colonies, 1760-1825," in Macmillan, *Canadian Business History: Selected Studies* (1972); M.L. Magill, "John H. Dunn and the Bankers," *OH* (1970), "William Allan, Pioneer Business Executive," in F.H. Armstrong, ed., *Aspects of Nineteenth-Century Ontario* (1974), and "The Failure of the Commercial Bank," in G. Tulchinsky, ed., *To Preserve and Defend: Essays on Kingston in the Nineteenth Century* (1976); K. Matthews and G. Panting, eds., *Ships and Shipbuilding in the North Atlantic Region* (1978); D. McCalla, *The Upper Canada Trade, 1834-1872: A Study of the Buchanans' Business* (1979), and "The Commercial Politics of the Toronto Board of Trade, 1850-1860," *CHR* (1969); L. Michel, "Le livre de compte (1784-1792) de Gaspard Maussue, marchand à Varennes," *HS* (1980); W.P.J. Millar, "George P.M. Ball: A Rural Businessman in Upper Canada," *OH* (1974); F. Ouellet, *Histoire de la Chambre de Commerce de Québec, 1809-1959* (1959), *Social and Economic History of Quebec, 1760-1850* (1980), *Lower Canada, 1791-1840* (1980), and "Dualité économique et changement technologique dans la vallée du Saint-Laurent, 1760-1850," *HS* (1976); R. Rice, "The Wrights of Saint John: A Study in Shipbuilding and

Shipping in the Maritimes, 1839-1885," in Macmillan, *Canadian Business History*; J.-C. Robert, "Un seigneur entrepreneur: Barthélemy Juliette et la fondation du village de l'Industrie, 1822-1850," *RHAF* (1972); E.W. Sager and L.R. Fischer, "Patterns of Investment in the Shipping Industries of Atlantic Canada, 1820-1900," *Acadiensis* (1979); D. Sutherland, "Halifax Merchants and the Pursuit of Development, 1783-1850," *CHR* (1978); G. Tulchinsky, *The River Barons: Montreal Businessmen and the Growth of Industry and Transportation, 1837-1853* (1977); Bruce Wilson, "The Enterprises of Robert Hamilton: A Study of Wealth and Influence in Early Upper Canada, 1776-1812" (Ph.D. thesis, University of Toronto, 1978); D.J. Wurtele, "Mossom Boyd, Lumber King of the Trent Valley," *OH* (1958); G. Wynn, *Timber Colony: A Historical Geography of Early Nineteenth Century New Brunswick* (1981); A.G. Young, *Great Lakes Saga: The Influence of One Family on the Development of Canadian Shipping on the Great Lakes, 1816-1937* (1965).

Industrial Canada

The onset of the "railway age" is generally acknowledged to constitute the beginning of widespread industrialization in Canada. The railway industry has been examined in numerous studies, although there are some surprising gaps in the existing literature. A brief list of the most important older studies and a more comprehensive compilation of recent work includes the following: G.G. Backler and T.D. Heaver, "The Timing of a Major Investment in Railway Capacity: CPR's 1913 Connaught Tunnel Decision," *Business History* (1982); P. Baskerville, "The Boardroom and Beyond: Aspects of the Upper Canadian Railroad Community" (Ph.D. thesis, Queen's University, 1973), "On the Rails: Trends in Canadian Railway Historiography," *American Review of Canadian Studies* (1977), and "Professional versus Proprietor: Power Distribution in the Railroad World of Upper Canada/Ontario, 1850-1881," *HP* (1978); P. Berton, *The National Dream* (1970) and *The Last Spike* (1971); R. Chodos, *The CPR: A Century of Corporate Welfare* (1973); A.W. Currie, *The Grand Trunk Railway of Canada* (1957); P.C. Dorin, *The Grand Trunk Western Railroad: A Canadian National Railway* (1977); S.J. Eadie, "Edward Wilkes Rathburn and the Napanee Tamworth and Quebec Railway," *OH* (1971); H. Fleming, *Canada's Arctic Outlet: A History of the Hudson Bay Railway* (1957); D. Greenberg, "A Study of Capital Alliances: The St. Paul and Pacific," *CHR* (1976); H.A.

Innis, *A History of the Canadian Pacific Railway* (1923); J. Konarek, "Algoma Central and Hudson Bay Railway: The Beginnings," *OH* (1970); W.K. Lamb, *History of the Canadian Pacific Railway* (1977); R.F. Leggett, *Railroads of Canada* (1973); A. Martin, *James J. Hill and the Opening of the Northwest* (1976); D. McCalla, "Peter Buchanan, London Agent for the Great Western Railway of Canada," in Macmillan, *Canadian Business History*; O.S. Nock, *The Algoma Central Railway* (1975); T.D. Regher, *The Canadian Northern Railway: Pioneer Road of the Northern Prairies, 1895-1915* (1976); G.R. Stevens, *Canadian National Railways* (1960, 1962); A. Tucker, *Steam into Wilderness: Ontario Northland Railway, 1902-1962* (1978); C. Wallace, "Saint John Boosters and the Railroads in the Mid-Nineteenth Century," *Acadiensis* (1976); B.J. Young, *Promoters and Politicians: The North-Shore Railways in the History of Quebec, 1854-1885* (1978).

Despite an increased interest in the social history of industrialization, Canadian historians have not yet paid much attention to the emergence and development of the modern corporation. For those with an interest in the corporate elite, business-government relations, the financial system, and industrial development, the following list of recent studies should prove helpful: T.W. Acheson, "The Social Origins of Canadian Industrialism: A Study in the Structure of Entrepreneurship, 1880-1910" (Ph.D. thesis, University of Toronto, 1971); D. Alexander, *The Decay of Trade: An Economic History of the Newfoundland Saltfish Trade, 1935-65* (1977); C. Armstrong, "Making a Market: Selling Securities in Atlantic Canada before World War I," *Canadian Journal of Economics* (1980); R. Armstrong, "L'industrie de l'amiante au Québec, 1878-1929," *RHAF* (1979); S. Baptie, *First Growth: The Story of British Columbia Forest Products Limited* (1975); M. Bliss, *A Living Profit: Studies in the Social History of Canadian Business, 1883-1911* (1974) and *A Canadian Millionaire: The Life and Business Times of Sir Joseph Flavelle, Bart. 1858-1939* (1978); J.A. Blyth, "The Development of the Paper Industry in Old Ontario, 1824-1867," *OH* (1970); G.W.S. Brooks, "Edgar Crow Baker: An Entrepreneur in Early British Columbia," *BCS* (1976); J.M.S. Careless, "Development of the Winnipeg Business Community, 1870-1890," *Transactions of the Royal Society of Canada* (1970); W. Clement, *The Canadian Corporate Elite* (1975) and *Continental Corporate Power* (1977); P. Cook, *Massey at the Brink* (1981); J. Deverell, *Falconbridge* (1975); R. Durocher and P.-A. Linteau, eds., *Le 'Retard' du Québec et l'infériorité économique des Canadiens-français* (1971); N.F. Dreisziger, ed., *Mobilization for Total War* (1981); A. Finkel, *Business and Social Reform in the Thirties* (1979); B. Forster, "The Coming of the National Policy: Business, Government and the Tariff, 1876-1879," *JCS* (1979); D. Frank, "The Cape Breton Coal Industry and the Rise and Fall of the British Empire Steel Corporation," *Acadiensis*(1977); D.T. Gallacher, "Men, Money, Machines: Studies Comparing Colliery Operations and Factors of Productions in British Columbia's Coal Industry to 1891" (Ph.D. thesis, University of British Columbia, 1979); G. Gervais, "Le commerce de détail au Canada, 1870-1880," *RHAF* (1980); J.D. Gibson and J. Schull, *The Scotiabank Story: A History of the Bank of Nova Scotia, 1832-1982* (1982); P. Gillis, "The Ottawa Lumber Barons and the Conservation Movement, 1880-1914," *JCS* (1974); J. Gilmour, *Spatial Evolution of Manufacturing in Southern Ontario, 1851-1891* (1972); E. Gould, *Oil: The History of Canada's Oil and Gas Industry* (1976); J. Hamelin and Y. Roby, *Histoire économique du Québec, 1851-1896* (1971); B.G. Hoskins, "Hiram Walker and the Origins and Development of Walkerville, Ontario," *OH* (1971); P.-A. Linteau, "Quelques réflexions autour de la bourgeoisie québécoise, 1850-1914," *RHAF* (1975), and *Maisonneuve* (1981); L.R. Macdonald, "Merchants Against Industry: An Idea and its Origins," *CHR* (1975); D. MacKay, *Empire of Wood: The MacMillan Bloedel Story* (1982); D. Macgillivray, "Henry Melville Whitney comes to Cape Breton: The Saga of a Gilded Age Entrepreneur," *Acadiensis* (1979); I. Macpherson, *Each for All* (1979); D. McCalla, "Tom Naylor's *A History of Canadian Business, 1867-1914*: A Comment," *HP* (1976); J. McCallum, *Unequal Beginnings: Agriculture and Economic Development in Quebec and Ontario until 1870* (1980); L.D. McCann, "The Mercantile-Industrial Transition in the Metal Towns of Pictou County, 1857-1931," *Acadiensis* (1981); R.A.J. McDonald, "Business Leaders in Early Vancouver, 1886-1914" (Ph.D. thesis, University of British Columbia, 1977); D. Mcdowall, "Steel at the Sault: Sir James Dunn and the Algoma Steel Corporation, 1906-56" (Ph.D. thesis, Carleton University, 1978); T. Naylor, *The History of Canadian Business, 1867-1914* (1976) and "Trends in the Business History of Canada, 1867-1914," *HP* (1976); H.V. Nelles, *The Politics of Development: Forests, Mines and Hydro-electric Power in Ontario, 1849-1941* (1974) and "Public Ownership of Electrical Utilities in Manitoba and Ontario," *CHR* (1976); E.P. Neufeld, *The Financial System of Canada: Its Growth and Development* (1972) and *A Global Corporation: A History of the International Development of Massey-Ferguson Limited* (1969); J. Niosi, "La Laurentide (1887-1928): pionnière du papier journal au Canada," *RHAF* (1975) and *Canadian Capitalism* (1980); C. Nish and R. Choquette, *Banque canadienne nationale, 1874-1974: cent ans d'histoire* (1974); E.B. Ogle, *Long Distance Please: The Story of The TransCanada Telephone System* (1978); D.G. Paterson, "European Financial Capital and British Columbia: An Essay on the Role of the Regional Entrepreneur," *BCS* (1974); G. Piédalue, "Les groupes financiers et la guerre du papier au Canada, 1920-30," *RHAF* (1976) and "Les groupes financiers au Canada, 1900-30: étude préliminaire," *RHAF* (1976); G. Porter and R. Cuff, eds., *Enterprise and National Development* (1972); T.D. Regehr, "A Backwoodsman and an Engineer in Canadian Business: An Examination of Entrepreneurial Practices in Canada at the Turn of the Century," *HP* (1977); J. Richards and L. Pratt, *Prairie Capitalism: Power and Influence in the New West* (1979); Y. Roby, *Les Québécois et les investissements américains, 1918-1929* (1976); P.E. Roy, "Direct Management from Abroad: The Formative Years of the British Columbia Electric Railway," *Business History Review* (1973); R. Rudin, "A Bank Merger unlike the Others: The Establishment of the Banque Canadienne Nationale," *CHR* (1980); D. Smith and L. Tepperman, "Changes in the Canadian Business and Legal Elites, 1870-1970," *Canadian Review of Sociology and Anthropology* (1974); P. Smith, *The Treasure-Seekers: The Men Who Built Home Oil* (1978); G.H. Stanford, *To Serve the Community: The Story of Toronto's Board of Trade* (1975); G. Taylor, "Charles F. Sise, Bell Canada, and the Americans: A Study of Managerial Autonomy, 1880-1905," *HP* (1982); G.W. Taylor, *Timber: History of the Forest Industry in B.C.* (1975); T. Traves, *The State and Enterprise: Canadian Manufacturers and the Federal Government, 1917-31* (1979) and "Business-Government Relations in Canadian History," *History and Social Science Teacher* (1982); G. Tulchinsky, "Recent Controversies in Canadian Business History," *Acadiensis* (1978); A. Tupper and C.B. Doern, *Public Corporations and Public Policy in Canada* (1981); J.-P. Wallot, *Joseph-Edmund McComber: Mémoirs d'un bourgeois de Montréal, 1874-1949* (1980); J.F. Whiteside, "The Toronto Stock Exchange to 1900: Its Membership and the Development of the Share Market" (M.A. thesis, Trent University, 1979); M. Wilkins, *The Emergence of Multinational Enterprise: American Business Abroad from the Colonial Era to 1914* (1970) and *The Maturing of Multinational Enterprise: American Business Abroad from 1914 to 1970* (1974); B.J. Young, *George-Etienne Cartier: Montreal Bourgeois* (1981).

Notes

Introduction

1. David S. Macmillan, ed., *Canadian Business History: Selected Studies, 1497-1971* (Toronto, 1971); Glenn Porter and Robert Cuff, eds., *Enterprise and National Development: Essays in Canadian Business and Economic History* (Toronto, 1972).

2. Alan Wilson, "Problems and Traditions of Business History: Past Examples and Canadian Prospects," in Macmillan, ed., *Canadian Business History*.

3. Gregory S. Kealey and Peter Warrian, eds., *Essays in Canadian Working Class History* (Toronto, 1976), pp. 7-8.

4. José Igartua, "The Merchants and Négociants of Montreal, 1750-1775: A Study in Socio-Economic History" (Ph.D. thesis, University of Wisconsin, 1974); John Bosher, "A Quebec Merchant's Trading Circle in France and Canada: Jean-André Lamaltie before 1763," *HS* (1977).

5. Kari Levitt, *Silent Surrender: The Multinational Corporation in Canada* (Toronto, 1970).

6. Christopher Armstrong, "Making a Market: Selling Securities in Atlantic Canada before World War I," *Canadian Journal of Economics* (1980); John F. Whiteside, "The Toronto Stock Exchange to 1900: Its Membership and the Development of the Share Market" (M.A. thesis, Trent University, 1979); Michael Bliss, *A Canadian Millionaire: The Life and Business Times of Sir Joseph Flavelle, Bart., 1858-1939* (Toronto, 1978).

7. R.T. Naylor, "Trends in the Business History of Canada, 1867-1914," *HP* (1976); D. McCalla, "Tom Naylor's *A History of Canadian Business, 1867-1914*: A Comment," *HP* (1976)

8. Tom Traves, "Business-Government Relations in Canadian History," *The History and Social Science Teacher* (1982).

9. See also Graham D. Taylor, "Charles F. Sise, Bell Canada, and the Americans: A Study of Managerial Autonomy, 1880-1905," *HP* (1982).

Chapter 1 McCalla, Nineteenth-Century Business World

1. Peter C. Newman, *Flame of Power* (Toronto, 1959), p. 12.

2. Gustavus Myers, *A History of Canadian Wealth*, vol. I, 2nd ed. (Toronto, 1972), *passim*; T. Naylor, *The History of Canadian Business, 1867-1914* (Toronto, 1975), I, p. xx.

3. This paper necessarily draws on a very selective range of potentially relevant sources; for a good review of recent literature in Canadian business history, see Christopher Armstrong, "Recent Books in Canadian Business History," *History and Social Science Teacher*, XIV (1978-79), pp. 171-7.

4. But see G. Kealey, *Toronto Workers Respond to Industrial Capitalism, 1867-1892* (Toronto, 1980), for an excellent account of the complex transition to a larger and more modern industrial structure in Toronto after about 1860.

5. A.D. Chandler, Jr., *The Visible Hand: The Managerial Revolution in American Business* (Cambridge, Mass., 1977), pp. 81-187. For a Canadian account paying some attention to issues of railroad management, see Peter Baskerville, "The Boardroom and Beyond: Aspects of the Upper Canadian Railroad Community" (Ph.D. thesis, Queen's University, 1973), pp. 207-93.

6. On this transition, see Michael Bliss's outstanding work, *A Canadian Millionaire* (Toronto, 1978), pp. 110-37 and *passim*; also Paul Craven, *"An Impartial Umpire": Industrial Relations and the Canadian State, 1900-1911* (Toronto, 1980), pp. 90-110, 375-80.

7. John F. Whiteside, "The Toronto Stock Exchange to 1900: Its Membership and the Development of the Share Market" (M.A. thesis, Trent University, 1979).

8. See also, on this transition, David Coombs, "The Emergence of a White Collar Workforce in Toronto, 1895-1911" (Ph.D. thesis, York University, 1978).

9. T.W. Acheson, "The Great Merchant and Economic Development in Saint John, 1820-1850," *Acadiensis*, VIII, 2 (Spring, 1979), p. 27. See also D. Sutherland, "Halifax Merchants and the Pursuit of Development, 1783-1850," *CHR*, LIX (1978), p. 11.

10. Eric Sager and Lewis Fischer, "Patterns of Investment in the Shipping Industries of Atlantic Canada, 1820-1900," *Acadiensis*, IX, 1 (Fall, 1979), p. 43. See also D. Alexander and G. Panting, "The Mercantile Fleet and its Owners, Yarmouth, Nova Scotia, 1840-1889," *Acadiensis*, VII, 2 (Spring, 1978), pp. 19-28.

11. David Alexander, "Some Introductory Thoughts on Entrepreneurship," in Lewis Fischer and Eric Sager, eds., *The Enterprising Canadians: Entrepreneurs and Economic Development in Eastern Canada, 1820-1914* (St. John's, 1979), pp. 3-4. See also Barry Supple, "A Framework for British Business History," in Supple, ed., *Essays in British Business History* (Oxford, 1977), pp. 12-15. Of course, under more modern business conditions it is possible for the entrepreneur to remain in an area but for his capital to leave.

12. H.C. Pentland, "Further Observations on Canadian Development," *Canadian Journal of Economics and Political Science*, XIX (1953), p. 410. The context of this note makes clear that "promoters" is used very much analogously with "entrepreneur."

13. For example, J.G. Simcoe to George Ross, Navy Hall, 21 October 1794, in E.A. Cruikshank, ed., *The Correspondence of Lieut. Governor John Graves Simcoe, III, 1794-5* (Toronto, 1925), pp. 38-9. See also Lillian Gates, *Land Policies of Upper Canada* (Toronto, 1968), pp. 35-6.

14. D. McCalla, *The Upper Canada Trade, 1834-1872* (Toronto, 1979), pp. 151-5. Regarding the structure of the timber trade, see Graeme Wynn, *Timber Colony: A Historical Geography of Early Nineteenth Century New Brunswick* (Toronto, 1981), pp. 113-37; A.R.M. Lower, *Great Britain's Woodyard: British America and the Timber Trade, 1763-1867* (Montreal, 1973), pp. 139-57.

15. For a few examples of the importance of the theme of failure and insecurity, see Dale Miquelon, *Dugard of Rouen: French Trade to Canada and the West Indies, 1729-1770* (Montreal, 1978), pp. 147-50; Michael Katz, *The People of Hamilton, Canada West: Family and Class in a Mid-Nineteenth Century City* (Cambridge, Mass., 1975), pp. 176-208; Michael Bliss, *A Living Profit: Studies in the Social History of Canadian Business, 1883-1911* (Toronto, 1974), pp. 139-40.

16. D. McCalla, "The Decline of Hamilton as a Wholesale Centre," *OH*, LXV (1973), pp. 247-54.

17. Dale Miquelon, ed., *Society and Conquest: The Debate on the Bourgeoisie and Social Change in French Canada, 1700-1850* (Toronto, 1977); Fernand Ouellet, *Lower Canada, 1791-1840: Social Change and Nationalism* (Toronto, 1980), pp. 2-20; also F. Ouellet, "Dualité économique et changement technologique au Québec (1760-1790)," *HS*, IX (1976), pp. 258-9, 296.

18. Bruce Wilson, "The Enterprises of Robert Hamilton: A Study of Wealth and Influence in Early Upper Canada: 1776-1812" (Ph.D. thesis, University of Toronto, 1978), p. 96.

19. McCalla, *The Upper Canada Trade*, pp. 38-9.

20. Paul-André Linteau and Jean-Claude Robert, "Land Ownership and Society in Montreal: An Hypothesis," in G. Stelter and A. Artibise, eds., *The Canadian City: Essays in Urban History* (Toronto, 1979), pp. 17-36. See also G. Tulchinsky, *The River Barons: Montreal Businessmen and the Growth of Industry and Transportation, 1837-53* (Toronto, 1977), p. 17.

21. John McCallum, *Unequal Beginnings: Agriculture and Economic Development in Quebec and Ontario until 1870* (Toronto, 1980).

22. R.C.B. Risk, "The Golden Age: The Law about the Market in Nineteenth-Century Ontario," *University of Toronto Law Journal*, XXVI (1976), pp. 307-58; Risk, "The Nineteenth-Century Foundations of the Business Corporation in Ontario," *University of Toronto Law Journal*, XXIII (1973), pp. 270-306.

23. For example, C. Armstrong and H.V. Nelles, "Private Property in Peril: Ontario Businessmen and the Federal System, 1898-1911," in G. Porter and R. Cuff, eds., *Enterprise and National Development* (Toronto, 1973), p. 20.

24. For such internecine business-political conflicts, see, for example, Peter Baskerville, "Entrepreneurship and the Family Compact: York-Toronto, 1822-1855," *Urban History Review*, IX, 3 (February, 1981), pp. 15-34.

25. J.K. Johnson, "John A. Macdonald," in J.M.S. Careless, ed., *The Pre-Confederation Premiers* (Toronto, 1980), pp. 197-245, with quotation from p. 212; see also Johnson's "John A. Macdonald, The Young Non-Politician," *CHAR* (1971), pp. 138-53. For Quebec, see, for example, Brian Young,

Promoters and Politicians: The North Shore Railways in the History of
Quebec 1854-85 (Toronto, 1978), pp. 138-44; Young, George-Etienne Cartier:
Montreal Bourgeois (Montreal, 1981). For a Maritime example, see Carman
Miller, "Family, Business and Politics in Kings County, N.S.: the Case of F.W.
Borden, 1874-1896," Acadiensis, VIII, 2 (Spring, 1978), pp. 60-75.

Chapter 2 Miquelon,
Havy and Lefebvre of Quebec

1. PAC, MC 24, L 3, Baby Collection, pp. 643-4 (letter of Lamaletie), 5 juillet 1745.
2. Rapport de l'Archiviste de la Province de Québec (1939-40), pp. 1-154, Quebec Census, 1744; Archives nationales, Paris (AN), 62 AQ(Fonds Dugard), Havy à Dugard, La Rochelle, 10 février 1759.
3. Phillipe Wolff, "L'Etude des économies et sociétés avant l'ère statistique," in Charles Samarin, ed., L'Histoire et ses méthodes (Paris, 1961), p. 852.
4. AN, Archives des Colonies (AC), C11A, v. 93.25, Bigot au Ministre, 3 octobre 1749.
5. On Pascaud, Dictionary of Canadian Biography (Toronto, 1969), II, p. 508.
6. "Approbation d'une Assemblée des marchands . . ." (6 octobre 1740), Edits et ordonnances: Revus et corrigés d'après les pièces originales déposées aux Archives Provinciales (Québec, 1855), II, pp. 554-5.
7. D.B. Miquelon, "Robert Dugard and the Société du Canada of Rouen, 1729-1770" (Ph.D. thesis, University of Toronto, 1973), Chap. III and passim.
8. AN, 62 AQ 36, Havy à Dugard, La Rochelle, 14 février 1761.
9. Ibid., 40, receipt, 18 juillet 1734; 36, Dugard à Havy, 14 juillet 1760.
10. Ibid., 31, Havy à Dugard, La Rochelle, 10 février, 19 mai, 11 juin 1759.
11. Ibid., 36, Havy à Dugard, La Rochelle, 5 juillet 1760.
12. Ibid., Havy à Dugard, La Rochelle, 16 juin 1761. See note 65.
13. PAC, Baby Collection, pp. 820-3, 7 mai 1746.
14. Ibid., p. 618, 11 juin 1748.
15. Ibid., pp. 592-5, 4 mai 1745.
16. Ibid., pp. 500-1, novembre 1743; p. 1153, 5 novembre 1748; pp. 759-64, 26 novembre 1745; AN, 62 AQ 40, François Havy son compte courant avec Dugard, 1733-57.
17. PAC, Baby Collection, Havy and Lefebvre letters to Guy, passim.
18. Ibid., pp. 1044-7, 20 juillet 1747.
19. Ibid., pp. 853-4, 17 juin 1746.
20. AN, AC, C11A, v. 78, 2, Hocquart au ministre, 8 octobre 1742.
21. Per-cent increases on various kinds of merchandise – dry goods, hardware, and provisions – may be averaged and the relative importance of each in a total figure determined in terms of the proportion of the cargo comprised by each category. See Miquelon, "Robert Dugard," pp. 128-9, 155, for tables based on data from Société historique de Montréal (SHM), Collection Pierre Guy, factures, esp. item 24; AN, 62 AQ 41, 14e cargaison, Aller, factures.
22. AN, AC, C11A, v. 91, p. 103, Reflection particulière du Cugnet . . . .
23. SHM, Collection Pierre Guy, factures; PAC, Baby Collection, pp. 548-1102;

Archives du Séminaire de Québec (ASQ), Polygraphie, 24 and *passim*.

24. For example, ASQ, Polygraphie, 24, 10-10E, Messieurs du séminaire doivent aux Havy et Lefebvre; SHM, Collection Pierre Guy, p. 84 and *passim*; Archives du Québec (AQ), Archives judiciaire de Québec (AJQ), Etude Dulaurant, 23 octobre 1743, facture de Monfort.

25. SHM, Collection Pierre Guy, factures; compare with AN, 62 AQ 41, 14e cargaison, factures.

26. AN, AC, C11A, v. 66, pp. 171-202.

27. While goods were often imported to fit the needs of particular customers, whose bale marks appear in the invoices, Dugard always supplied these goods and recipients always paid the invoice inflation plus the *bénéfice*.

28. PAC, Baby Collection, pp. 752-8, 12 novembre 1745; pp. 918-20, 4 octobre 1746.

29. *Ibid.*, pp. 524-7, 7 octobre 1744.

30. *Ibid.*, pp. 981-3, 6 mars 1747; pp. 987-8, 11 mars 1747 and *passim*.

31. AN, AC, C11A, v. 77, p. 143, Beauharnois au Ministre, 1 novembre 1742.

32. *Ibid.*, v. 67, pp. 109-44, Résponse au mémoire du roy, 1737.

33. AQ, AJQ, Etude Barolet, nos. 729, 1066; Etude Dulaurant, 3 octobre 1736, 23 octobre 1742, 15 septembre, 26 octobre 1743, 13 août 1747; Etude J. Pinguet, 5 septembre 1743; Etude Saillant, 8 septembre, 25 octobre, 6 novembre 1753, 18 septembre 1754.

34. ASQ, Polygraphie 24 et Séminaire de Québec, Grand Livre, 1737-40.

35. AN, 62 AQ 40, Comptes de gestion à Québec, 1730-38. The accounts for these years list the notes accepted for each year as well as previous debt returned. Unfortunately, the same information is not available for the years 1739-42 for which condensations made by Dugard are alone extant. All computations concerning debt and debtors are based upon these accounts.

36. See note 33 above.

37. AN, 62 AQ 40, Dépouillement des achapts fait à Québec en 1743.

38. PAC, Baby Collection, pp. 893-6, Québec, 11 septembre 1746.

39. *Ibid.*, pp. 543-4, Lamaletie à Guy, 1 janvier 1745.

40. *Ibid.*

41. AN, 62 AQ 40, Comptes de gestion à Québec, 1730-44; Compte de balance de Havy et Lefebvre, Québec, 15 juillet 1746. Many private merchants' bills also passed between Canada and France. The quantity and importance of these instruments has yet to be determined.

42. Miquelon, "Robert Dugard," Appendix A, provides short histories of each of the company ships.

43. A.J.E. Lunn, "Economic Development in New France, 1713-1760" (Ph.D. thesis, McGill University, 1942), Chap. 10, for a good survey of bounties and shipbuilding; AN, AC, C11A, v. 51, p. 53, Beauharnois et Hocquart au Ministre, 25 octobre 1729.

44. Miquelon, "Robert Dugard," Chap. VII, provides a full discussion of the company's West Indian trade and the extent to which it was tied in with Canadian trade. See also my biographical sketch, Léon Fautoux, in *Diction-*

ary of Canadian Biography, III (Toronto, 1974). Of particular interest are the letters of Havy and Lefebvre and Robert Dugard to M. de la Croix, intendant at Martinique, 30 May 1743 and 20 August 1743 in AN, AC, C8A, v. 55, p. 340.

45. AN, 62 AQ 40, Comptes de gestion à Québec, 1730-41, and Compte général de balance, 15 juillet 1746.

46. Correspondence between Hocquart (AC, C11A) and Maurepas (AC, B), but summarized in Lunn, "Economic Development," p. 477.

47. Jean Hamelin, *Economie et société en Nouvelle-France* (Québec, 1960).

48. This may be traced in the correspondence of Beauharnois and Hocquart with Maurepas printed in A. Shortt, *Documents relating to Canadian Currency, Exchange and Finance during the French Period*, 2 vols. (Ottawa, 1925).

49. AN, 62 AQ 40, Comptes de gestion à Québec, 1733, 1734.

50. Shortt, *Documents*, II, p. 655, Hocquart à Maurepas, 10 octobre 1734.

51. Lunn, "Economic Development," pp. 456, 464-5.

52. Hamelin, *Economie et société*, p. 61; also, AN, AC, C11A, letters of Hocquart *passim*; Lunn, "Economic Development," pp. 444-9, and *passim*.

53. AN, AC, C11A, v. 80, Hocquart au Ministre, 25 octobre 1743.

54. AN, AC, B, v. 67, p. 145v (28 décembre 1738); v. 77, p. 55, Ministre à Dugard, 13 février 1743.

55. AN, AC, C11A, v. 80, p. 9, Hocquart au Ministre, 15 octobre 1743.

56. Miquelon, "Robert Dugard," pp. 245-51, 256-60.

57. AN, 62 AQ 35, France fils à Dugard, Paris, 12 mars 1747.

58. AN, 62 AQ 40, Extrait de la lettre des Sr Havy et Lefebvre, écrit à Québec le 3 novembre 1747. There is no trace of the crucial letter from Dugard except this extract of the reply.

59. *Ibid.*, Messieurs Havy et Lefebvre de Québec, leur compte courant pour la gestion des cargaisons, 1731-57; *ibid.*, Havy à Dugard, La Rochelle, 19 avril 1757.

60. *Ibid.*, Havy à Dugard, La Rochelle, 16 juillet 1747.

61. PAC, Baby Collection, pp. 691-2, 789-91, 1020-2, 1057-8, 1059-61, 1142-3, 1148-50 (letters to Pierre Guy, 1745-48); AQ, AJQ, Etude Dulaurant, 4 juin 1748; Etude Panet, 19 août 1751.

62. *Ibid.*, Etude Saillant, 17 septembre 1754, 7 octobre 1752; AQ NF 11, Jug. et Del. du Con. Sup., arrêt, 11 septembre 1752.

63. AQ, AJQ, Etude Dulaurant, 10 novembre 1746; AN, 62 AQ 31, Havy à Dugard, La Rochelle, 20 mai 1760.

64. Lunn, "Economic Development," Appendix, pp. 466-7.

65. AN, 62 AQ 40, Comptes de gestion à Québec, 1737-38. It is difficult to credit Havy's assertion in Havy à Dugard, La Rochelle, 16 juin 1761 (62 AQ 31) that "tout Letems que Jay Esté avotre service qui a esté depuis 1732 Jusquen et compris lannée 1748 Jene Travaillois Pas non plus que Le defuns lefebvre Pour Mon Compte." None of the vessels built and employed in the sealing enterprises are debited as Société du Canada assets. Oil sent to France as return cargo (see cargo account items in 62 AQ 41) always appears as having been sold to the company by some partner of Havy and Lefebvre, e.g., Sr

Volant, Fornel et Cie, etc. The present interpretation is therefore that the sealing stations were undertakings by which Havy and Lefebvre stood to gain or lose for their own account.

66. P.G. Roy, *Inventaire des pièces sur la côte de Labrador*, 2 vols. (Québec, 1940, 1942), II, pp. 50, 51, 56, 151; I, p. 293 (Acte de Société from AQ, AJQ, Etude Barolet, 3 mai 1737). On sealing ventures at Baie des Châteaux and Baie des Esquimaux, see my biographical sketches of Louis Bazil and Jean-Louis Fornel in DCB, III.

67. AQ, AJQ, Etude La Tour, Acte de Société, 17 mai 1740, published in Roy, *Inventaire*, II, p. 177.

68. *Ibid.*, II, p. 229; I, p. 90; AC, C11A, v. 92, p. 259, Representations Respectueuses, sd; AQ, NF 17, Registres de l'Amirauté de Québec, II (1749-56), Laudiance des Criées tenant par Extrord^re le mercredy vingt quatre avril 1754 deux heures de relevé.

69. AQ, Pièces judiciaires et notariales no. 4129, published in Roy, *Inventaire*, II, p. 352.

70. The exact location of Baie des Esquimaux is in doubt, but a probable present-day identification is Hamilton Inlet.

71. Roy, *Inventaire*, II, pp. 234, 235-8, 244-5, 249-55; I, pp. 91-2, 99-101.

72. *Ibid.*, II, pp. 88, 259-61; AN, AC, C11A, v. 100, p. 337, Mémoire sur l'exploitation des Traittes . . . .

73. *Ibid.*, Mémoire sur l'exploitation . . . .

74. AN, 62 AQ 31, Havy à Dugard, La Rochelle, 21 janvier 1756.

75. *Ibid.*, 19 avril 1757.

76. *Ibid.*

77. *Ibid.*, 10 février 1759. La Galissonière was not alone in thus interpreting the strategic significance of Canada.

78. PAC, Baby Collection, pp. 1697-1701, Havy à Baby frères, 12 février 1759.

79. AN, 62 AQ 31, Havy à Dugard, La Rochelle, 16 septembre 1758.

80. PAC, Baby Collection, pp. 2010-13, S. Jauge à Fr Baby, Bordeaux, 15 mai 1763.

81. AN, 62 AQ 31, Havy à Dugard, La Rochelle, 11 juin 1759.

82. *Ibid.*, 20 mai 1760.

83. *Ibid.*, 27 décembre 1759.

84. PAC, Baby Collection, Lefebvre à Dargenteuil, Québec, 13 novembre 1760.

85. AQ, AJQ, Etude Panet, 10 octobre 1760, Procuration de Jean Lefebvre agissant pour la société de Havy et Lefebvre à François Levesque.

86. AN, 62 AQ 36, Havy à Dugard, La Rochelle, 17 janvier 1761.

87. PAC, Baby Collection, pp. 1989-91, Havy à Baby, Bordeaux, 16 avril 1763.

88. *Ibid.*, pp. 1931-6, S. Jauge à F. Baby, Bordeaux, 4 février 1763.

89. *Ibid.*, pp. 2010-13, 15 mai 1763.

90. *Ibid.*, pp. 2445-7, Thouron frères aux Baby frères, La Rochelle, 6 mars 1767. The above letter gives no precise date; however, Professor J. Bosher has kindly communicated to me Havy's *acte de sépulture* from the registers in the Archives départementales de la Gironde (Bordeaux), giving the date as stated and Havy's age as sixty-seven. But the age given by Havy in the Quebec census

of 1740 is to be preferred to this information as Havy presumably supplied it himself. Professor Bosher's own research in the baptismal records of Bolbec, the town he has discovered to have been Havy's birthplace, invalidates the Bordeaux date.

91. *Ibid.*, pp. 970-4, Havy et Lefebvre à Guy, 8 février 1747.
92. ASQ, Polygraphie 24, 10 B, 1011C, 36 K; CI1A, v. 57, p. 156, Hocquart au Ministre, 15 octobre 1732; *ibid.*, v. 76;, pp. 318-45, Mémoire sur le Commerce du Canada, 1741; v. 73, p. 377, Hocquart au Ministre, 2 novembre 1740.
93. AN, 62 AQ 31, Havy à Dugard, La Rochelle, 19 mai 1759.
94. PAC, Baby Collection, pp. 1989-91, Havy à Baby, 16 avril 1763.
95. *Ibid.*, pp. 711-15, 5 octobre 1745.
96. *Ibid.*, pp. 829-33, 19 mai 1746. They were less impressed by the glittering profits of war than Guy Frégault, "Essai sur les Finances canadiennes," *Le Siècle canadien* (Montréal, 1968).
97. AN, 62 AC 31, Havy à Dugard, La Rochelle, 11 juin 1759.
98. PAC, Baby Collection, pp. 1053-5, Havy et Lefebvre à Guy, Québec, 20 août 1747.
99. Miquelon, "Robert Dugard," pp. 69-70.
100. Pierre Dardel, *Navires et marchandises dans les ports de Rouen et du Havre au XVIIIe siècle* (Paris, 1936), pp. 155, 423.

Chapter 3 McKay,
Capital and Labour in the Halifax Baking
and Confectionery Industry

1. Karl Marx, *Capital* (New York, n.d.), p. 338 and Chaps. 14, 15.
2. Raphael Samuel, "The Workshop of the World: Steam Power and Hand Technology in mid-Victorian Britain," *History Workshop Journal*, 3 (Spring, 1977), pp. 6-72.
3. In some of these industries the work force itself was largely imported. In Halifax cotton mills, for example, imported skilled workers were organized but the increasingly native unskilled work force was not.
4. See Gregory S. Kealey, "Artisans Respond to Industrialism: Shoemakers, Shoe Factories and the Knights of St. Crispin in Toronto," *HP* (1973), pp. 137-57. In Lynn, Mass., the transition was stretched out over a long period, and involved the borderline case of the manufacturer hiring labour and working alongside his employees with his family. Alan Dawley, *Class and Community: The Industrial Revolution in Lynn, Massachusetts* (Cambridge, Mass., 1976).
5. This highly schematic outline draws from Wayne Roberts, "Artisans, Aristocrats and Handymen: Politics and Unionism among Toronto Skilled Building Trades Workers, 1896-1914," *L/LT*, 1 (1976), pp. 92-121; Joanne Burgess, "L'industrie de la chaussure à Montréal: 1840-1870 – le passage de l'artisanat à la fabrique," *RHAF*, 31 (September, 1977), pp. 187-210; Gregory S. Kealey, "'The Honest Workingman' and Workers' Control: The Experience of Toronto Skilled Workers, 1860-1892," *L/LT*, 1 (1976), pp. 32-68.

6. It seems self-evident that at no time during "the making of the Canadian working class" (1850-1914) was there a serious possibility of generalized class conflict, and that this is the central problem of labour history that must be explored. Such an absence of national class conflict made Canada unusual among the industrializing countries.

7. J. Othick, "The cocoa and chocolate industry in the nineteenth century," in D.J. Oddy and D.S. Miller, eds., *The Making of the Modern British Diet* (London, 1976), pp. 77-90.

8. See William G. Panschar, *Baking in America*. I. *Economic Development* (Evanston, 1956), pp. 81-3, for a discussion of the biscuit and cracker trade. Biscuits originated more as medicinal goods than as articles for pleasurable consumption. See T.A.B. Corley, "Nutrition, technology and the growth of the British biscuit industry, 1820-1900," in Oddy and Miller, eds., *Modern British Diet*, pp. 13-25.

9. Gregory S. Kealey, *Working Class Toronto at the Turn of the Century* (Toronto, 1973), p. 22, shows a diet for a working-class girl, her mother, and two sisters, with an expenditure per week of 85¢ on bread and 15¢ on potatoes, as against 25¢ on meat. See also Terry Copp, *The Anatomy of Poverty: The Condition of the Working Class in Montreal 1897-1929* (Toronto, 1974), Appendix A. Bread in relation to the tariff is discussed in the *Acadian Recorder*, 11 October 1895, 10 October 1893, 29 March 1890. (Newspapers cited in the notes were published in Halifax unless otherwise noted.)

10. *Census of Canada*, 1871, Table III: R.F. Banks, "Labour Relations in the Baking Industry Since 1860: With Special Reference to the Impact of Technical and Economic Change on Union Administration and Bargaining Procedure" (Ph.D. thesis, University of London, 1965), Chap. 1; Panschar, *Baking in America*, Chaps. 2, 3.

11. *Morning Journal and Commercial Advertiser*, 26 October 1860: *Acadian Recorder*, 23 September 1893.

12. For the traditional bread economy, see Sidney and Beatrice Webb, "The Assize of Bread," *The Economic Journal*, 14 (June, 1904), pp. 196-218; for Halifax bread controls, see *The Halifax City Charter with Ordinances and By-Laws* (Halifax, rev. ed., 1914), Part XIV, Section 948, "Inspection and Measuring." For discussion of the application of these controls, see *Acadian Recorder*, 16 February 1885; *Report of Royal Commission on the Relations of Labour and Capital* (RCLC), Nova Scotia Evidence (Ottawa, 1889), J.W. Moir, p. 14, Lewis Archibald, p. 180; *Acadian Recorder*, 28 November 1896, 14 December 1894, 30 January 1897; Halifax City Council Minutes, Mss., Microfilm at the Public Archives of Nova Scotia (PANS), Reel 10, 29 January 1897. An interesting trial of a baker for selling light-weight bread is to be found in the *Morning Chronicle*, 14 August 1875. For adulteration, see John Burnett, "The History of Food Adulteration in Great Britain in the Nineteenth Century, With Special Reference to Bread, Tea and Beer" (Ph.D. thesis, University of London, 1958). Canadian legislation may be consulted in the Statutes of Canada, 37 Vic., Cap. 3, 1874.

13. Details of the distribution of local bread come from J.L. Martin, *The Story of Dartmouth* (Dartmouth, 1957), p. 347; *Acadian Recorder*, 2 July 1898; PANS, Moirs Papers, MG3, vol. 1866, nos. 72, 74 (licences to sell bread in Dartmouth). A useful discussion of oven design is presented in J.R. Seville, "The Baker's Oven," *Arkady Review* (1955), pp. 18-20, 30-4, 63-8. Information on the Halifax and Dartmouth Master Bakers' Association is drawn from *Acadian Recorder*, 19 June 1891.

14. This description of traditional craft mixing is drawn from George Read, *The Baker, Including Bread and Fancy Baking with Numerous Receipts* (London, n.d. [c. 1850]). For Ebenezer Stevens, father of the Stevens Patent Dough Making Machine, see his *A Voice from the Bakehouse* (London, 1861); John Burnett, "The Baking Industry in the Nineteenth Century," *Business History*, 5 (June, 1962), pp. 106-7. Samuel, "The Workshop of the World," is unduly sceptical of the impact of this machine, which became very common in both Britain and North America.

15. See the ad of W.C. Moir explicitly mentioning the machine: *British Colonist*, 26 March 1864.

16. The method used in scanning directories was to rely on business directories for years in which these were available and general listings for years in which no business directories appeared. It was impossible to include confectioners in this research because they could not be sorted out from the proprietors of corner candy shops. Bakers were taken to be petty proprietors when two addresses were given: the frequent "h do" notation (house ditto) was taken to indicate a small master operating out of his own home, whereas one address indicated a journeyman. Data from the 1860's are treated separately because the directories cited in Table 3 are less frequent and of uneven quality for that decade. Those consulted for the 1860's were Hutchinson's *Halifax Business Directory* for 1863, Hutchinson's *Nova Scotia Directory* for 1866-67, and McAlpine's *Nova Scotia Directory* for 1868-69.

17. See Keith Johnston, "The Halifax Drink Trade, 1870-1895" (Honours thesis, History Department, Dalhousie University, 1977), pp. 10, 12, for instances of women managing breweries.

18. I call it Moirs throughout this paper, for reasons of simplicity. It was variously called Moir & Co., Moir, Son and Company, and Moirs, Limited.

19. 1871 manuscript census, Halifax West and Halifax East, Schedule 6, Return of Industrial Establishments (PAC, microfilm).

20. This represents all the probate records of handicraft bakeries, which included reasonably complete inventories, located by searching each listing in the directories.

21. *Acadian Recorder*, 7 August 1888.

22. An analysis of the impact of the military on the city's economy may be found in C.S. Mackinnon, "The Imperial Fortresses in Canada: Halifax and Esquimault, 1871-1906" (Ph.D. thesis, University of Toronto, 1965). When Moirs asked the Colonial Office to allow the free importation of flour, a puzzled official commented, "I should have thought that taking 2,000 barrels of flour to Canada was like carrying coals to Newcastle" (p. 160).

23. For Allen, see Manuscript Records, R.G. Dun and Company, Baker Library, Harvard Business School, vol. 11 (Halifax), p. 568; *Halifax Citizen*, 7 January, 4 April 1868. For O'Brien, see Halifax County Probate Court, Estate of M.J. O'Brien, Warrant of Appraisement, 1888, no. 3668. O'Brien was not included in the manuscript census of 1871.

24. Assessment Book, City of Halifax, 1830, p. 5, PANS, RG 35, Series "A," vol. 2, no. 7; *British Colonist*, 24 March 1868; *Halifax Citizen*, 18 April 1868; *Herald*, 23 September 1875; Halifax County Probate Court, Estate of J.J. Scriven, Warrant of Appraisement, 1876, no. 2349.

25. [Scriven's Ltd.], *Over a Century in the Bread Baking Business. Scriven's of Halifax, Canada, 1821-1921* (n.p. [Halifax], n.d. [1921]); *Acadian Recorder*, 29 December 1897.

26. *Acadian Recorder*, 10 August 1881, 29 December 1897; Assessment Book, City of Halifax, 1823, p. 31, PANS, RG 35, Series "A," vol. 1, no. 5; Halifax County Probate Court, Estate of John Liswell, Warrant of Appraisement, no. 2910. O'Malley's bakery is the subject of a historical sketch in the *Chronicle-Herald*, 3 February 1959. This is a borderline case: although the bakery became an important manufactory in the twentieth century, it is difficult to say when the transition occurred, and at any rate it was certainly after the labour developments discussed later in this essay.

27. General accounts of the firm include G.A. White, *Halifax and Its Business* (Halifax, 1876), pp. 79-80; Elizabeth Hiscott, "Moirs: A Pot of Gold and a Giant," *Atlantic Advocate* (August, 1976), pp. 59-63.

28. PANS, Vertical Mss. File, Cook Collection, Power of Administration of Bara Moir, widow of Alexander Moir, 1819; Cook Family Genealogical Chart, Stack 15, no. 101. Benjamin Moir was the son of a Scottish armourer in the dockyard who came to Halifax in the 1780's. For the size of the business in 1845, see Halifax County Probate Court, Estate of Benjamin Moir, Warrant of Appraisement, 1845, no. 132.

29. White, *Halifax*, pp. 79-80; Manuscript Records, R.G. Dun and Company, vol. 12, p. 694.

30. The history of the Bedford enterprises is very complicated and cannot be fully discussed here. See "An Act to incorporate the Bedford Grain Importation, Milling and Manufacturing Company, Limited," *Statutes* of Nova Scotia, 40 Vic., Cap. 81, 1877; "An Act to amend the Act to incorporate . . .," *ibid.*, 43 Vic., Cap. 52, 1880; "An Act to revive and continue the Act to incorporate . . ., *ibid.*, 44 Vic., Cap. 54, 1881.

31. "Report of Edward Willis, on the Manufacturing Industries of Certain Sections of the Maritime Provinces," Canada, *Sessional Papers*, 48 Vic., no. 37, 1885, pp. 40-1.

32. White, *Halifax*, p. 80; Moirs Papers, vol. 1865, nos. 57-9, 62; vol. 1866, nos. 103-8; vol. 1867, no. 2; vol. 1866, nos. 5-6 (transactions with Halifax Co. lumbermen). See also [Halifax Board of Trade], *The City of Halifax, The Capital of Nova Scotia, Canada* (Halifax, 1908), p. 66.

33. The traditional date given for the shift to confectionery is 1873. However, White does not mention confectionery in his account of 1876, and the firm did

not advertise confectionery products to any great extent in the 1870's. Thus, there would seem to be a case for locating the shift some time at the end of the 1870's. Moir's comments to Edward Willis also support the contention that the National Policy was more favourable to confectionery than flour milling or bread-baking.

34. See Kenneth Leslie's poem to James Moir for an appreciation of Moir's concern for high quality controls and innovation: "I used to love to watch his inward mind / rove, as he slowly chewed a grain of cacao, / to Java, Venezuela, or Ceylon, / tasting at once its source, appraising it. . . . I never knew that purity was passion / until I saw this gaunt and gray-beard man." Kenneth Leslie, "The Candy Maker," in *The Poems of Kenneth Leslie* (Ladysmith, 1971), p. 24. A good description of the firm in 1898 may be found in the *Acadian Recorder*, 22 December 1898.

35. Petition of W.C. Moir, 1865, in PANS, Petitions of Trade and Commerce. Moir wanted to have duties returned to him that he had paid on the imported machinery.

36. *Reporter*, 2 January 1864; White, *Halifax*, p. 80; *Acadian Recorder*, 16 June 1891, 5 October 1892. See also the references to James W. Tester and Co. of Montreal (Moirs Papers, vol. 1866, p. 33). It is also possible that Moir was in contact with Smith & Hand of New York, "manufacturers of Confectioners machinery," or so we may assume from a stray letterhead in the Moirs Papers, vol. 1866, no. 43.

37. Moirs Papers, vol. 1866, no. 4, Memo to Close Account, Moir & Co., 30 March 1872; *Morning Chronicle*, 6 August 1881; *Acadian Recorder*, 13, 20 August 1881; *Herald*, 13 August 1881; Deed of Assignment, W.C. Moir and Wife and Jas. W. Moir to James R. Graham, 14 September 1881, Moirs Papers, vol. 1865, no. 67. For Moirs and banks, see *ibid.*, vol. 1867, nos. 7, 12; vol. 1864, no. 25, Memorandum of Agreement, 30 April 1903; vol. 1866, [no. 45], Moirs Limited to Eastern Trust, Mortgage to Secure Bonds; vol. 1864, nos. 63-5, resolutions concerning agreement with Eastern Trust.

38. Deed of Assignment, W.C. Moir and Wife and Jas. W. Moir to James R. Graham, 14 September 1881, Schedule A.

39. *Acadian Recorder*, 30 June 1898, 22 December 1896. In a letter from Moirs to the mayor and city council, asking for the continuation of tax concessions, Moir argued that "The great development of the Canadian North West has naturally created a big market for all classes of manufactured goods. We are now shipping the products of our factories throughout the whole of the Dominion as far as the Pacific Coast." However, Moir noted that the firm was handicapped by high freight rates and the slow delivery of products. Moirs Papers, vol. 1864, no. 48, letter of 3 March 1911.

40. *Acadian Recorder*, 22 December 1896. G.W. Mackinlay sold his bread route in the south end to Moirs in 1896 (Moirs Papers, vol. 1864, no. 17), and Richard Pearce sold his Star Bakery to Moirs in the same year.

41. On the subject of municipal bonusing in Halifax, see Larry McCann, "Staples, Urban Growth and the Heartland-Hinterland Paradigm: Halifax as an Imperial Outpost, 1867-1914," paper presented at the Canadian Urban History

Conference, Guelph, 1977, p. 35; "An Act relating to the assessment of Manufacturing Industries in the City of Halifax," *Statutes* of Nova Scotia, 2 Edwd. VII, Cap. 49, 1902. For Moirs' relationship with the city, see "An Act to amend Chapter 76, Acts of 1903, entitled 'An Act to enable the City of Halifax to exempt Moir, Son and Company from certain taxes,'" *Statutes* of Nova Scotia, 3 & 4 Edwd. VII, Cap. 58, 1904. On water rates (important for a firm that consumed 4,235,375 gallons in 1907), see PANS (Warehouse), City of Halifax Papers, RG 35-102, Series 40, City Engineer's Papers, 1880-1909; Moir to Board of Works, 4 August 1884; Reports of City Engineer, 30 August 1899 to 28 April 1907, no. 633, Reports re Moir's Limited Water Rate.

42.   The list was published in the *Acadian Recorder*, 16 June 1891, in connection with the fire at the factory.

43.   *Acadian Recorder*, 22 May 1897, 23 November 1896.

44.   Occupational diseases included phthsis, bronchitis, and pneumonia. For an early discussion, see W.A. Guy, *The Case of the Journeymen Bakers* (London, 1860). Fumes in Halifax: RCLC, S. McCarthy, p. 166, Joseph Connors, p. 169, Philip Shears, p. 172, John Hogan, p. 173, Lewis Archibald, p. 180, John Cudihee, p. 182, J.W. Moir, p. 13. Industrial accidents: *Unionist*, 11 September 1868; *Evening Express*, 11 September 1868, 18 February 1874; *Acadian Recorder*, 31 October 1889, 14 June 1900. Moirs paid Walter Daly $200 and Robert Walker $100 in compensation for accidents and as a release from further obligation: Moirs Papers, vol. 1866, no. 89, "Release – Walter Daly to James W. and W.C. Moir, 15 October 1892"; *ibid.*, vol. 1864, no. 22, "Release – Robert Walker to Moir Son & Co. and James W. Moir," 1901.

45.   For details of bakers' struggles in Hamilton, see Robert Storey, "Industrialization in Canada: The Emergence of the Hamilton Working Class, 1850-1870s" (M.A. thesis, Dalhousie University, 1975), pp. 115-20; Bryan D. Palmer, "Most Uncommon Common Men: Craft Culture and Conflict in a Canadian Community, 1860-1914" (Ph.D. thesis, State University of New York at Binghamton, 1977), pp. 376-81. The theme of "white slavery" was raised in Hamilton as an insult to striking journeymen. It was more commonly evoked by journeymen themselves to describe their working conditions, as in this poem in the union newspaper, *Bakers' Journal* (New York), 1 September 1894:

> 'Tis six at night, – see! who goes there
> With faltering steps and looks of care,
> His eyes half closed and visage wan –
> An object of pity to gaze upon?
> Who is he, and what can his calling be,
> He looks so haggard and pale to see!
> 'Tis the Baker, who toils both night and day
> In heat and steam, for his humble pay.
>
> . . . United be, and spare no pains, –
> The white slave yet shall break his chains.

46.   RCLC, James Moir, p. 12, S. McCarthy, p. 166, Charles Beamish, p. 168,

Richard Hogan, p. 171. The poem of Peter Connolly is in the *Bakers' Journal*, 29 August 1891.

47. RCLC, James Moir, pp. 12-14, S. McCarthy, pp. 166-7, Charles Beamish, pp. 168-9, Richard Hogan, p. 171, John Hogan, p. 173, Henry Naylor, p. 174, Lewis Archibald, p. 179.

48. Recognition of the bakers as a special case dates back to the English Bakehouse Regulation Act in 1863. A report on bakehouse legislation in Canada can be found in the *Labour Gazette*, 1 (January, 1901), pp. 247-8. The emphasis of all such legislation was the curbing of night-work by juveniles. The international situation (with reports on virtually every industrial country) is documented in the International Labour Conference, Sixth Session, Geneva, June, 1924, *Report IV, Report on Night Work in Bakeries* (Geneva, 1924). Nova Scotia told the International Labour Office that "Inasmuch as, with one exception, there are no large bakeries in this Province, it is doubtful if there is any necessity for legislation on this matter." The citation from the *Canadian Baker and Confectioner* is taken from the *Bakers' Journal*, 11 February 1893. I have been unable to locate a good nineteenth-century run of this Canadian trade periodical.

49. A boy was sentenced to St. Patrick's home for three years for stealing nuts from the firm; another was arrested in 1890 for stealing two loaves of bread valued at 15¢ (he testified that he gave part of the bread, which was stale anyway, to the horses). *Acadian Recorder*, 5 October 1889; *Morning Chronicle*, 27 August 1890.

50. RCLC, J.W. Moir, p. 14, Lewis Archibald, p. 180.

51. Coroner's Inquests, Inquisition on the Body of Charles Brunt, PANS, RG 41, Box 37 (1864), 19 May 1864.

52. RCLC, Joseph Larkins, pp. 176-7; *Morning Chronicle*, 10 April 1888.

53. These estimates are drawn from lists of the executive members in *Constitution and Bye-Laws of the Journeymen Bakers' Friendly Society, of Halifax and Vicinity* (Halifax, 1869); *Acadian Recorder*, 24 April 1882, 26 March 1883, 4 January 1886, 16 January 1889, 29 January, 15 July 1890, 13 January 1891, 16 January 1893; *Morning Chronicle*, 30 January 1890.

54. See Kenneth G. Pryke, "Labour and Politics: Nova Scotia at Confederation," *HS*, 4 (November, 1970), pp. 33-55, for a discussion of the emergence of the Halifax craft unions in the 1860's and early 1870's.

55. *Constitution and Bye-Laws, passim.*

56. PANS, MG 1, John R. Willis Papers, "To the Master Bakers of Halifax," printed petition of the Journeymen Bakers' Friendly Society (1868). The surviving copy of this document reveals how keen the bakers were to gain public support; it was sent to John Willis, alderman, from John Kew, the union president, with the inscription, "To John R. Willis, The Mechanics friend . . . ."

57. *British Colonist*, 4, 8 April 1868.

58. *Halifax Reporter*, 9 April 1868; *Presbyterian Witness*, 11 April 1868.

59. *Halifax Citizen*, 16 April 1868; *Halifax Reporter*, 23 April 1868; *Christian Messenger*, 15 April 1868; *Acadian Recorder*, 18 April, 2 May 1868.

60. *Trades Journal* (Stellarton), 28 July 1880.

61. *Constitution and Bye-Laws, passim.*

62. *Acadian Recorder*, 6 January 1873.

63. *Constitution and Bye-Laws, passim.*

64. *Acadian Recorder*, 6 January 1873.

65. *Trades Journal*, 28 July 1880.

66. The ATU was founded in 1882, with its primary base in the building trades, although the bakers were among the earliest unions to affiliate. Its early functions seem to have been confined to securing a hall for workingmen's meetings, but it later expanded its activities, both by serving as a support group for crafts on strike and by entering municipal politics.

67. See the obituary in *Acadian Recorder*, 8 October 1913. Archibald was born in Country Harbour, Guysborough County. He was often president of the ATU, and died in dire poverty. His directory address is given in 1892-93 as 202 Barrington, the same address as Mechanic's Hall, the ATU headquarters. He became a small master baker in about 1895, and in 1899 entered the employ of Scriven's. *Directories*, 1892-1913.

68. See Michael A. Gordon, "The Labor Boycott in New York City, 1880-1886," *Labor History*, 16 (Spring, 1975), pp. 185-229, for the evolution of this tactic; and Sidney G. Tarrow, "Lochner versus New York: A Political Analysis," *Labor History*, 3 (Fall, 1964), pp. 277-312, for the social and legal framework of both bakers' boycotts and the demand for protective legislation.

69. P.J. McGuire visited the city in 1884 and recommended the boycott to Halifax trade unionists. *Morning Chronicle*, 24 January 1884.

70. *Acadian Recorder*, 13 August 1884.

71. *Ibid.*, 13 September 1884.

72. *Trades Journal*, 24 September, 22, 29 October 1884.

73. *Morning Chronicle*, 23 October 1884.

74. *Acadian Recorder*, 23 September 1884.

75. *Ibid.*, 16 October 1884.

76. *Trades Journal*, 29 October 1884.

77. *Acadian Recorder*, 20 October 1884.

78. *Trades Journal*, 19 November 1884.

79. The information on Knights of Labor affiliation is courtesy of Senator Eugene Forsey, whose source is *The Tailor*. I have been unable to locate this local assembly elsewhere. *If* the bakers indeed affiliated with the Knights, this affiliation was of very short duration and of no practical importance to labour struggles.

80. The first local notice I have found for the union is *Acadian Recorder*, 29 January 1890, but this story says the union had been in existence for at least a year.

81. Founded in New York City in 1884, the union had from its earliest days stressed legislative action as a remedy for the ills of the craft. By 1887 the union contained over eighty locals. It had a large number of socialists in leadership positions, and under the editorship of Henry Weisman, its newspaper carried an overtly Marxist line. Low dues and the inherent difficulty of organizing sweated labour put the union in decline in the 1890's. See Tarrow,

"Lochner versus New York"; John Laslett, "Reflections on the Failure of Socialism in the American Federation of Labor," *Mississippi Valley Historical Review*, 50 (March, 1964), pp. 634-51; Laslett, "Socialism and the American Labor Movement: Some New Reflections," *Labor History*, 8 (Spring, 1967), pp. 136-55.

82. *Acadian Recorder*, 13 August 1884.

83. *Herald*, 14 November 1884.

84. RCLC, Lewis Archibald, pp. 179-81.

85. *Acadian Recorder*, 20 October 1884.

86. *Herald*, 14 November 1884.

87. *Acadian Recorder*, 13 August 1884.

88. *Morning Chronicle*, 13 September 1884.

89. *Acadian Recorder*, 20 October 1884.

90. *Herald*, 14 November 1884.

91. RCLC, Lewis Archibald, p. 180.

92. *Acadian Recorder*, 23 July 1889, 21 July 1891; *Morning Chronicle*, 24 July 1890, 21 July 1892.

93. *Baker's Journal*, 24 May 1890.

94. Small bakers in this negotiation said they were willing to concede but agreed to follow the lead of the larger employers, who dominated the Master Bakers' Association. *Morning Chronicle*, 10 May 1890.

95. *Acadian Recorder*, 28 January 1891.

96. PANS, MG 20, Box 332, Minutes of the Halifax Typographical Union, Book 1, meetings of 7 February, 7 March 1891; *Acadian Recorder*, 22, 28 January, 10, 11 February 1891.

97. In the Labour Day Parade of 1892 only thirty members marched; in 1894 the union did not appear at all, but there were separate floats for baking and confectionery firms. The union failed to acknowledge receipt of $50 sent by the international union in 1891. At the meeting of Local 89 in November, 1892, the union appointed a committee to "meet and find out the correct number of members in good standing." The listing disappears from the union newspaper with the 14 October 1896 issue. *Bakers' Journal*, 9, 16 May 1891, 26 November, 31 December 1892; *Bakers' Journal and Deutsche-Americkanische Backer-Zeitung*, 14 October 1896.

98. *Herald*, 1 October 1904.

99. See in particular R.Q. Gray, *The Labour Aristocracy in Victorian Edinburgh* (Oxford, 1976); H.F. Moorhouse, "The Marxist theory of the labour aristocracy," *Social History*, 3 (January, 1978), pp. 61-82, for an epistemological critique; and Gregor McLennan, *Marxism and the Methodologies of History* (London, 1982), chapter ten, for a qualified defence.

100. See David M. Gordon, Richard Edwards, and Michael Reich, *Segmented Work, Divided Workers: The historical transformation of labour in the United States* (Cambridge, 1982).

Chapter 4 Frost,
The "Nationalization" of the Bank of Nova Scotia

1. Adam Shortt, *History of the Bank of Nova Scotia* (Halifax, 1900); Bank of Nova Scotia, *The Bank of Nova Scotia, 1832-1932* (Toronto, 1932); Victor Ross, *The Canadian Bank of Commerce*, 2 vols. (Toronto, 1920); Royal Bank of Canada, *Fiftieth Anniversary of the Royal Bank of Canada* (Montreal, 1919). For the history of Canadian banking, see R.M. Breckenridge, *The Canadian Banking System* (New York, 1895); B.E. Walker, *A History of Banking in Canada* (Toronto, 1909); B.H. Beckert, *The Banking System of Canada* (New York, 1929); E.P. Neufeld, *The Financial System of Canada* (Toronto, 1972). Also useful is Merrill Denison, *Canada's First Bank: A History of the Bank of Montreal*, 2 vols. (Montreal, 1966).

2. James M. Cameron, "The Pictou Bank," *Nova Scotia Historical Quarterly*, 6 (June, 1976), pp. 119-42; J.T. Croteau, "The Farmers' Bank of Rustico," *Dalhousie Review*, 36 (Summer, 1956); W.A. Harrison, "The Maritime Bank of the Dominion of Canada, 1872-1887" (M.A. thesis, University of New Brunswick, 1970).

3. T.W. Acheson, "The National Policy and the Industrialization of the Maritimes, 1880-1910," *Acadiensis*, I (Spring, 1972), pp. 3-28.

4. R.T. Naylor, *The History of Canadian Business, 1867-1914* (Toronto, 1975), I, pp. 118-25, 149-50, 156-64, 178-80.

5. The present study focuses on the "flow of funds" through the Bank of Nova Scotia's branch system, an approach made possible by the existence of a very complete set of statistical records for each of the bank's branches. I would like to thank the Bank of Nova Scotia Archives, Toronto, for permitting me to examine these records for the period of this study. A more extended report on this research is contained in the author's "Principles of Interest: The Bank of Nova Scotia and the Industrialization of the Maritimes, 1880-1910" (M.A. thesis, Queen's University, 1978).

6. Shortt, *History of the Bank of Nova Scotia*; historical abstracts, Bank of Nova Scotia Archives (BNSA).

7. BNSA, "Circular 483," 15 January 1892, "Rules and Regulations," 1885, 1898, 1902.

8. Both Acheson and Naylor imply that the region's industrial development would have been considerably enhanced if the larger Halifax banks had engaged in longer-term lending. However, this conclusion appears to ignore findings about the structure of industrial finance in Britain and the United States, and also to underestimate considerably the importance of short-term lending or working capital in industrial finance. Historians of the Industrial Revolution have come to recognize that working capital normally constituted one-half, and frequently much more, of the total capital of industrial enterprises. Working capital paid for raw materials, wages, and the transportation of goods to market, thus freeing up the shareholders' equity for further investment. See Rondo Cameron *et al.*, *Banking in the Early Stages of Industrialization: A Study in Comparative Economic History* (London,

1967); Sidney Pollard, "Fixed Capital in the Industrial Revolution in Britain," *Journal of Economic History*, XXIV (1964), pp. 299-314.

9. Information compiled from G.A. White, *Halifax and Its Business* (Halifax, 1876); Phyllis Blakeley, *Glimpses of Halifax, 1867-1900* (Halifax, 1949); H.J. Morgan, *Canadian Men and Women of the Time* (Toronto, 1912); Probate Court Records, Halifax; Public Archives of Nova Scotia, Biography Files.

10. *Morning Herald* (Halifax), 2 August 1883.

11. BNSA, Cashier's Correspondence Book, 8 December 1883.

12. Acheson, "Industrialization of the Maritimes," pp. 8-9; Naylor, *History of Canadian Business*, I, p. 162; BNSA, Directors' Minute Book, abstract, 17 November 1880, Cashier's Correspondence Book, 8 November, 19 January 1884.

13. BNSA, Thomas Fyshe to J.B. Morgan, 28 July 1882.

14. BNSA, Cashier's Correspondence Book, 19 November 1883. See also Peter DeLottinville, "The St. Croix Cotton Manufacturing Company and Its Influence on the St. Croix Community, 1880-1892" (M.A. thesis, Dalhousie University, 1979).

15. BNSA, Cashier's Correspondence Book, 9 November 1883.

16. *Ibid.*, 24 February 1884. See also Acheson, "Industrialization of the Maritimes"; James M. Cameron, *Industrial History of New Glasgow District* (New Glasgow, 1961).

17. BNSA, Cashier's Correspondence Book, 25 February 1884.

18. *Ibid.*, 31 September, 4 March 1883; J.B. Forgan, *Recollections of a Busy Life* (New York, 1924), p. 55.

19. BNSA, Statistical Records, 1881-1914 (BNS Statistics), calculations by the author.

20. The rest of the bank's Maritime lending activity up to 1884 took place in what might be referred to as staples-producing areas. This group included the bank's branches at Charlottetown and Summerside, Prince Edward Island, and they accounted for about 13 per cent of the bank's loans at this time. Of the other branches, the most important were located at Woodstock, Newcastle, and Chatham, New Brunswick. All three branches were involved in the lumber trade and related activities in their vicinities and together they accounted for 40 per cent of the loans in this group. Total average loans for these three branches in 1884 were $346,818, deposits were only $83,615, and the ratio of loans to deposits was 4.14:1, thus, more than $280,000 of unemployed funds had to be brought from elsewhere to meet local needs. BNS Statistics, "Woodstock," "Chatham," "Newcastle."

21. Edward J. Chambers, "Late Nineteenth Century Business Cycles in Canada," *Canadian Journal of Economics and Political Science*, XXX (1964), pp. 391-412; *Monetary Times*, 9 September 1881, p. 809; BNSA, "Circular 59," 9 November 1881, "Circular 100," 30 November 1882.

22. BNSA, "Circular 110," 5 February 1883. See also BNS Circulars, 1880-83; BNSA, Cashier's Correspondence Book, Fyshe to Edward Trout, 21 February 1884; House of Commons, *Debates*, 1880, pp. 44, 102, 195, 217, 218, 284, 286.

23. BNSA, "Annual Statement, 1882-1883," Cashier's Correspondence Book, 1883.

The list included a variety of businesses, including grocers, dry goods merchants, booksellers, boot and shoe makers, printers, tailors, victuallers, and druggists, from almost every town where the Bank of Nova Scotia maintained an agency.

24. Forgan, *Recollections*; BNSA, Directors' Minute Book, abstract, 27 November 1883, Fyshe to Forgan, 21 January 1884, Fyshe to Robert Steven, 20 February 1884.

25. For Fyshe's comments on "business conditions" in 1884, see BNSA, Fyshe to Edward Trout, 21 February 1884, Fyshe to S.A. White, 29 September 1884, "Circular 160," 4 March 1884, Fyshe to George MacLeod, 11 March 1884.

26. BNSA, Fyshe to S.A. White, 29 September 1884. For comments on the Bremner and Hart failure, see *Acadian Recorder* (Halifax), 15, 16 July 1884; *Novascotian* (Halifax), 5 July 1884.

27. BNSA, "Annual Statement," 31 December 1884.

28. BNSA, "Circular 194," 7 April 1885, "Rules and Regulations," 1885.

29. PAC, Records of the Department of Finance, vol. 3038, no. 2893, Fyshe to Charles Tupper, 20 April 1887.

30. *Ibid.*, vol. 2000, no. 591, J.M. Courtney to Fyshe, 15 June 1887.

31. Fyshe wrote to several financial experts who had experience with this type of investment. See BNSA, Fyshe to James Goldie, 7 January 1884, Fyshe to James Burnett, 21 January 1884, Fyshe to F.G. Webster, 24 March 1884. For a complete listing of these bonds, see Fyshe to Adam Burns, 12 March 1885.

32. Shortt, *History of the Bank of Nova Scotia*, author's calculations.

33. BNSA, "Annual General Meeting, Report," 18 February 1885, Cashier's Correspondence Book, 26 August 1885.

34. See D.L.C. Galles, "The Bank of Nova Scotia in Minneapolis, 1885-1892," *Minnesota History* (Fall, 1971), p. 271; BNSA, Directors' Minute Book, abstract, 17 February 1886.

35. BNSA, J.B. Forgan to Fyshe, 1 June 1886.

36. BNS Statistics, "Minneapolis"; BNSA, Fyshe to T.V. Macdonald, 7 September 1888, Cashier's Correspondence Book.

37. BNSA, Fyshe to James Burnett, 20 May 1886, Fyshe to John S. MacLean, 10 August 1887, "Circular 62," 12 January 1882.

38. BNSA, Fyshe to T.V. Macdonald, 31 May, 27 November 1888, 4 June 1889, Cashier's Correspondence Book; BNS Statistics, "Montreal."

39. BNSA, "Circular 266," 31 March 1887, Fyshe to John Paton, 12 March, 3 June 1889; PAC, Records of the Department of Finance, vol. 3074, no. 5241.

40. BNSA, Cashier's Correspondence Book, 31 December 1883, Fyshe to Jim Robinson, 10 March 1884, Fyshe to S.A. White, 29 September 1884, Fyshe to J.M. Robinson, 8 January 1886; BNS Statistics, "Saint John."

41. DeLottinville, "The St. Croix Cotton Manufacturing Company"; BNSA, Cashier's Correspondence Book, 8 December 1883, 27 August 1885, Fyshe to S.A. White, 5 January 1884; BNS Statistics, "St. Stephen."

42. BNSA, Cashier's Correspondence Book, 27 February 1885, 18, 27 December 1884; BNS Statistics, "Moncton."

43. *Acadian Recorder*, 17 July, 2 August 1888; BNSA, Fyshe to John Doull, 8 August 1888, Fyshe to T.V. Macdonald, 7 September 1888.

44. BNSA, Fyshe to S.M. Brookfield, 3 June 1889, Fyshe to B.H. Calkin, 31 July 1889; *Morning Chronicle*, 7 August 1890; *Daily Echo* (Halifax), 13 January 1891.

45. *Census of Canada*, 1901; BNS Statistics, "Amherst."

46. *Census of Canada*, 1901; BNS Statistics, "New Glasgow."

47. BNSA, Fyshe to Graham Fraser, 3 November 1887; BNS Statistics, "New Glasgow."

48. BNS Statistics, calculations by the author.

49. BNSA, "Circular 535," 28 June 1893, "Circular 638," 4 April 1896.

50. BNSA, "Branches," Yarmouth #12, 1892, Agent to Fyshe, 7 April, 16 July 1892, Fyshe to Agent, 9 February 1895, McLeod to Agent, 21 September 1897.

51. BNSA, McLeod to Agent, 20 July 1897.

52. BNSA, McLeod to Agent, 23 February 1898. Fyshe left to join the Merchants' Bank of Canada in Montreal, but little is known about this transition.

53. BNS Statistics, "Saint John"; BNSA, McLeod to Board, 28 May 1900. This letter refers to an inspection report filed on 7 April 1898.

54. McLeod did not expect Robertson to accept the seat; he wanted only to "bring the firm closer to the bank": BNSA, McLeod to Board, 19 September 1900.

55. BNS Statistics, "Saint John."

56. *Census of Canada*, 1901; Acheson, "Industrialization of the Maritimes"; Cameron, *Industrial History of New Glasgow*; BNS Statistics, "New Glasgow." It should be noted, however, that there is some difficulty in making direct comparisons of 1890 and 1900 census data as the definition of industrial establishments in 1900 excluded most enterprises employing less than five people. On New Glasgow, see also L.D. McCann, "The Mercantile-Industrial Transition in the Metal Towns of Pictou County, 1857-1931," *Acadiensis*, X (Spring, 1981), pp. 29-64.

57. *Census of Canada*, 1901. Evidence of these accounts can be found in BNSA, H.C. McLeod to Board, 25 June 1906; BNS Statistics, "Amherst." On the industrial development of Amherst, see Nolan Reilly, "The General Strike in Amherst, Nova Scotia, 1919," *Acadiensis*, IX (Spring, 1980), pp. 56-77.

58. *Census of Canada*, 1901; BNSA, McLeod to Board, 10 October 1901; BNS Statistics, "Sussex."

59. Galles, "The Bank of Nova Scotia in Minneapolis"; BNSA, Daniel Waters pro. H.C. McLeod to Board, 7 August 1908; BNS Statistics, "Chicago."

60. BNS Statistics, "Montreal." In 1894 Fyshe sent W.E. Stavert, the agent in Kingston, to the Bahamas to look over the prospects there. He concluded that the limited trade of those islands offered the bank little incentive, unless all other banking competition was eliminated. See BNSA, W.E. Stavert to Thomas Fyshe, 11 December 1894.

61. BNS Statistics, "Kingston."

62. *Monetary Times*, 14 December 1894, p. 766, 21 December 1894, p. 797.

63.   BNSA, Directors' Minute Book, abstract, 12 December 1894.

64.   BNS Statistics, "St. John's," "Harbour Grace"; Naylor, *History of Canadian Business*, II, p. 255.

65.   Unfortunately, the official reason for moving the general office, as recorded in the Directors' Minute Books, was not available. Before McLeod became general manager in 1897 he had worked in Amherst, Minneapolis, and Chicago, and it is conceivable that between 1897 and 1900 he began to find that Halifax was too distant from important financial markets.

66.   BNS Statistics, calculations by the author.

67.   *Ibid.*, "Montreal."

68.   BNSA, McLeod to Board, 24 September 1901.

69.   BNSA, H.A. Flemming to McLeod, 23 October 1903.

70.   BNSA, McLeod to Board, 2 January 1904; BNS Statistics, "Winnipeg."

71.   See N.S.B. Gras, *Business and Capitalism: An Introduction to Business History* (New York, 1939), pp. 268-9; BNSA, "Circular 927," 23 November 1903, "Arrangements with Correspondents and Customers," August, 1904, p. 135, nos. 25-30.

72.   BNSA, McLeod to Board, 18 December 1905, 30 March 1906, 7 August 1908, 26 July 1909 (nos. 242, 243, 250, 286, 401); BNS Statistics, "Chicago."

73.   BNSA, McLeod to Board, 14 March 1901, 5 April, 6 November 1906; BNS Statistics, "Jamaican branches." For the bank's relationship with the United Fruit Company, see BNSA, McLeod to Board, 6 November 1906.

74.   BNS Statistics, "Cuba."

75.   Three of the new board members were lawyers. John Y. Payzant, president of the bank from 1899 to 1918, was also president of the Empire Trust Company and the Nova Scotia Fire Insurance Company, and vice-president of Stanfield's Woollens, Halifax Electric Tramway, and the Nova Scotia Telephone Company; however, his other interests included Great West Life Insurance, Westinghouse Electric, General Electric, and some Trinidad utilities. Hector McInnes, who joined the board in 1900, was president of Eastern Trust and of the Nova Scotia Savings, Loan and Building Society; he was also at various times a director of Nova Scotia Car Works, Dominion Coal, North America Life Insurance, Hollingsworth and Whitney, and Brandram Henderson. Robert L. Borden, who also joined the board in 1900, was a prominent Halifax corporation lawyer and a director of Nova Scotia Telephone and Eastern Trust. In addition to these lawyer-businessmen, the new directors also included a group of five industrialists. Charles Archibald, whose family had owned a coal-mining and shipping firm in Cape Breton that was absorbed by Dominion Coal, was involved in several Caribbean utility companies as well as Scotia Steel, Dominion Iron and Steel, and Stanfield's. George S. Campbell owned a Halifax shipping firm, was a director of Nova Scotia Fire Insurance, Nova Scotia Building Society, Silliker Car, Empire Trust, and Stanfield's, and had sizable holdings in Canadian Pacific Railway, Canada Steamship Lines, and Eastern Trust. J. Walter Allison, who headed the Dartmouth firm of John P. Mott and Company, manufacturers of chocolate and spices, was also a director of Stanfield's, Scotia Steel, Nova Scotia Fire Insurance, Acadia

Sugar Refining, and Nova Scotia Savings, Loan and Building Society. Nathaniel Curry and J.H. Plummer, who both joined the board in 1910, were figures of national standing in Canadian business. Curry had been president of the Amherst company, Rhodes, Curry, which merged into Canadian Car and Foundry in 1909, and his membership on the board was probably most important for his Montreal business connections. Plummer was also important for his contacts outside the region, as he was closely tied to the Canadian Bank of Commerce and the Dominion Iron and Steel Company. The data were compiled from Morgan, *Canadian Men and Women of the Time*; W.R. Houston, ed., *Directory of Directors in Canada, 1912* (Toronto, 1912); BNSA, "Directors"; Probate Court Records, Halifax; and Public Archives of Nova Scotia, Biography Files.

76. See David Frank, "The Cape Breton Coal Industry and the Rise and Fall of the British Empire Steel Corporation," *Acadiensis*, VII (Autumn, 1977), pp. 3-34; Acheson, "Industrialization of the Maritimes."
77. BNSA, H.A. Flemming (Board Secretary) to McLeod, 19 July 1901, no. 73.
78. BNSA, "Circular 867," 5 November 1901.
79. BNSA, H.A. Richardson to Board, 21, 27, 30 July 1910. This was an advance to the directors but not necessarily to the company itself.
80. BNS Statistics, "New Glasgow."
81. BNSA, McLeod to Board, 13 June 1910; BNS Statistics, "Stellarton."
82. BNS Statistics, "North Sydney."
83. *Census of Canada*, 1911; BNS Statistics, "Amherst."
84. Reilly, "The General Strike in Amherst"; BNSA, McLeod to Board, various dates, 25 June 1906 to 17 November 1909.
85. BNSA, McLeod to Board, 23 April, 21 November 1901; C.M. Wallace, "Saint John, New Brunswick (1800-1900)," *Urban History Review* (June, 1975), pp. 12-21.
86. *Census of Canada*, 1911; BNS Statistics, "Saint John." The account of the Maritime Nail Works went to the Merchants' Bank of Canada when it opened in Saint John: BNSA, H.A. Richardson to Board, 26 October 1910.
87. BNSA, McLeod to Manager, 2 March 1901, Alex Robertson pro. G.M. to Manager, 16 January 1903, McLeod to Manager, 10 May 1907, McLeod to Manager, 14 November-13 December 1901 (nos. 61, 62, 64, 68, 75), McLeod to Board, 13, 15 November 1901, Branch Correspondence, Yarmouth.
88. *Morning Herald*, 26-31 March 1900; *Acadian Recorder*, 26-31 March 1900; *Census of Canada*, 1911; BNS Statistics, "Halifax."
89. *Census of Canada*, 1911; BNSA, McLeod to Board, 12 July 1905; BNS Statistics, "Campbellton."
90. BNSA, McLeod to Board, 12, 19 September 1904; BNS Statistics, "Sussex."
91. BNS Statistics, calculations by the author.
92. BNS Statistics, "Maritime Banks." The following list summarizes the rise and fall of banking in the Maritime Provinces:
Bank of New Brunswick, 1820-1913 (amalgamated with Bank of Nova Scotia)
Halifax Banking Company, 1825-1908 (amalgamated with Canadian Bank of Commerce)

Charlotte County Bank of New Brunswick, 1825-1865 (liquidated)
Bank of Nova Scotia, 1832-
Westmorland County Bank of New Brunswick, 1854-1862 (liquidated)
Central Bank of New Brunswick, 1834-1862 (failed)
St. Stephen's Bank, 1836-1910 (failed)
City Bank of St. John, 1830-1839 (amalgamated with Bank of New Brunswick)
Bank of Prince Edward Island, 1856-1881 (failed)
Union Bank of Halifax, 1856-1910 (amalgamated with Royal Bank)
Bank of Yarmouth, 1859-1905 (failed)
Farmers' Bank of Rustico, 1862-1892 (failed)
Union Bank of Prince Edward Island, 1864-1883 (amalgamated with Bank of Nova Scotia)
People's Bank of Halifax, 1864-1905 (amalgamated with Bank of Montreal)
People's Bank of New Brunswick, 1864-1907 (amalgamated with Bank of Montreal)
Commercial Bank of Windsor, 1864-1902 (amalgamated with Union Bank of Halifax)
Merchants' Bank of Halifax, 1869-1901 (Royal Bank)
Summerside Bank, 1866-1901 (amalgamated with Bank of New Brunswick)
Exchange Bank of Yarmouth, 1869-1903 (amalgamated with Bank of Montreal)
Merchants' Bank of Prince Edward Island, 1871-1906 (amalgamated with Canadian Bank of Commerce)
Bank of Acadia, 1872-1873 (failed)
Bank of Liverpool, 1872-1879 (failed)
Maritime Bank of Canada, 1872-1887 (failed)
Pictou Bank, 1874-1887 (failed)

Chapter 5 Lowe,
Administrative Revolution in the Canadian Office

1. David Lockwood, *The Blackcoated Worker* (London, 1966), p. 36.
2. Ida R. Hoos, *Automation in the Office* (Washington, 1961), p. 79; Lockwood, *The Blackcoated Worker*, pp. 92-4; Jon M. Shepard, *Automation and Alienation: A Study of Office and Factory Workers* (Cambridge, Mass., 1971), p. 8.
3. Carl Dreyfuss, *Occupation and Ideology of the Salaried Employee*, 2 vols., trans. Eva Abramovitch (New York, 1938), I, p. 113.
4. See Alfred D. Chandler, Jr., *The Visible Hand: The Managerial Revolution in American Business* (Cambridge, Mass., 1977).
5. Herbert A. Simon, "Decision-Making and Administrative Organization," in R.K. Merton *et al.*, eds., *Reader in Bureaucracy* (New York, 1952), p. 185.
6. C. Wright Mills, *White Collar: The American Middle Classes* (New York, 1956), p. 189.
7. Our evidence is limited to the Canadian office; however, there is good reason to believe that the argument we present can also explain the development of modern administration in other advanced capitalist countries. See Chandler,

The Visible Hand; Lockwood, *The Blackcoated Worker*; Harry Braverman, *Labor and Monopoly Capital: the Degradation of Work in the Twentieth Century* (New York, 1974); Mills, *White Collar*; Emil Lederer, *The Problem of the Modern Salaried Employee: Its Theoretical and Statistical Basis*, trans. E.E. Warburg (New York, 1937).

8. Reinhart Bendix, *Work and Authority in Industry* (Berkeley, 1974), p. 211.

9. Graham S. Lowe, "Women, Work and the Office: The Feminization of Clerical Occupations in Canada, 1901-1931," *Canadian Journal of Sociology*, 5 (1980).

10. Hugh Armstrong and Pat Armstrong, *The Double Ghetto: Canadian Women and Their Segregated Work* (Toronto, 1978), p. 20.

11. Lowe, "Women, Work and the Office."

12. The First World War, which occurred in this decade, influenced the formation of the contemporary office in two important respects. In the first place, the tremendous demands of the war economy for goods and services sparked rapid industrial expansion. This in turn produced a boom in clerical employment, as office staffs swelled. And second, severe labour force disruptions, as many male workers enlisted, accelerated the shift toward female clerical employment. See Lowe, "Women, Work and the Office."

13. *Ibid.*

14. Graham S. Lowe, "The Administrative Revolution: The Growth of Clerical Occupations and the Development of the Modern Office in Canada, 1911-1931" (Ph.D. thesis, University of Toronto, 1979), p. 190.

15. *Ibid.*, p. 184.

16. This wage pattern seems to be standard in advanced capitalist societies. Research in the U.S. by Braverman and Burns and in Britain by Lockwood documents how the growth of the white-collar sector of the labour force has been marked by a relative decline in clerical wages. See Braverman, *Labour and Monopoly Capital*; Robert K. Burns, "The Comparative Economic Position of Manual and White-Collar Employees," *Journal of Business*, 27 (1954), pp. 257-67; Lockwood, *The Blackcoated Worker*.

17. Lowe, "Women, Work and the Office." This is consistent with broad labour force trends. In 1971, the average income of women doing paid work was about half that of men: Hugh Armstrong and Pat Armstrong, "The Segregated Participation of Women in the Canadian Labour Force, 1941-71," *Canadian Review of Sociology and Anthropology*, 12 (1975), p. 371.

18. *Work in America*, Report of a Special Task Force to the U.S. Secretary of Health, Education and Welfare prepared by the W.E. Upjohn Institute for Employment Research (Cambridge, Mass., 1973), p. 38; James W. Rinehart, *The Tyranny of Work* (Don Mills, Ont., 1975), p. 92; Evelyn Nakano Glenn and Roslyn L. Feldberg, "Degraded and Deskilled: The Proletarianization of Clerical Work," *Social Problems*, 25 (1977), pp. 52-64.

19. See Max Weber, *From Max Weber: Essays in Sociology*, trans. and ed. H.H. Gerth and C.W. Mills (New York, 1958); Weber, *The Theory of Social and Economic Organization* (New York, 1964).

20. Bendix, *Work and Authority in Industry*, p. 2.

21. See Chandler, *The Visible Hand*; Daniel Nelson, *Managers and Workers: Origins of the New Factory System in the United States, 1880-1920* (Madison, Wis., 1975).

22. Braverman, *Labor and Monopoly Capital*, p. 107.

23. William Henry Leffingwell, *Scientific Office Management* (Chicago, 1917). While Taylorism was undoubtedly the label most commonly attached to attempts to rationalize the labour process, it was only one strategy in the broad "thrust for efficiency" that took root after 1900. The term "scientific management" includes, then, a variety of systematic programs initiated by management to inject order and efficiency into the organization and execution of work. See Bryan Palmer, "Class, Conception and Conflict: The Thrust for Efficiency, Managerial Views of Labour and the Working Class Rebellion, 1903-22," *Radical Review of Political Economics*, 7 (1975), pp. 31-49.

24. *Industrial Canada*, July, 1905, p. 843.

25. Bank of Nova Scotia, *The Bank of Nova Scotia, 1832-1932* (Toronto, 1932).

26. See Samuel Haber, *Efficiency and Uplift: Scientific Management in the Progressive Era, 1890-1920* (Chicago, 1964).

27. Lowe, "The Administrative Revolution."

28. Life Office Management Association, Proceedings of Annual Conference, 1924, p. 8.

29. Lowe, "Women, Work and the Office."

30. Mills, *White Collar*, p. 195.

31. Shepard, *Automation and Alienation*, p. 63.

32. Lowe, "Women, Work and the Office."

33. O.J. Firestone, "Canada's Economic Development, 1867-1952," paper prepared for the Third Conference of the International Association for Research in Income and Wealth, Castelgandolfo, Italy, 1953, p. 160.

34. Kenneth Buckley, *Capital Formation in Canada, 1896-1930* (Toronto, 1974), p. 4; Robert Craig Brown and Ramsay Cook, *Canada 1896-1921: A Nation Transformed* (Toronto, 1976), pp. 83-4.

35. Herbert Marshall, F.A. Southard, and K.W. Taylor, *Canadian-American Industry* (Toronto, 1976), p. 18.

36. Firestone, "Canada's Economic Development," p. 152.

37. *Ibid.*, p. 156.

38. International Labour Office, "The Use of Office Machinery and Its Influence on Conditions of Work for Staff," *International Labour Review*, 36 (1937), p. 513.

39. James Poapst, "The Growth of the Life Insurance Industry in Canada, 1909-47" (M.Comm. thesis, McGill University, 1950), p. 14.

40. See E.P. Neufeld, *The Financial System of Canada* (Toronto, 1972); Sun Life Assurance Co. Archives, Montreal, Personnel File no. 2.

41. Meredith G. Rountree, *The Railway Worker: A Study of the Employment and Unemployment Problems of the Canadian Railways* (Toronto, 1936), p. 12.

42. Bank of Montreal, *The Service Industries*, Study No. 17, Royal Commission

on Canada's Economic Prospects, 1956, p. 128.

43. J.C. Weldon, "Consolidation in Canadian Industry, 1900-1948," in L.A. Skeoch, ed., *Restrictive Trade Practices in Canada* (Toronto, 1966), p. 233.

44. See Herbert A. Simon, *Administrative Behaviour*, 3rd ed. (New York, 1976); Luther Gulick, "Notes on the Theory of Organization," in L. Gulick and L. Urwick, eds., *Papers on the Science of Administration* (New York, 1937).

45. Herbert Kaufman, "The Administrative Function," in David Sills, ed., *International Encyclopedia of the Social Sciences*, vol. 1 (New York, 1968), p. 61.

46. Weber, *Essays in Sociology*; Weber, *The Theory of Social and Economic Organization*.

47. Weber, *Essays in Sociology*, p. 214.

48. See Martin Albrow, *Bureaucracy* (London, 1970); Peter M. Blau, *The Dynamics of Bureaucracy*, rev. ed. (Chicago, 1963); Robert K. Merton, "Bureaucratic Structure and Personality," in Merton *et al.*, eds., *Reader in Bureaucracy*.

49. Gulick, "Notes on the Theory of Organization."

50. Joseph A. Litterer, "Systematic Management: Design for Organizational Recoupling in American Manufacturing Firms," *Business History Review*, 37 (1963), p. 370.

51. George A. Theodorson and Achilles G. Theodorson, *A Modern Dictionary of Sociology* (New York, 1969), p. 335.

52. See Braverman, *Labor and Monopoly Capital*; Palmer, "Class, Conception and Conflict."

53. Stephen A. Marglin, "What Do Bosses Do?: The Origins and Functions of Hierarchy in Capitalist Production," Harvard Institute of Economic Research, Discussion Paper No. 222, 1971.

54. Braverman, *Labor and Monopoly Capital*.

55. Litterer, "Systematic Management"; see also Nelson, *Managers and Workers*.

56. David Landes, *The Unbound Prometheus: Technological Change and Industrial Development in Western Europe from 1750 to the Present* (Cambridge, 1969).

57. Braverman, *Labor and Monopoly Capital*, p. 301.

58. See Braverman, *Labor and Monopoly Capital*; F.B. Cooley, *Frederick W. Taylor, Father of Scientific Management*, 2 vols. (New York, 1923); Lyndall P. Urwick, *The Life and Work of Frederick Winslow Taylor* (London, 1957); Nelson, *Managers and Workers*.

59. James W. Rinehart, "Contradictions of Work-Related Attitudes and Behaviour: An Interpretation," *Canadian Review of Sociology and Anthropology*, 15 (1978), p. 6.

60. William A. Rushing, "The Effects of Industry Size and Division of Labour on Administration," *Administrative Science Quarterly*, 12 (1967), pp. 273-95; Stewart Melman, "The Rise of Administrative Overhead in the Manufacturing Industries of the United States, 1899-1947," *Oxford Economic Papers*, New Series 3 (1951), pp. 62-112.

61. Allan M. Murdoch and J. Rodney Dale, *The Clerical Function: A Survey of*

Modern Clerical Systems and Methods (London, 1961), p. 2.

62. Life Office Management Association, Proceedings of Annual Conference, 1927, p. 188.

63. Homer J. Hagedorn, "The Management Consultant as Transmitter of Business Techniques," *Explorations in Entrepreneurial History*, 7 (1955), p. 167; Leffingwell, *Scientific Office Management*, p. 5.

64. Leffingwell, *Scientific Office Management*, pp. 35, 111, 109.

Chapter 6 Traves,
The Political Economy of the Automobile Tariff

1. Dominion Bureau of Statistics, *Automobile Statistics for Canada, 1932*. (DBS did not distinguish between automobile and truck registration so the ratios given are somewhat distorted.) Mira Wilkins and Frank E. Hill, *American Business Abroad: Ford and Six Continents* (Detroit, 1964), p. 442; General Motors of Canada Limited, Domestic and Export Production, 1908-31 December 1972 (provided courtesy of General Motors of Canada Ltd.). It should be noted that the first figure cited here (61.7) was obtained by adjusting GM's data to take account of exports. I used the industry average of exports to total production (31.1 per cent) as a correction factor. In the case of both the figures cited here, it was necessary to count trucks as automobiles. Trucks averaged 16.8 per cent of total production for the period 1920-30.

2. PAC, Tariff Commission, 1920 Papers, vol. 8, file 23, pp. 4288-9, testimony by W.P. Shillington, Studebaker Corp., 30 November 1920.

3. DBS, *Canada Year Book, 1929* (Ottawa, 1929), pp. 416-17; *Industrial Canada*, October, 1925, pp. 59, 75. The development of the auto industry also had a significant impact on the sources of provincial government revenues. In 1921 revenues from motor vehicle licences and gasoline taxes accounted for only $3.4 million of total provincial revenues in Canada of $90.4 million (3.7 per cent), but by 1930 these sources accounted for $43.4 million of total tax revenues of $173.8 million (25 per cent). J.H. Perry, *Taxes, Tariffs and Subsidies* (Toronto, 1955), p. 238, table 18.

4. Tariff Commission, 1920 Papers, pp. 4321-2, testimony of W.R. Campbell, Ford Motor Co. of Canada, 30 November 1920.

5. Advisory Board on Tariff and Taxation (ABTT), *Record of Public Sittings, Iron and Steel*, Hearings of 12 December 1929, 22, 23 January 1930, vol. 3, Automobiles and Parts, testimony of T.A. Russell, Willys-Overland Co., p. 44.

6. *Financial Post*, 25 November 1921. The complete tariff for all classes of imports prior to 1926 was 22.5 per cent, 30 per cent, 35 per cent. After the change the complete tariff was 12.5 17.5, 20 on cars valued at retail at not more than $1,200 and 15, 25, 27.5 on cars valued at retail at more than $1,200. The duty, however, was charged against the wholesale price, not the retail value.

7. In the 1925 federal election the Liberals won 101 seats, the Conservatives 116,

the Progressives 26, and others 2. The Conservatives won 46 per cent of the national popular vote while the Liberals captured only 40 per cent. M.C. Urquhart and K.A.H. Buckley, *Historical Statistics of Canada* (Toronto, 1965), pp. 618, 620. The Liberals, however, decided to retain office and to meet Parliament, and for a short period this tactic was successful.

8. PAC, W.L.M. King Papers, Transcript Diaries, vol. 20, p. G4085, 17 November 1924, and pp. G4185-6, 16 March 1925; Correspondence, MG26J1, vol. 113, p. 96263, J.W. Carruthers to King, 13 November 1925, vol. 133, p. 133428, Hon. P.C. Larkin, High Commissioner to London, to King, 17 April 1926.

9. PAC, Arthur Meighen Papers, vol. 134, file 168(1), p. 80774, Chas. T. Todd, director, J.H. Todd & Sons, Ltd., Victoria, B.C., to Dr. S.F. Tolmie, MP, 26 April 1926.

10. King Papers, Correspondence, vol. 139, p. 118211, King to W.E.N. Sinclair, MPP, 1 August 1926.

11. C.H. Aikman, *The Automobile Industry in Canada*, McGill University Economic Studies, no. 8 (Toronto, 1926), p. 39. Though Robb himself was not very sympathetic to this position it is suggestive that he adopted this line in response.

12. See, for example, *Industrial Canada*, October, 1927, p. 97.

13. *Ibid.*, May, 1926, p. 39; King Diaries, vol. 21, 1926, p. G4503, 23 April 1926; Correspondence, vol. 128, p. 108992, C.M. Bowman to King, 2 June 1926.

14. Quoted in Wilkins and Hill, *American Business Abroad*, p. 132.

15. See, for example, ads in the *London Free Press*, 28 April 1926; *Globe* (Toronto), 24 April 1926.

16. In the case of Ford, "the record of the company shows that 72% of its earnings since incorporation has been reinvested in the business." PAC, ABTT Papers, vol. 49, file 134-6, Supplementary memorandum to be presented to the ABTT, 22 January 1930. A study of the inter-corporate directorship links between the auto companies and other business interests revealed that only Willys-Overland, a small company, had significant ties to leaders of the Toronto business community. The boards of the other companies were made up of local management and U.S. parent company representatives.

17. King Diaries, vol. 21, p. G4444, 18 February 1926. Gundy was one of the leading financiers of the 1920's. For biographical data and a list of his business activities, see B.M. Greene, ed., *Who's Who in Canada, 1928-29* (Toronto, 1929), pp. 369-70.

18. King Diaries, vol. 21, p. G4450, 23 February 1926.

19. *Ibid.*, vol. 17, p. G3861, 13 April 1923.

20. Quoted in Aikman, *Automobile Industry*, p. 41. Ford's position on the tariff was unique among American automobile manufacturers. It reflected both his business strategy and his ideological commitment to free trade. Given his place in the popular imagination of the twenties, however, despite his isolation, Ford's comments had a tremendous impact. By 1931, the executives of Ford Canada had prevailed upon Henry Ford to the point where he agreed to refrain from commenting on Canadian tariff policy against their wishes.

Wilkins and Hill, *American Business Abroad*, p. 132.

21. King Papers, Correspondence, vol. 128, pp. 108843-6, Hon. G.H. Boivin to King, 1 May 1926.

22. *News*, 25 (22 April 1926), p. 12; Aikman, *Automobile Industry*, p. 26.

23. By the early 1920's over 80 per cent of all Canadian automobile exports went to imperial markets. See T.C. Byrnes, "The Automotive Industry in Ontario" (M.A. thesis, University of Toronto, 1951), pp. 68-9; Sun Life Assurance Company, *The Canadian Automotive Industry*, study prepared for the Royal Commission on Canada's Economic Prospects (Ottawa, 1956), p. 11.

24. King Diaries, vol. 21, p. G4498, 16 April 1926. The tariff on agricultural implements had been cut by more than half in 1924 to nominal rates of 5 per cent, 7.5 per cent, 10 per cent: see O.J. McDiarmid, *Commercial Policy in the Canadian Economy* (Cambridge, Mass., 1946), p. 264. King Papers, Correspondence, vol. 133, p. 113469, King to Larkin, 14 May 1926.

25. For an example of business hostility to the industry, see Public Archives of Ontario, G.H. Ferguson Papers, RG3, General Correspondence, file 1926 (automobile industry), memo to Ferguson from Hon. William H. Price, provincial treasurer, 14 May 1926. "In discussing this important question with a number of life long Conservatives, businessmen, I find a total lack of sympathy with the auto manufacturers . . . ."

26. King Papers, Correspondence, vol. 128, p. 108983, Bowman to King, 30 April 1926 (Bowman's son was an auto parts manufacturer in Owen Sound, Ont.); vol. 139, pp. 118201-2, Sinclair to King, 24 April 1926.

27. *Ibid.*, vol. 128, pp. 108846-7, Boivin to King, 1 May 1926; Diaries, vol. 21, p. G4513, 8 May 1926.

28. O.J. McDiarmid, "Some Aspects of the Canadian Automobile Industry," *Canadian Journal of Economics and Political Science*, 6 (1940), p. 262. Automobiles entering under the British preference were automatically granted the exemption from the excise tax as well, but such imports were a negligible factor in the industry. King Papers, Correspondence, vol. 137, p. 116649, T.A. Russell, president, Automotive Industries of Canada, to Robb, 5 June 1926.

29. King Papers, Correspondence, vol. 128, pp. 108843-6, Boivin to King, 1 May 1926.

30. ABTT Papers, vol. 48, file 134-3, Circular no. 565C, file no. 126453, Department of Customs and Excise, 26 January 1927.

31. Meighen Papers, vol. 134, file 168(1), pp. 80822-3, Meighen to F. Tolputt, 21 June 1926. Since the excise tax applied only to imports, Meighen contended that it had become a duty. Though only 5 per cent, the tax was taken on the duty value plus the duty so that it amounted effectively to an extra 6 per cent protection for domestic producers.

32. ABTT, *Iron and Steel* (note 5 above), Russell, p. 44; King Papers, Memoranda and Notes, vol. 135, file 1086, p. C98509. There is no author cited but internal evidence indicates fairly clearly that this memo was prepared by the DBS.

33. PAC, R.J. Deachman Papers, MG30D104, vol. 2, file 1, p. 45, "Auto Price Comparison," 3 January 1928; ABTT, *Iron and Steel*, testimony of H.A.

Brown, General Motors of Canada, pp. 22, 31, Russell, pp. 44, 47.

34. Sun Life, *Automotive Industry*, pp. 173, 16, table 7.

35. ABTT, *Iron and Steel*, testimony of R.T. Herdegen, Galt Art Metal Co. Ltd., p. 146.

36. DBS, *Automobile Statistics*. Of course, the government's tariff policy did not *cause* increased automobile consumption. One could argue that the industry would have sold more cars and provided more jobs during the boom period if the tariff had not been reduced, but such counter-factual hypotheses, while interesting, are historically irrelevant since they completely ignore the socio-political context of the industry's development.

37. There appear to have been two causes for these increased imports. First, the number of low-priced cars had increased and many smaller American producers were now more competitive with the industry leaders. The second reason is related to the first in that the reduced tariff allowed these American exporters to sell their vehicles at a lower price in Canada than heretofore. For the extent of increased low-price competition, see James Dalton, "What Will Ford Do Next?" *Motor* (May, 1926), collected in A.D. Chandler, Jr., *Giant Enterprise: Ford, General Motors and the Automobile Industry* (New York, 1964). pp. 104-11. On the face of it these increased imports suggest that prices under the new tariff were no longer artificially high, but changing consumption patterns that stressed style as well as price might also account for part of this increase.

38. ABTT Papers, vol. 48, file 134-3, data prepared by Professor H.R. Kemp, University of Toronto. These figures for capacity include both truck and auto production, as do the utilization figures.

39. Wilkins and Hill, *American Business Abroad*, p. 442; GM Domestic and Export Production (see note 1 above for additional comments).

40. See A.D. Chandler, Jr., *Strategy and Structure* (Cambridge, Mass., 1962); Chandler, *Giant Enterprise*; Chandler and Stephen Salsbury, *Pierre S. Du Pont and the Making of the Modern Corporation* (New York, 1971).

41. William T. Hogan, *Economic History of the Iron and Steel Industry in the United States* (Lexington, Mass., 1971), III, p. 1019, table 29-16.

42. Chandler, *Giant Enterprise*, p. 16.

43. It has been argued that the American low-price market became saturated before the Canadian market, and that the continental application of a commercial strategy aimed to minimize price competition and substitute product differentiation as the basis of competition in the auto industry had the effect of limiting the potential size of the Canadian market. The evidence cited for this view is the higher ratio of population to autos in Canada than in the U.S., a ratio that income differentials between the two countries alone do not explain. See J.C.S. Grimshaw, "Problems and Policies of Labour and Management in the Automobile Industry in Relation to Prices, Competitive Conditions and Industrial Structure" (M.A. thesis, University of Toronto, 1946), pp. 241-3.

44. ABTT, *Iron and Steel*: the directions from the Minister of Finance are printed

in full on p. 15; ABTT Papers, vol. 49, file 134-6, memo presented to the ABTT, 12 December 1929, and supplementary memo to be presented to the ABTT, 22 January 1930.

45. *Ibid.*, memo of 22 January 1930, p. 8.

46. Tariff Commission, 1920 Papers, p. 4320, Campbell. In 1927 the Canadian content of Ford cars was: touring, 72.3 per cent; runabout, 71.5; coupe, 63.3; two-door, 64.2; four-door, 61.6; chassis, 78.7; truck chassis, 78.1. ABTT Papers, vol. 49, file 134-6, E.R. Musselman, Ford Motor Co., to W.H. Moore, board chairman, 11 June 1929, file 134-7, Professor J.A. Coote to Moore, 20 August 1929.

47. ABTT Papers, vol. 49, file 134-6, memo, Musselman, undated but clearly posted 22 January 1930; see also file 134-8, memo, General Motors of Canada, Ltd., 12 December 1929; ABTT, *Iron and Steel*: letters from parts manufacturers supporting the anti-import plan are reprinted on pp. 94-5; letters and telegrams from import dealers are reprinted on p. 90; consumer opposition is recorded on p. 53.

48. ABTT, *Iron and Steel*, p. 55 (Campbell), p. 54 (Studebaker).

49. Prior to the election the King government was on the edge of announcing favourable tariff changes, but the political manoeuvrings around this issue fell apart at the last moment. See King Diaries, vol. 26, p. G5670, 12 March, p. G5740, 2 June, p. G5742, 3 June 1930.

50. DBS, *Automobile Statistics*. Russell's influence on Conservative leaders is apparent in both the Meighen Papers and the Bennett Papers. Greene, *Who's Who in Canada, 1930-31* (Toronto, 1932), p. 1592 (re Ryckman).

51. PAC, R.B. Bennett Papers, MG26K, vol. 734, file T-100-A, pp. 449077-341 (see also vol. 735, file T-100-A), p. 449067, R.D. Morand, MP, to Sir George Perley, Acting Prime Minister, 23 October 1930.

52. *Ibid.*, vol. 736, file T-100-A, pp. 450787-8, Ryckman to Bennett, 9 February 1931; vol. 735, file T-100-A, p. 449999, T.A. Russell to Bennett, 20 February 1931.

53. *Ibid.*, vol. 735, p. 450791, Bennett to Russell, p. 449961, Bennett to J.H. Fortier, both 18 February 1931.

54. *Ibid.*, p. 450035, H.A. Brown to Bennett, 28 February 1931.

55. DBS, *Automobile Statistics*, Motor Vehicle Manufacturers' Association, "Background on the Canada-U.S. Automobile Products Agreement" (mimeo.), p. 8.

56. Michael Bliss, "Canadianizing American Business: The Roots of the Branch Plant," in I. Lumsden, ed., *Close the 49th Parallel* (Toronto, 1970).

57. See, for example, D.G. Creighton, "The Decline and Fall of the Empire of the St. Lawrence," *CHAR* (1969), p. 21.

Chapter 7 Taylor,
The Case of Canadian Industries Limited, 1928-1948

1. House of Commons, *Debates*, 1944, vol. II, pp. 1763-9.

2. Statement by Wendell Berge, Assistant Attorney General, U.S. Department of Justice, 10 January 1944, in Jasper Crane Papers, Box 1036, Records of E.I. du Pont de Nemours Co., series II, part 2, Eleutherian Mills Historical Library, Greenville, Del. Hereafter referred to as Crane Papers.
3. United States vs. Imperial Chemical Industries, E.I. du Pont de Nemours Co., Inc. *et al.*, 100 *Federal Supplement* (1951), pp. 504, 557-64.
4. Few critical studies of multinational enterprise have dealt specifically with issues of internal management relations in detail, but for representative comments see Richard J. Barnet and Ronald E. Müller, *Global Reach: The Power of the Multinational Corporations* (New York, 1974), pp. 42-4; Kari Levitt, *Silent Surrender: The Multinational Corporation in Canada* (Toronto, 1970), pp. 83-9. Detailed studies of the internal management of multinational companies in recent years include J.M. Stopford and I.T. Wells, Jr., *Managing the Multinational Enterprise: Organization of the Firm and Ownership* (New York, 1972); M.Z. Brooke and H.L. Remmers, *The Strategy of Multinational Enterprise: Organization and Finance* (London, 1970). See also A.E. Safarian, *Foreign Ownership of Canadian Industry* (Toronto, 1973), pp. 50-70.
5. See I.F. Haber, *The Chemical Industry, 1900-1930* (London, 1971), pp. 9-33, 135-49, 173-83, 291-318, on the commercial and technological development of the chemical industry in this period. On the tradition of international cartels in chemicals, see G.W. Stocking and M.W. Watkins, *Cartels in Action: Case Studies in International Business Diplomacy* (New York, 1946), pp. 418-29.
6. "Canadian Industries Ltd. and Predecessor and Associated Companies," in Accession 1460, Box 32, Records of E.I. du Pont de Nemours Co., series II, part 2. See also W.J. Reader, *Imperial Chemical Industries: A History*, 2 vols. (London, 1970, 1974), I, pp. 196, 211-12.
7. Herbert Marshall, Frank Southard, and Kenneth Taylor, *Canadian-American Industry: A Study in International Investment* (New Haven, 1936), pp. 82-4; A.D. Chandler, Jr., and Stephen Salsbury, *Pierre S. Du Pont and the Making of the Modern Corporation* (New York, 1971), pp. 477, 567-8; Reader, *Imperial Chemical*, II, pp. 212-13.
8. Stocking and Watkins, *Cartels*, pp. 438-50; Chandler and Salsbury, *Pierre S. Du Pont*, pp. 570-1; Reader, *Imperial Chemical*, II, pp. 13-21.
9. United States vs. Imperial Chemical Industries, E.I. du Pont de Nemours Co., Inc. *et al.*, trial records, Govt. Exhibit 15, AT 4134, Govt. Exhibit 18, AT 4138, Govt. Exhibit 21, AT 2570-A, Govt. Exhibit 24, AT 4206. (Hereafter U.S. vs. ICI, Records.) The trial transcript and records were deposited by the Du Pont corporation at Eleutherian Mills Historical Library.
10. Reader, *Imperial Chemical*, II, p. 212.
11. "Canadian Industries Ltd. and Predecessor and Associated Companies."
12. Transcript of meeting, Montreal, 16 September 1932, U.S. vs. ICI, Records, Govt. Exhibit 816, AT 4337, testimony of H. Greville-Smith, vice-president, Canadian Industries Ltd., 17 May 1950, U.S. vs. ICI, Trial Transcript, pp. 2078-9.

13. Canadian Industries Ltd., Annual Reports, 1928, 1943.

14. Minutes of meeting at Nobel House, London, 29 April 1924; U.S. vs. ICI, Records, Govt. Exhibit 48, AT 4379.

15. Notes on discussion at Walter Carpenter's house, 3 October 1940, Crane Papers, Box 1043.

16. Jasper Crane, Du Pont foreign relations committee, to Walter S. Carpenter, Jr., president, Du Pont, 2 March 1942, Carpenter to Sir Harry McGowan, chairman, Imperial Chemical Industries Ltd., 15 May 1942, Crane Papers, Box 1034.

17. McGowan of Nobel had observed of the Canadian directors of CIL's predecessor company that "they should clearly understand that their nomination comes from Nobel's." Reader, *Imperial Chemical*, I, p. 211.

18. In 1934-36, the CIL management committee, which included the president and vice-president, Purvis and Huggett, and the heads of the four groups of divisions, consisted of four men from ICI and its subsidiaries, and two from Du Pont. Canadian Industries Ltd., Annual Report, 1935.

19. Reader, *Imperial Chemical*, II, 212-13; *Dictionary of National Biography, 1941-1950* (London, 1959), pp. 700-2.

20. George Huggett, vice-president, CIL, to J. Thompson Brown, executive committee, Du Pont, 14 November 1939, Crane Papers, Box 1034; testimony of Wendell R. Swint, foreign relations committee, Du Pont, 6 June 1950, U.S. vs. ICI, Trial Transcript, p. 2992.

21. William Richter, Du Pont Fabrics and Finishes Dept., to Jasper Crane, foreign relations committee, Du Pont, 24 November 1930, Crane Papers, Box 1034.

22. Reader, *Imperial Chemical*, II, p. 214; minutes of meeting, Wilmington, Del., 19 October 1937, U.S. vs. ICI, Records, Govt. Exhibit 881, AT 3748-A.

23. Arthur B. Purvis, president, CIL, to Sir Harry McGowan, 15 October 1928, minutes of meeting, New York, 23 October 1928, U.S. vs. ICI, Records, Govt. Exhibit 772, ICI, Govt. Exhibit 774, ICI; Chandler and Salsbury, *Pierre S. Du Pont*, p. 569.

24. Memorandum on CIL and Arthur B. Purvis, October-November, 1939, Crane Papers, Box 1034.

25. Memorandum regarding Practices and Procedures to be followed with respect to Export Sales, CIL foreign relations committee, 23 February 1948, U.S. vs. ICI, Records, Defense Exhibit D-673, CIL; Agreement between ICI and CIL, 19 August 1948; *ibid.*, Defense Exhibit D-743, ICI. These agreements were part of a general restructuring of relations between Du Pont and ICI ending all cross-licensing arrangements and the system of exclusive regional licences except in certain fields. The final consent decree in the case of U.S. vs. ICI *et al.* in 1952 eliminated these arrangements as well. See Reader, *Imperial Chemical*, II, pp. 437-41.

26. Memorandum: Dividend Policy of Canadian Industries Ltd., 30 April 1941, Crane Papers, Box 1034; U.S. vs. ICI, Records, Defense Exhibit D-664, CIL. It should be noted that a substantial part of the capital for establishment of Defense Industries Ltd. was provided by the Canadian government.

27. John K. Jenney, assistant director, Foreign Trade Development Division, Du
     Pont, to Du Pont foreign relations committee, n.d. [1941], Crane Papers, Box
     1034. Ironically, ICI had first raised this possibility in 1935, but had been
     persuaded by Du Pont to endorse the stock bonus program as preferable to
     cash bonuses. Minutes of meeting, London, 17 June 1935, U.S. vs. ICI,
     Records, Govt. Exhibit 846, AT 3085-A.
28. Minutes of meeting, Montreal, 2 October 1928, *ibid.*, Govt. Exhibit 173, ICI;
     minutes of meeting, Wilmington, Del., 12 October 1928, *ibid.*, Govt. Exhibit
     174, AT 3646.
29. Minutes, Du Pont foreign relations committee meeting, 6 October 1928,
     ibid., Govt. Exhibit 190, AT 3641; minutes of meeting, Montreal, 4 December
     1930, Crane Papers, Box 1034.
30. Robert Salmon, ICI chemicals group, to Jasper Crane, 27 February 1931,
     Crane to Purvis, 6 March 1931, Purvis to Crane, 19 March 1931, I.W. Haslett,
     ICI cellulose group, to Crane, 27 April 1931, Crane Papers, Box 1034. ICI held
     shares in Allied Chemical through an investment by one of its predecessor
     companies, Brunner, Mond, in Solvay Process Co., which merged with four
     other firms in 1920 to form Allied. In 1928, ICI sold most of its Allied shares to
     the French chemical company, Solvay et Cie., but retained a small amount,
     equal to less than 1 per cent of Allied's issued capital. Despite this participa-
     tion, relations between ICI and Allied were never very cordial. The initial steps
     that led to the establishment of ICI in 1926 were the result of a breakdown in
     merger negotiations between Brunner, Mond and Allied. See Reader, *Imperial
     Chemical*, II, pp. 15, 35-7, 49-50.
31. H.J. Mitchell to Lammot du Pont, 11 June 1934, Crane Papers, Box 1039.
32. Sir Harry McGowan to Lammot du Pont, 11 June 1934, *ibid.*
33. W.R. Swint, foreign relations committee, Du Pont, to Lammot du Pont, 10
     July 1934, *ibid.*, Box 1034; G.W. White, president, ICI (New York), to L.J.
     Greenwood, foreign relations department, ICI, 28 February 1936, U.S. vs. ICI,
     Records, Govt. Exhibit 853, ICI; Arthur H. Purvis to Lammot du Pont, 15
     September 1936, *ibid.*, Govt. Exhibit 858, ICI.
34. Agreement between ICI, Du Pont, CIL, 1 December 1936, *ibid.*, Govt. Exhibit
     868, AT 1701.
35. F.A. Wardenburg, Du Pont Ammonia Dept., to Jasper Crane, 25 January
     1938, Crane Papers, Box 1037. W.R. Swint, foreign relations committee, to
     M.G. Tate, ICI (New York), 28 November 1938, *ibid.*, Box 1034. Minutes of
     meeting, Wilmington, Del., 19 October 1937, U.S. vs. ICI, Records, Govt.
     Exhibit 881, AT 3748-A.
36. E.J. Barnsley, ICI (New York), to Lord Melchett, 13 October 1939, *ibid.*, Govt.
     Exhibit 715, ICI.
37. W.R. Swint to George Huggett, president, CIL, 21 November 1945, J.H.
     Wadsworth, ICI foreign relations department, to Huggett, 11 December 1945,
     ibid., Defense Exhibits D-665, D-668, ICI. Testimony of Herbert H. Lank,
     vice-president, CIL, 18 May 1950, U.S. vs. ICI, Trial Transcript, p. 2122.
38. Testimony of Walter S. Carpenter, Jr., 8 June 1950, *ibid.*, p. 3218.
39. Lammot du Pont to executive committee, Du Pont, 29 June 1927, U.S. vs. ICI,

Records, Defense Exhibit D-755, DP. Walter S. Carpenter, Jr., to Du Pont departments, 1 July 1927, *ibid.*, Govt. Exhibit 177, ICI.

40. Carpenter to L. du Pont, 18 August 1927, Carpenter to Arthur H. Purvis, 4 August 1927, Purvis to Carpenter, 25 October 1927, *ibid.*, Defense Exhibits D-770, D-772, D-773, DP. See also Reader, *Imperial Chemical*, II, p. 216.

41. John K. Jenney to W.R. Swint, 8 March 1932, Crane Papers, Box 1034

42. G.W. White, president ICI(New York), to H. Greville-Smith, cellulose group, CIL, 11 August 1932, U.S. vs. ICI, Records, Defense Exhibit D-852, ICI.

43. H. Greville-Smith, memorandum, Isobutanol Prices to CIL, 13 July 1936, R.W. McClelland, Du Pont Ammonia Dept., to Jasper Crane, 22 July 1936, Greville-Smith to Crane, 4 August 1936, Crane to Greville-Smith, 7 August 1936, Greville-Smith to Crane, 27 January 1938, Crane Papers, Box 1034.

44. J.K. Jenney to W.R. Swint: Data on CIL Purchases from Major Stockholders, 8 January 1940, *ibid.*, Box 1034; U.S. vs. ICI, Records, Defense Exhibit D-792, CIL, schedules A-1, A-2; testimony of H. Greville-Smith, 17 May 1950, U.S. vs. ICI, Trial Transcript, pp. 2035-6.

45. W.R. Swint to George Huggett, 21 November 1945, U.S. vs. ICI, Records, Defense Exhibit D-782, DP.

46. Reader, *Imperial Chemical*, II, pp. 416-17.

47. See Alfred D. Chandler, Jr., *Strategy and Structure: Chapters in the History of Industrial Enterprise* (Cambridge, Mass., 1962), pp. 104-11, on Du Pont's decentralization. In the case of ICI, decentralization was enhanced by the fact that the two major elements of the company were drawn from quite different industrial and cultural backgrounds. See Reader, *Imperial Chemical*, II, pp. 71-4.

Contributors

Douglas McCalla is a professor in the history department at Trent University and the author of *The Upper Canada Trade, 1834-1872: The Buchanan Business.*

Dale Miquelon is a professor of history at the University of Saskatchewan and the author of *Dugard of Rouen: French Trade to Canada and the West Indies, 1729-1770.*

Ian McKay recently completed his doctorate in history at Dalhousie University on the social history of the Nova Scotia coal fields.

James D. Frost studied history at McGill, Queen's, and Dalhousie Universities. He is currently working for the Halifax-Dartmouth Port Development Commission.

Graham S. Lowe is a professor of sociology at the University of Alberta.

Tom Traves teaches history and is Dean of Arts at York University. He is the author of *The State and Enterprise: Canadian Manufacturers and the Federal Government, 1917-31.*

Graham D. Taylor is a professor of history at Dalhousie University and author of *The New Deal and American Indian Tribalism.*

THE CANADIAN
SOCIAL HISTORY SERIES

Terry Copp,
*The Anatomy of Poverty: The Condition of the Working Class
in Montreal 1897-1929*, 1974.

Michael Bliss,
*A Living Profit: Studies in the Social History
of Canadian Business, 1883-1911,* 1974.

Gregory S. Kealey, Peter Warrian, Editors,
Essays in Canadian Working Class History, 1976.

Alison Prentice,
*The School Promoters: Education and Social Class
in Mid-Nineteenth Century Upper Canada*, 1977.

Susan Mann Trofimenkoff and Alison Prentice, Editors,
*The Neglected Majority:
Essays in Canadian Women's History*, 1977.

John Herd Thompson,
The Harvests of War: The Prairie West, 1914-1918, 1978.

Donald Avery,
*"Dangerous Foreigners": European Immigrant Workers
and Labour Radicalism in Canada, 1896-1932*, 1979.

Joy Parr, Editor,
Childhood and Family in Canadian History, 1982.

Howard Palmer,
*Patterns of Prejudice:
A History of Nativism in Alberta*, 1982.

Tom Traves, Editor,
Essays in Canadian Business History, 1984.